Towards European Science

Dynamics and Policy of an Evolving European Research Space

Edited by

Linda Wedlin

Associate Professor, Uppsala University, Sweden

Maria Nedeva

Professor of Science and Innovation Dynamics and Policy, University of Manchester, UK

Edward Elgar
PUBLISHING

Cheltenham, UK • Northampton, MA, USA

Published by
Edward Elgar Publishing Limited
The Lypiatts
15 Lansdown Road
Cheltenham
Glos GL50 2JA
UK

Edward Elgar Publishing, Inc.
William Pratt House
9 Dewey Court
Northampton
Massachusetts 01060
USA

A catalogue record for this book
is available from the British Library

Library of Congress Control Number: 2015950504

This book is available electronically in the **Elgar**online
Business subject collection
DOI 10.4337/9781782545514

ISBN 978 1 78254 550 7 (cased)
ISBN 978 1 78254 551 4 (eBook)

Typeset by Servis Filmsetting Ltd, Stockport, Cheshire
Printed and bound in Great Britain by TJ International Ltd, Padstow

Contents

Contributors

Bleiklie, Ivar, Professor, Department of Administration and Organization Theory, University of Bergen, Norway.

Braun, Dietmar, Professor, Institut d'Etudes Politiques, Historiques, et Internationales, University of Lausanne, Switzerland.

Cruz-Castro, Laura, Senior Researcher, Spanish National Research Council, CSIC, Institute of Public Goods and Policies (IPP), Spain. Head of the Department of Science and Innovation, CSIC.

Enders, Jürgen, Professor, School of Management, University of Bath, UK.

Engwall, Lars, Professor Emeritus, Department of Business Studies, Uppsala University, Sweden.

Gornitzka, Åse, Professor, Department of Political Science, and Research Professor at Arena Centre for European Studies, both at University of Oslo, Norway. Adjunct Professor, Department of Administration and Organization Theory, University of Bergen, Norway.

Hedmo, Tina, Senior Lecturer, Department of Business Studies, Uppsala University, Sweden.

Jonkers, Koen, Deputy Head of Unit of the Innovation Systems Analysis Unit of DG JRC of the European Commission. Previously researcher at the Spanish National Research Council, CSIC, Institute of Public Goods and Policies (IPP), Spain.

Lepori, Benedetto, Head of Unit on Performance and Management of Research and Higher Education Institutions, University of Lugano, Switzerland.

Luukkonen, Terttu, Chief Advisor, The Research Institute of the Finnish Economy, Finland.

Mathisen Nyhagen, Gigliola, Researcher, Uni Research Rokkan Center, Norway.

Nedeva, Maria, Professor of Science and Innovation Dynamics and Policy at Manchester Business School, the University of Manchester, UK.

Sanz-Menéndez, Luis, Research Professor, Spanish National Research Council, CSIC, Institute of Public Goods and Policies (IPP), Spain. Chair of Committee for Scientific and Technological Policy (CSTP) at the OECD (2007–2015).

Wedlin, Linda, Associate Professor, Department of Business Studies, Uppsala University, Sweden.

Abbreviations

ALLEA	ALL European Academies
BFUG	Bologna Follow Up Group
CERN	European Organisation for Nuclear Research
CIRAD	Centre de coopération Internationale en Recherche Agronomique pour le Développement
CNRS	Centre National de la Recherche Scientifique
COST	European Co-operation in Scientific and Technical Research
CSIC	Spanish National Research Council
DLO	Netherlands Organr for Agricultural Research
EARTO	European Association of Research and Technology Organisations
EASAC	European Academies Science Advisory Council
EC	European Commission
ECA	European Consortium for Accreditation
EFA	European Funding Area
EHEA	European Higher Education Area
EIT	European Institute of Innovation and Technology
ELSF	European Life Sciences Forum
EMBL	European Molecular Biology Laboratory
EMBO	European Molecular Biology Organisation
ENQA	European Network for Quality Assurance
EQAR	European Quality Assurance Register for Higher Education
ERA	European Research Area
ERC	European Research Council
ERCEA	European Research Council Executive Agency
ERCEG	European Research Council Expert Group
ESF	European Science Foundation
ESG	Standards and Guidelines for Quality Assurance in the European Higher Education Area
ESIB	European Student Information Bureau
EUA	European University Association
EURAB	European Research Advisory Board

EURASHE	European Association of Institutions in Higher Education
EURATOM	European Atomic Energy Community (also EAEC)
EUROHORCS	European Heads of Research Councils
FEAM	Federation of European Academies of Medicine
FEBS	Federation of European Biochemical Societies
FP	Framework Programme
IAA	International Association of Academies
IAC	InterAcademy Council
IAMP	InterAcademy Medical Panel
IAP	InterAcademy Panel on International Issues
ICSU	International Council for Science
IFS	International Foundation for Science
INIA	Instituto Nacional de Investigación y Tecnologia Agraria y Alimentaria
INRA	l'Institut National de la Recherche Agronomique
IRC	International Research Council
IRI	Independent Research Institute
JIIP	Joint Institute for Innovation Policy
JPI	Joint Programming Initiative
JTI	Joint Technology Initiatives
MOC	mission-oriented research centre
MPG	Max Planck Gesellschaft/Max Planck Society
NFA	National Funding Agency
NSF	National Science Foundation
OMC	open method of coordination
PRC	public research centre
PRO	public research organisation
PSR	public sector research
REA	Research Executive Agency
RTO	research technology organisation
STAC	Science and Technology Advisory Council (to the European Commission)
TEEP	Transnational European Evaluation Program
TNO	Netherlands Organisation for Applied Scientific Research
UAI	Union Académique Internationale
VTT	Technical Research Centre of Finland

Preface

The idea for this volume emanated from an international research conference, and Nils Klim seminar, entitled "Challenges for European Science", held at Uppsala University in 2009, where several of the contributors to this volume participated. The conference was co-hosted with the Holberg Prize, University of Bergen, Norway and with additional financial support from the Jan Wallander and Tom Hedelius Foundation and the Swedish Research Council (VR). Some of the research work for the conference and for this volume was carried out (by Linda Wedlin) in relation to a research project financed by RJ (P2005-1189:1).

We are grateful for this financial and organisational support, which created a starting point for this collaborative work. We are equally grateful to all the participants at the conference, who made us see the importance of the European developments in science and research policy and its many implications. We would also like to extend our sincere gratitude to all our contributors, without whose work and patience this volume would not have been.

Linda Wedlin
Maria Nedeva

1.   Towards European science: an introduction

Linda Wedlin and Maria Nedeva

INTRODUCTION

> Over the past seven years, the European Union has had to deal with the worst financial and economic crisis since the last century. We have managed to overcome the existential threat to the Euro area and we have developed our Europe 2020 strategy for smart, sustainable and inclusive growth, with a strong focus on science, research and innovation.
>
> The European Union remains the largest knowledge factory in the world: it accounts for almost a third of global science and technology production. And despite the crisis, Europe and its Member States have managed to maintain this competitive knowledge position.
>
>   . . .
>
> I am a firm believer that science, engineering and technology are vital for the health of our society, economy and environment. We must look to the future, to anticipate and prepare for new developments rather than react to them. (EC 2014; STAC report: 1)

This is the opening by the then European Commission president José Manuel Barroso in commenting on the report, "The Future of Europe is Science", presented to him by his Science and Technology Advisory Council (STAC) in 2014. The report was presented and further discussed at a high-level conference with the same title, convened in Lisbon in early October 2014. It is part of the promotion and further elaboration of Horizon 2020, the new Framework Programme (FP) for research for the EU, guiding the EU research and innovation funding for the years 2014 to 2020. With nearly €80 billion of funding available over these seven years, it is the biggest EU Research and Innovation program ever (EC 2015a). At a time when the overall EU budget has shrunk slightly, this program provides an increase of the funding base for science, innovation and research by nearly 30 per cent compared to its precursor, the 7th Framework Programme (FP 7).

There is little doubt that science and research has become an important policy area in the European context in recent years, not least within the

1

EU. The past decade, since the early 2000s, has implied a steadily growing interest in these issues, and an intensification of policy discussions and initiatives to promote science, research and knowledge development within the EU (see for instance Chou and Gornitzka 2014). One of the starting points for these discussions has been the concept of the ERA, the European Research Area, launched in 2000 to present a new vision for knowledge development and growth within the union. The main aim, as it is expressed by the European Commission, is to create a "European market for research", where knowledge, researchers and technology can circulate freely within the Union. While early analyses of the development of the ERA suggest that the initiative had a somewhat rocky start (Edler 2003; de Elera 2006), we know now that the concept and its ideas have survived. Originally a vision for 2010, it was recently renewed and is now included as one of the centrepieces of the Europe 2020 strategy (European Council 2012).

During this time, the ideas of the ERA and its ensuing policy initiatives have endured one of the more turbulent times in the history of the European Union: the global financial crisis of 2008 and the economic, political and social challenges of the union that followed. Thus despite significant financial pressures and economic recession in several member countries, spending on science, innovation and research has increased. Furthermore, the period since the launch of the ERA has been characterised by a large increase in the number and scope of policy initiatives in the area of science and research policy (Chou and Gornitzka 2014), as well as a significant focus on new policy ideals and rhetoric (Erkilää and Piironen 2014). Supported by a transnational policy discourse of higher education and research – stressing the functional role of science and education for economic competitiveness and growth (see e.g. King 2009) – the EU has taken an increasingly prominent role in discussions about science and research as well as higher education (Corbett 2005; Keeling 2006). Through explicit links to political reform agendas of the European project, most notably the Lisbon and the Bologna processes respectively, the European Commission has established a firm position for itself in the policy discourse on higher education and research, as well as securing the influence of European-level objectives in the future development of these areas within the European Union (Keeling 2006: 203).

While the political rhetoric of the commitment to science and research is evident, recent developments show that this position is not unquestioned. In early 2015, the new president of the Commission, Jean-Claude Juncker, announced an "Investment Plan for Europe" for which he plans to invest in new infrastructure to help rebuild European economies in the wake of the crisis (see EC 2015b). His suggestion involves cutting €2.7 bn from the research, space and innovation budget – a proposal to which a large number of science organisations recently protested (EUA 2015). Not long before that, the EC president was also facing strong opposition to his decision to scrap the position of the Chief Scientific Advisor to the Commission, a decision that made science organisations across Europe heavily protest and question the intentions of the EU president to live up to his promises to protect the role of science in the developing European union context (Sense about Science 2014).

Despite these recent events, the notion of the ERA and the ideal of a common European market for science, research and education seems to persist, and the ideas and policy ideals have survived, and in some ways even thrived, during this critical period. Why has science and research policy become such a key issue and central concern for the EU? What does the expansion and elaboration of this new policy area – and the new policy mechanisms, tools and political rationales that follow along – really mean, and what does such a development entail?

This book will take issue with developments in European science and research policy and governance that have taken place over the past years. While most existing studies focus on the early years of the ERA and European initiatives (Edler et al. 2003), we will take a much-needed look also at the more recent developments and at what has proven to be more far-reaching and continuous efforts to construct a European research area. While significant attention has been paid to analysing contemporary policy developments in higher education and research, this research appears rather fragmented. These studies have focused on either specific national domains or the European level, and have analysed primarily policy initiatives and developments (e.g. Chou and Gornitzka 2014; Edler et al. 2003), the development and functioning of one or a small set of new governance mechanisms or policy programs (e.g. Edler et al. 2014; Luukkonen et al. 2006; Nedeva 2013), or have focused on the political dynamics of new policies and the role of "policy entrepreneurs" in driving change (Corbett 2005). In addition, most studies are linked to a singular analytical framework, most notably starting in political science approaches to governance, or in related areas such as law or science policy studies. This book is an attempt to build on these, and other, previous studies and move towards a synthesis of this knowledge area.

AIM OF THE BOOK

In this book, we aim to take the first steps towards a more comprehensive understanding of these developments, drawing out a framework for understanding not only new policy initiatives and governance systems, but also the potential implications of such changes on the essential relationship between science governance and research performing actors and organisations. Our starting point is that current transformations seem to go beyond the scope of a single and unified change towards what is often assumed to be a "multi-level" governance system of science in Europe (Edler et al. 2003; Chou and Gornitzka 2014). The change involves a transnational governance process, interacting with national efforts, but clearly also an attempt to create something new at the transnational level.

This "something" we analyse as the development of a European-level research space. A research space is defined as the funding and policy space of research activities and actors, within which the rules of knowledge production, knowledge legitimacy and knowledge use are negotiated (Nedeva 2013). Such a space thus holds the "essential" relationships between funding agencies, governance actors, and the researchers and research organisations of that space. These relations are essential to the extent that research practices are dependent on them for resources, support and legitimacy.

The transformation into a new research space thus involves many elements; it involves deeper integration and new political initiative for governance and funding, new means and modes of governing, accompanied by new policy ideals and rhetoric, and new ambitions and aspirations for a common European area for science and research. It also holds changes in interaction patterns, regulatory mechanisms and principles, but also a wider normative and cognitive change to the ideals, models and expectations for what research and science is, how it should be structured and governed, and what is expected of science and science organisations. It also holds changes to the research performing organisations and their researchers, and the relations between these actors and the wider policy and governance framework and actors. Thus, such changes implicate the development of a transnational space for science and research at the European level, holding what we can assume to be significant implications for science and research activities, actors and organisations.

In this book we are interested to explore the development of this European science space and what it means. The main aim is thus to explain how conditions for science are shaped at the transnational level, and what they mean for the organising of science. The following questions guide our work:

- Is a European-level research and science space developing and, if so, what does it entail?
- What are the implications of this development – for science and research and for the overall governance of the scientific field?

● What novel issues emerge in the analysis of the dynamics of interaction between the European and other research spaces?

Enhancing the understanding of the dynamics inherent in contemporary changes to European science governance is important for three main reasons. First, it is practically expedient: if we can better understand contemporary policy initiatives and their relation to changes in the overall structuring and organising of the scientific field, this knowledge can be used to enhance both the effectiveness and efficiency of policy and policy-making for science and research. Such knowledge is relevant to both policy-makers and the science policy experts and advisors that take part in forming science governance at the national as well as the European levels. Second, our study is of interest to scholars aiming to understand the dynamics of science systems more generally, and the inherently complex relationships between the governance, organisations of knowledge, and the epistemic properties of science and scientific activities. Third, a more elaborate understanding of the dynamics of science governance and organising in the European research space opens new avenues to understand the intertwined relations between research spaces at different levels of social aggregation: that is, how transnational research spaces interact with national, local or other regional research spaces. This suggests, also, that we can identify driving forces to change outside of political and policy-related domains, highlighting the role of the profession and the epistemic conditions of science as a driving force for an increasing transnational organisation of science and science policy.

STRUCTURE OF THE BOOK

We begin our exploration of the development of a European space for science and research by elaborating a framework for understanding the current shifts in European science policy and organisation, and the dynamics that this change may create in the field of science and research. Thus, in Chapter 2, we describe the current and past transformations of the European science space as a transition between two relatively stable and persistent stages of science support, from what we term an era of "Science in Europe" to the development of a coherent space that we term "European Science". This transition involves, we argue, three significant parts: 1) a change in the rationale for supporting research and building research capacity at the European level; 2) changes in the targets for policy intervention; and 3) a transformation of the organisational architectonics of the European science space. What this shift contains, and what it entails, is further elaborated in Chapter 2. What we can note here, however, is that this framework takes account not only of specific policy and governance mechanisms and initiatives being developed, but attempts to bring these changes into context to understand how these implicate the conditions for science and scientific activities and how these are continuously negotiated and revised. Building on the notion of "research spaces" elaborated by Nedeva (2013), we set out to explore the multifaceted relationships and interactions between governance, institutional context(s) and the organisations of science at different socio-political levels, for example, the national, the European and the global levels.

Our framework sets the stage for an increasing focus on the dynamics of change in contemporary governance of science and research. Particularly, we focus attention beyond the formal policy development process and the specific policy initiatives involved, to enhance understanding of the related and supporting developments in the wider European research space, as well as in related national – or other regional – research spaces. Our framework highlights the intertwined changes in rationales, governance mechanisms, and the organisational dynamics and structures that carry such changes with them.

Based on the distinction of the three factors involved in the transition from "Science in Europe" to "European Science" – policy rationales, target of intervention (particularly funding), and organisational architectonics – we explore the development and shape of the new European research and science space, and what it entails. The remaining chapters focus on each – or a combination – of these three factors. The chapters thus provide an overview, or an exclusive selection, of the kinds of processes and dynamics involved in the construction of a European research space, rather than an exhaustive list. Our contributors represent different research fields and analytical traditions, including political science, sociology of science, science and technology studies, and organisation studies. They are brought together here to begin the journey towards integration of this knowledge domain. Our selection of chapters is thus primarily intended to inspire, to guide and to illustrate the potential dynamics of a developing European research space, and to put focus on a new set of issues and a new agenda for the study of science dynamics and science policy developments.

We begin this journey into new empirical territory in Chapter 3, with an analysis of the development of a new rationale for science policy in Europe: the evolution of the concept of the ERA, the European Research Area. In this chapter Terttu Luukkonen explores the development and continued revision of the ERA concept over its first ten years. She shows how the agenda gradually has changed from being a policy for the promotion and development of science, to one where the role of science has become elevated to promote the social and economic development of Europe, thus serving the broader European Union agenda. In this way, the ERA concept has become a "science for policy" agenda. In her account of the changes, Luukkonen stresses the development of the ERA concept as an active and dynamic process, uncovering an interaction between the overall policy concept, and the more specific policy tools or mechanisms promoted within it. Particularly, the central role of the new funding mechanism, the ERC, is stressed, which was both an element in the ERA agenda but also contributed to shaping the subsequent policy agenda and legitimising the new policy rationale.

The centrality of the ERC for the development of the European research space is further elaborated in Chapter 4, where Dietmar Braun focuses attention to the role of the ERC as a new target for policy intervention in the developing space. He analyses here the dynamics of the evolving European Funding Area: the space where a multitude of funding agencies and mechanisms at both the national and the transnational levels interact to form a coherent whole. Braun directs attention to the dynamics and, potential or real, conflicts between the different actors and actor constellations in this developing space, exploring how the creation of the ERC alters the interactions and relations of actors in this space. Particularly the interaction between the national and the European research spaces is highlighted, as the ERC has opened new avenues for direct interaction between the European research community and European funding, thus in part bypassing the national level of funding support. This hosts one of the strengths but also one of the potential sources of conflict within the developing European space.

In Chapter 5 we turn our attention to the third aspect of change, the organisational architectonic of the European research space. In this chapter, Åse Gornitzka analyses the changes in the executive governance capacities of the European Commission (EC) that are forming the organisational backbone of the European research area. The EC is one of the central actors in this space, hosting debates of the ERA as well as organising the ERC. This chapter thus analyses the development of governance structures and procedures for hosting the new policy rationales of the EU in science policy, highlighting both the striking inertia in the governance system and the parallel signals of change in terms of the introduction of new research policy instruments developed outside or on the fringe of existing governance systems. Gornitzka discusses, from these developments, the possibilities and prospects of realising the policy imperative of a common European research space.

While Chapters 3 to 5 focus directly on each of the three notions of change – policy rationales, target of intervention and (the most policy relevant part of the) organisational architectonic – the remaining chapters of the volume broaden the view of the organisational dynamics of the new policy rationales and the influence of the changing policy targets. We here explore, in various ways, the interrelation between policy rationales – both European ones but also global ones inherent in the science and research fields more generally – and the changing forms of organising and organisation that both signifies the development of policy and policy rationales, and which may follow from such policy changes. The new funding mechanisms and policy target – the ERC – is a central but largely implicit aspect of such dynamics, which is evident from all the remaining chapters.

Linking directly on to where the previous chapter ended, Chapter 6 explores the interaction between the policy ambitions and agendas of the EC with other organisational actors and attempts to build a European science space. Here, Linda Wedlin and Tina Hedmo analyse the development of what is largely a global policy rationale for enhancing "quality" and "excellence" in higher education and research, and how this plays out in the European space. They analyse the development of two mechanisms for governance at the European level, the European Quality Assurance Register (EQAR) and the ERC, stressing the interaction between the EC and national governments and intergovernmental processes (such as the Bologna process), national funding agencies, national and transnational policy and interest organisations, scientific organisations and many others, in shaping new governance mechanisms and policy rationales for European science. By legitimising both the increasing role of the EU and other transnational attempts in governing European science, this policy rationale and the rhetoric of quality and excellence have become important elements in the evolving European research space.

In the following chapters, we elaborate on the role of research performing organisations and academic associations and their role in the European science space. First, in Chapter 7, Ivar Bleiklie, Gigliola Mathisen Nyhagen, Jürgen Enders and Benedetto Lepori reflect on the developing knowledge ideals and their implications for university organisation. Linking directly to the issue of quality assurance and measurements of excellence of the previous chapter, the authors here elaborate on the role of these mechanisms for university organisation. Arguing that the promoted knowledge ideals surrounding higher education and universities show evidence of standardisation as well as diversity, the universities are facing a complex set of models and ideas on which to react. Through the influence of funding arrangements, evaluations and other governance mechanisms, including those at the European level, a space has opened for a partly new set of actors in university organisation and management. Rather than simply more tightly managed, university hierarchies have thus been penetrated by influential academic elites that influence and shape knowledge organisation within universities. This has also opened new ways for universities to interact and build networks with other organisations in the evolving new, largely transnational, space for science.

Elaborating in part the arguments from the previous chapter, the next one, Chapter 8, explores the role and prominence of a particular kind of science organisation: the academies of science. These academies are to a large part learned societies organising the elites, and as such these have been a more or less central organising force in science almost since the Middle Ages. In this chapter Lars Engwall describes the emergence and expansion of the academies in Europe, and shows how these very recently have expanded and taken form as European-level cooperative bodies. Analysing the basic characteristics and functions of these academies, Engwall argues that these organisations have taken an increasingly important role in policy-making in the European science space. These academies have a dual role, as they partake in both "policy for science" and "science for policy" discussions (see also Chapter 3 for this distinction). As partakers in policy-making and debates, the academies are likely to have a continuing prominent role in the development of the European science space.

Following the exploration of the role of universities and of academies in the developing European space for science and research, we turn to a much less studied yet prominent form of organisation in the European landscape, namely research institutes. In Chapter 9, Laura Cruz-Castro, Koen Jonkers and Luis Sanz-Menéndez analyse the strategies employed by different kinds of research institutes to meet the challenges of internationalisation and, particularly, Europeanisation. Building an analytical framework for understanding how the organisational characteristics of public research organisations may influence the strategies chosen for internationalisation, the authors here suggest that internationalisation at the organisational level of public research institutes is dependent on the external autonomy and internal authority of the institutes. As most research institutes have limited organisational autonomy as well as managerial discretion, this seems to significantly limit the potential of strategic Europeanisation of such research organisations and, thus, likely constrain the further development of a coherent, fully transnational, European science field for these organisations.

The book ends with a concluding chapter, where we draw together the main findings of the previous chapters and discuss the interrelations between the three dimensions of change and the implications for understanding the creation of the new era of European science and a coherent European research space.

REFERENCES

Chou, M-H. and Gornitzka, Å. (2014). *Building the Knowledge Economy in Europe. New Constellations in European Research and Higher Education Governance.* Cheltenham, UK and Northampton, MA, USA: Edward Elgar.

Corbett, A. (2005). *Universities and the Europe of Knowledge: Ideas, institutions and policy entrepreneurship in European Community higher education policy, 1955–2005.* Basingstoke, UK: Palgrave Macmillan.

de Elera, Á. (2006). "The European research area: on the way towards a European Scientific Community?", *European Law Journal*, 12(5): 559–74.

EC (2014). "The Future of Europe is Science". A report of the President's Science and Technology Advisory Council (STAC), available at: https://ec.europa.eu/programmes/horizon2020/en/news/report-pres-barrosos-science-and-technology-advisory-council-stac-future-europe-science-oct2014 (Accessed on 5 June 2015).

EC (2015a). "What is Horizon 2020?", available at: https://ec.europa.eu/programmes/horizon2020/en/what-horizon-2020 (Accessed on 5 June 2015).

EC (2015b). "An investment plan for Europe", available at: http://ec.europa.eu/priorities/jobs-growth-investment/plan/docs/invest_in_europe_en.pdf (Accessed on 5 June 2015).

Edler, J. (2003). "Change in European R&D policy as a complex consensus building process", in Edler J., Kuhlman S. and Behrens M., (Eds.) *The Changing Governance of Research and Technology: The European Research Area.* Cheltenham, UK and Northampton, MA, USA: Edward Elgar.

Edler, J., Kuhlman, S. and Behrens, M. (Eds.) (2003). *The Changing Governance of Research and Technology: The European Research Area.* Cheltenham, UK and Northampton, MA, USA: Edward Elgar.

Edler, J., Frischer, D., Glanz, M. and Stampfer, M. (2014). "Funding individuals – changing organisations: The impact of the ERC on universities". *Research in the Sociology of Organizations*, 42: 77–109.

Erkkilä, T. and Piironen, O. (2014). "Shifting fundamentals of European higher education governance: Competition, ranking, autonomy and accountability". *Comparative Education*, 50(2): 177–91.

EUA (2015). "ERA Stakeholders Joint Statement on the European Fund for Strategic Investments (EFSI)", available at: http://www.eua.be/Libraries/Press/ERA_Stakeholders_-_Joint_Statement_on_EFSI.sflb.ashx (Accessed on 5 June 2015).

European Council (2012). "Conclusions on 'A reinforced European research area partnership for excellence and growth'", the Competitiveness Council Meeting, 11 December, available at: http://www.consilium.europa.eu/uedocs/cms_data/docs/pressdata/en/intm/134168.pdf (Accessed on 8 June 2015).

Keeling, R. (2006). "The Bologna Process and the Lisbon Research Agenda: The European Commission's expanding role in higher education discourse", *European Journal of Education*, 41(2): 203–23.

King, R. (2009). *Governing universities globally: Organizations, regulation and rankings.* Cheltenham, UK and Northampton, MA, USA: Edward Elgar.

Luukkonen, T., Nedeva, M. and Barré, R. (2006). "Understanding the Dynamics of Networks of Excellence", *Science and Public Policy*, 33(4): 239–52.

Nedeva, M. (2013). "Between the global and the national: Organising European Science", *Research Policy*, 42(1): 220–30.

Sense about Science (2014). "Scientific scrutiny in Europe is essential", Letter to President Juncker, available at: http://www.senseaboutscience.org/pages/maintain-cu-chief-scientific-advisor.html (Accessed on 5 June 2015).

2. From 'Science in Europe' to 'European Science'

Maria Nedeva and Linda Wedlin

INTRODUCTION

Research funding and support at the European level has a long history and can be traced back almost to the very beginnings of the European project. As early as the 1950s the idea of establishing a pan-European funding agency in the image of the National Science Foundation in the United States was in the air. Over the next couple of decades, European-level research organisations were established in very specific science areas, such as nuclear research (CERN) and molecular biology (EMBO). During the 1970s and the 1980s organisations seeking to coordinate national research efforts, such as the European Co-operation in Scientific and Technical Research (COST), the European Science Foundation (ESF) and Eureka were set up, and in the 1980s the Framework Programme (FP), largely supporting collaborative research at the more applied spectrum, was established.

In the wake of the twenty-first century, Europe embarked on an ambitious, large-scale project ideologically framed and politically justified by the concept of the European Research Area. This project 1) was associated with an overhaul of the European-level rationale for supporting research and building research capacity, 2) changed the target of policy intervention, and 3) transformed the organisational architectonics of the European research space and brought about new forms of policy and governance mechanisms.

Thus, in terms of the rationale for supporting and funding research at European level, this change was signalled by a general re-orientation from the coordination of national research to the integration of national public science systems (Breschi and Cusmano 2004; ERA Expert Group 2008; LERU 2007; Luukkonen et al. 2006; Luukkonen and Nedeva 2010). Furthermore, the target of policy intervention was extended to include more basic science and research. Transforming the organisation of research funding and support at European level was enacted by the implementation of a number of policy instruments aiming to enable further alignment of national funding spaces, albeit with varying levels of success (ERA-NETs, Technology Platforms, Networks of Excellence[1] and Integrated Projects, for instance). Even more importantly, a dedicated research-funding agency to support investigator-driven research, the European Research Council (ERC), was established.

In this chapter we advance the understanding of these far-reaching transformations by suggesting that they can be interpreted as the transition between two relatively stable and persistent stages of science support at the European level. One of these, defined by rationales for complementarity, support for research close to application, and organisations enabling mobility and coordinating national research effort, we term 'Science in Europe'. The other one, defined by rationales incorporating competition, policy including the support of basic research, and research funding organisations comparable to, and possibly competing with, those at the national level, we refer to as 'European Science'.

We posit that this transition from 'Science in Europe' to 'European Science' unfolds along the three dimensions mentioned above and marks a development that is characterised by increasing the level of commensurability between the European research space and national research spaces. This has serious implications for the complex relationships and interactions between the European level and national research spaces[2] generally and some of their parts in particular. For instance, it makes it possible for researchers and research organisations to bypass influences from their national research spaces by linking directly to opportunities offered by the European research space; it also means that mechanisms for policy learning across national boundaries gain effectiveness by having a shared point of comparison at European level.

Enhancing the understanding of the dynamics of this change – the transition of 'Science in Europe' to 'European Science' – is important in three distinct ways. First, it is practically expedient: understanding better the latest change in research support organisation at European level can lead to the improvement of the effectiveness and efficiency of policy, hence being of interest to both policy makers and science policy experts and advisors. Second, the study of the change processes enacted at European level can contribute to the understanding of the dynamics of the science system more generally and is of interest to scholars studying the complex relationships between the institutions and organisations of knowledge and its epistemic properties. And third, a more nuanced understanding of the transformations affecting the European research space can improve the understanding of the complex interaction between research spaces at different levels of social aggregation, for example, European, national and regional, and aid policy analysis.

We begin by recapping key conceptual developments addressing the transformation of the European research space; following that we outline the approach we use in some detail. Next, we characterise the two distinct stages of development of the European research space and explicate the mechanisms of transition from one to the other. We conclude by outlining some of the important implications of this transition for policy, the European and national research spaces, research funding, research organisations and research fields.

EUROPEAN-LEVEL DYNAMICS: KEY NOTIONS AND APPROACHES

Important as they are, the changes affecting the European-level research space have not gone unnoticed and have attracted the interest of scholars from several research fields that study the science system, policy and governance, and broader developments at European level. For instance, the process of organising science at the European level has been detailed by valuable historical accounts (Guzzetti 1995; Morange 1995; Krige 2006). It is also being discussed under the banner of 'Europeanisation' of research (van der Meulen 2002; Trondal 2002; Olsen 2002; Borras and Edler 2014).

Other scholars, sharing more analytical focus, have discussed the transformation of the European research space: a) in the context of the generally increasing interest towards science and research and the imperatives of the knowledge society; b) as part of a broader political agenda for further integration at European level; and c) as part of the overall trend towards globalisation and global governance forms.

In the context of the generally increasing interest towards science and research, and the imperatives of the knowledge society, the argumentation for an EU focus on science and research follows the ideas and rhetoric of the 'knowledge society'. Thus following the development observed in many national contexts since the 1990s, there is an increasing prominence of a new rationale for supporting science and science policy development. It is a rationale that places science as an important element in the promotion of economic, social and cultural growth and prosperity for the general benefit of society. This development has been amply elaborated in studies of innovation systems, where concepts such as 'Triple Helix' (Etzkowitz and Leydesdorff 2000) and 'Mode 2 knowledge' (Gibbons et al. 1994; Nowotny et al. 2001), are used to point to the increasing links between universities, political bodies and industry.

With this, research and science policy has also become closely interlinked with innovation strategies and policies (Eklund 2007), linking together science with industry, business and other innovation system actors. This has not only increased the interest of governments in issues relating to research and innovation, but has also increased the political attention for science policy and governance more generally. Some claim, even, that science policy has become the new 'defense policy' of developed nations (see also Engwall, Chapter 8, *infra*).

In this perspective, the EU rhetoric and argumentation for science and research can be interpreted as following along these lines, as it has become increasingly linked to a broader development of the EU as a political and economic unit as well as to innovation, technological development and general economic growth. As mentioned above, the ERA concept was launched in 2000 and became closely linked to the ambitions and rationales set out in the Lisbon 2000 convention of heads of states: to become 'the most competitive and dynamic knowledge-based economy in the world' by 2010 (Lisbon European Council 2000). Similarly connected to the Single Market Act encouraging the free movement of persons, goods and services within the union, the ERA was framed as the Fifth Freedom: the free circulation of researchers, knowledge and technology across Europe. In the renewed ERA visions in 2010, this policy area has also become more closely intertwined with debates on innovation and technological development, as it has become a key feature aimed to fulfil the mission of an 'Innovation Union' by 2020. Still today, the ERA vision is prominent in the policy discourse, now described as an 'open space for knowledge and growth' (ERA website 2015). Thus we can posit that, following what has been observed for the higher education discourse (Keeling 2006), the European Commission has taken an increasingly prominent role in the discourse on research and science policy in Europe, aided clearly by the ideals and the policy rhetoric of the 'knowledge society'.

The fact that issues of science and research systems and their integration, development and change become linked to broader political agendas and rationales, such as the Lisbon Agenda, can also be taken as a sign of a further integration at European level (Chou and Gornitzka 2014). Thus, such integration takes shape as a widening political agenda and mandate in many areas, and witnessed in the large number of policy initiatives, funding arrangements, research programmes, policy coordination and control mechanisms instigated at the European level (Maassen and Olsen 2007; Luukkonen and Nedeva 2010). Analysing this deepening integration of research and science policy, and its related processes in higher education, a recent volume by Chou and Gornitzka (2014) highlights the vertical and horizontal dynamics of this process. In this perspective, vertical tensions exist between European processes and national interests and perspectives, and horizontal tensions exist between different sectors and policy areas.

Such dynamics, they argue, shape a multi-faceted and complex integration process, with the result being an area characterised by 'mixed modes of governance' and without a clear and stable supranational logic of integration present (Chou and Gornitzka 2014: 22).

Despite resistance and significant inertia in the process of integration in science (Banchoff 2002), the area of science policy and research governance has followed, in principle, a general elaboration of the forms for collaboration, integration and interaction across the EU. This is expressed, for instance, in the wider scope of EU policy involvement for many areas inscribed in the new and revised Treaties (Sandholz and Stone Sweet 1998). In this sense, developments in science policy and research governance follow closely those of other policy areas, such as those in higher education (cf. e.g. Corbett 2005).

A third possibility to interpret the development of a European science and research agenda is that it is an expression of globalisation and the development of a transnational governance system. Increasing shares of governance activities in many areas of society are taking place between and across nations, and new means as well as modes of regulation develop in the transnational setting (Djelic and Sahlin-Andersson 2006). These processes are often also multi-level in character – taking shape in interaction between transnational actors and process, and national or local ones (Djelic and Quack 2003). In this context, the EU is an important supranational actor that forms regulatory principles and practices, and takes an increasingly important role in governance of many societal areas (Stone Sweet et al. 2001).

Rather than a shift in authority away from the nation states, or a redistribution of authority and control over research and science policy from the nation state to the transnational and European arena (Mazza et al. 2008; Gornitzka et al. 2007), European developments can be interpreted as transnational governance efforts that supplement or add to an increasingly complex governance structure for this field (Hedmo and Wedlin 2008). In such a system, national efforts to govern interact with transnational and European efforts, and these are strongly interdependent. Through soft regulatory measures, voluntary policy coordination mechanisms (such as the Open Method of Coordination, see Keeling 2006 and Gornitzka 2014 for higher education and research), and networking tools (such as the Networks of Excellence, see Luukkonen and Nedeva 2010), European efforts rely heavily on national participation and coordination (for examples from the early ERA developments, see Edler et al. 2003). In this sense, this constitutes the development of a multi-level governance system in which a wide set of European efforts and actors become interlinked.

These perspectives, valuable as they are, have one common deficiency: while they contribute greatly towards describing the changes taking place, and even go some way towards offering a useful analysis of the changing conditions of research governance and policy at European level, they have limited analytical power. There are two main reasons for this. First, they attempt to understand an empirical phenomenon by using other empirical objects, for example, they attempt to understand the fundamental change of European-level support for science by using politically derived notions like 'integration' and 'the knowledge society'. And second, these accounts are fragmented and focus on different aspects of the European-level support for research, for example, governance, policy instruments, structures, rationales and organisations.

More recently, two complementary and analytically interesting notions aiming to aid the understanding of the ongoing science and research space dynamics at European level have gone some way towards remedying these issues. One of these, proposed by Borras and Edler (2014), construes the dynamics of socio-technical and innovation systems in terms of a three-pillar framework. These are:

1) the pillar of the 'opportunity structures and capable agents' comprising historically specific openings for change provided by the interplay of institutional arrangements and the social agents that have the capacity to navigate complex contexts and mobilise these openings for social change;
2) the pillar of the instruments of change consisting of the different policy and governance instruments that develop, and are used, in the process of change; and
3) the pillar of legitimacy that offers the perspective through which to question (and frame) issues around uncertainty, trust and acceptance.

The other analytical perspective, espoused by Nedeva (2013), frames the continuous change of science and research policy and organisation at European level as the sequential attempts to resolve the inherent tension between the global nature of research fields (as knowledge communities and knowledge pools) and the localised research spaces as expressed by funding, organisational and governance arrangements. This tension, it's been argued, is inherent to the science and research system; it cannot be solved but is continuously alleviated. How this inherent tension is resolved is historically specific but it generally demands that the research space is extended in some way to a higher level of social aggregation.

In the next part of this chapter, building on these notions regarding the science and research dynamics at European level, we set out the framework used for the purposes of this work and apply it to the analysis of the latest changes and their implications.

FROM 'SCIENCE IN EUROPE' TO 'EUROPEAN SCIENCE'

Extending the notions aiming to explain the latest change of the science and research space at European level, we propose that these mark the transition between two relatively stable and persistent stages, that is, the transition from 'Science in Europe' to 'European Science'. Our focus is on outlining these stages, unpacking the difference and the dimensions of change, and pointing to some important implications of this transition for science and national and transnational research policy, research organisations and knowledge communities. While questions around the mechanisms, causes and reasons for this change are very important, they will not be discussed here.

We approach these research tasks by making the following assumptions. First, we concur with Nedeva (2013) that the tension between global research fields and largely national research spaces creates an inherent tension that is continuously alleviated by extending the research space: the development of a science and research support infrastructure at European level is an empirical expression of that.

Second, we recognise that the change sequence that the European-level infrastructure for support of science and research has undergone – and continues to experience – is historically specific and predicated on opportunity (or openings for new sequences to develop) and the politicking and hegemony of group and individual actors, and enacted through the development and mobilisation of a variety of instruments. These factors make the change of large social systems, like the European-level science and research space, for instance, very difficult to capture in a way that allows for systematic, analytical comparison. This difficulty can be offset by identifying relatively persistent stages of development (and functioning) and unpacking the transition between them.

And third, these relatively persistent stages of functioning of large social systems ought to be identified and described. For several decades now, the notion of national research/innovation systems has dominated the analysis of the policy context for science and research (Freeman 1987; Lundvall 1992; Nelson 1993; Rip and Van der Meulen 1995). While this notion has been useful through its claim that research and innovation are generated within specific social system(s), it is largely descriptive and its usefulness is confined to particular geographical domains (the description of the

North European contexts for research and innovation) and socio-political domains (for example, it enabled policy to refocus from science to innovation and to account for the complex relationships between varied socio-cultural domains). This notion, however, has very limited analytical clout (Boden et al. 2004) and doesn't afford the methodological clarity necessary for the analytical comparison of multi-faceted (and multi-level) science and research spaces.

This is why we endeavour to characterise distinct science and research spaces by using three essential dimensions, noted in the introduction: 1) the dimension of the policy and governance rationale(s) or the 'ideology' of science systems (Nedeva and Boden 2006); 2) the dimension incorporating the rules and arrangements around funding science and research; and 3) the dimension consisting of the characteristics of the organisations framing the science and research space and the relationships between them (Nedeva and Jacob 2012; Nedeva et al. 2014). These dimensions, on the one hand, characterise science and research spaces and, on the other, channel the change processes that affect them.

In other words, to detect empirically the transformation of any large social system – like the European research space or national research spaces – one ought to register changes along the three dimensions set out above. It is also true that change of large social systems while empirically expressed in the change of social structures, organisations and rules would be impossible to enact without the change of rationale(s): after all, we do structure our social world according to our beliefs and enact these beliefs according to our motivations.

There are two advantages, we believe, to this approach. One, the change ceases to be 'one thing after another' or even a collection of loosely associated change processes. We are looking for patterns. And two, our approach is integrative in the sense that it brings together change of ideology (rationales), change of organisation and structures, and change of governance. Framing the transformation through the transition between two distinct stages of organising of the European research funding space also opens a set of issues to be explored; this sets the starting point for a different research programme.

In the sections that follow, we characterise the two stages of development and organisations of the support for science and research at European level – the stage we refer to as 'Science in Europe' and the one we term 'European Science' – using these three dimensions in a somewhat more specific form. Hence, we focus on the a) change of policy rationale for the support of science at European level; b) the change of the target for policy intervention; and c) the change of organisational architectonic.

'Science in Europe': Key Characteristics

Policy rationale(s) for the support of science and research

The 'Science in Europe' stage of European-level support for science and research was ideologically founded upon three key assumptions.

First, traditionally, European policy was shaped by the 'principle of subsidiarity' (re-affirmed in 1992 by the Treaty of Maastricht) stating that the EU could act only in cases where action by individual countries was insufficient. In the context of science and research this translated into an objective for 'strengthening the scientific and technological bases of Community industry' through promoting cooperation. As usefully summarised by Stampfer (2008), the European added value was generally perceived to be subsidiarity, additionality and complementarity.

Second, there appeared to be an explicit assumption that the 'added value' of the EU, namely its coordination of national policies for science and research, would be achieved by developing funding and support instruments to enable the collaboration of scientists and researchers from different parts of Europe. Consequently, a number of policy instruments were set up to target explicitly increasing collaboration amongst scientists from different countries, and between scientists and industry (Georghiou 1998). This also enabled intensive collaboration within Europe and the emergence of a European research community (Wagner and Leydesdorff 2005).

And third, the assumption that Europe is 'good in science but not so good at the application of its results' dominated the policy arena and the discussions of scientific elites for several decades and manifested in the guises of the 'European paradox' or the 'gap argument'. In brief, the 'European paradox', a re-incarnation of the 'UK paradox' (fashionable in the 1970s), stated that Europe is a world leader in science and research, but was lagging behind in the industrial and economic exploitation of scientific ideas (Pavitt 2000; Dosi et al. 2006).

These rationales underpinning European-level policy for science and research had clear implications for the target of policy intervention and for the way in which this was organised.

Target of policy intervention

These policy rationales helped give rise to a highly fragmented European science and research policy. It focused either on a specific kind of research, for example, European-level support was targeted at applied research, thus lessening the perceived importance of publicly funded fundamental research for the industrial and economic future of Europe (Sharp 1997; Pavitt 2000). As Sharp put it, Europe was 'focused largely on supporting technology (application) whereas support for basic science rests firmly with member states' (Sharp 1997: 203).

European level support for research, and a variety of policy instruments, also targeted some specific social conditions for research, such as collaboration and networking. This translated into multinational agreements that opened the space for specific large-scale scientific endeavours and infrastructures, as in particle physics, organisations the functions of which were to enable the coordination of national effort in research, and multiple research programmes funding research collaboration and research close to application.

Organisational architectonic
Organisation building for the support of science and research at the stage of Science in Europe occurred in what can be seen as three different waves. The first wave of European-level science and research organisations consisted of the establishment of large, transnational facilities in two very specific areas, namely nuclear research and molecular biology. In 1952 CERN (The European Organization for Nuclear Research) was established as an inter-governmental organisation. This was followed in 1957 by EURATOM, marking an important point in the building of the European Communities (Guzzetti 1995). Then in 1964 the European Molecular Biology Organization (EMBO) was set up, followed in 1974 by the establishment of its pan-European 'laboratory' (the EMBL), initially supported by the Swiss government (Morange 1995).

These organisations shared two characteristics: (1) they provided research facilities and/or (2) they enabled the mobility of scientists in very specific research fields like particle physics and molecular biology. For instance, according to the Convention by which CERN was established, its mission was to:

> [P]rovide for collaboration among European States in nuclear research of a pure scientific and fundamental character . . . The Organization shall have no concern with work for military requirements and the results of its experimental and theoretical work shall be published or otherwise made generally available (CERN Convention 1953).

Functionally, CERN was a crystallising mechanism for the integration of the European nuclear physics research community. Structurally, it is the 'ego' in a star-like network with relationships to national governments, national research funders and national research communities. However, it didn't, and still doesn't, have any obvious connections to European science policy or governance organisations.

Representing the second wave, the 1970s witnessed the establishment of what Gronbaek refers to as 'diffuse' organisations (Gronbaek 2003). These include the European Co-operation in Scientific and Technical Research (COST) established in 1971 and the ESF set up in 1974. These organisations are different from the ones discussed above in that they include all fields of research, including the social sciences. At the same time, both organisations were designed to provide platforms for cross-national cooperation rather than to support science at European level. Their missions and objectives are difficult to pinpoint, their core practices variable and their structural position similar to those of CERN and the EMBO.

The ESF as an organisational structure, for example, was built around membership by national funding agencies. Initially it had 42 member academies and research councils in 15 European countries; over the years its membership has expanded and stood at 78 organisations in 30 countries (ESF website).[3] The ESF's mission statement perfectly illustrates its 'diffuse' character:

> The European Science Foundation provides a common platform for its Member Organizations in order to: Advance European research; Explore new directions for research at the European level' (ESF website).

In parallel, different European Community research programmes continued to exist or to emerge. Nevertheless '[g]reat disorder reigned in Community research affairs at the beginning of the 1980s' (Guzzetti 1995: 83). There was no overall European policy on science and technology. National governments generally guarded their sovereignty and opposed any further extension of the role of the Community in science and technology. All programmes had to be approved separately and unanimously by the Council of the European Parliament. Only in 1983 did a way to offset this emerge with the establishment of the Framework Programme (FP) that brought all research programmes in technological fields under the same heading. This, then, represents the third wave of organisation building in the Science in Europe era.

Originally, the overarching mission of the FP was to 'enhance the competitiveness of European industries by raising their technological level' (Luukkonen 2002: 437). The main instrument to achieve this was to develop and implement targeted programmes funding collaborative R&D projects. Collaboration was encouraged across geographical locations, research domains and between research and industry.

Peterson and Sharp (1998) have indicated that the model for, and the underlying principles of, the FP were based on developments in Japan that were perceived to be effective in enabling companies to raise their know-how and solve generic research and technical problems. Sharp has also convincingly argued that the most noteworthy feature of the FP, and European research policy more generally, was its focus on supporting technology and application, whereas support for basic science was left to member states (1997). Although the mission of the FP has undergone sequential iterations and has been expanded to incorporate a wide range of aims, including broadly social ones such as cohesion, job creation and migration and social mobility, its applied research orientation has remained.

In a nutshell, 'Science in Europe' is a period during which a partial and fragmented science and research system developed; this complemented national science, research and innovation arrangements while avoiding competitions with them at any cost. Hence, European-level research policy and funding arrangements generally had limited effects on universities, research institutes and national funding agencies, and landscapes. Multi-goal arrangements in this setting presented a variety of difficulties for the measurement and attribution of impact. Last but not least, the European-level science and research landscape wasn't commensurate with national-level spaces in two important aspects: it didn't support and develop a European research base, and it didn't, as a rule, include explicitly European-level research performing organisations.

'European Science': Key Characteristics

Policy rationale for the support of science and research

This stage of development of the European-level science and research space is founded on rationales that are substantively different than the rationales of the 'Science in Europe' stage; these rationales also made possible the transformation of the funding rules (target of intervention) at European level and enabled the establishment of the European Research Council (ERC).

First and foremost, the understanding of 'European added value' shifted from focusing on coordination to incorporating competition. Our research shows that this re-framing was absolutely critical to the establishment of the ERC. Informally attributed to A. Mitsos (the then Director General of EC DG Research), this shift was captured by the ERC Expert Group (ERCEG, chaired by F. Mayor) as follows:

> Until now European added value has been defined as the collaboration of research teams in different countries. It is now time to bring a new definition of added value, one that incorporates the principle of allowing a researcher in any European state to compete with all other researchers on the basis of excellence. Competition in order to achieve real excellence in research should become an

essential part of a new, forward looking definition of European added value. (ERCEG 2003: 4)

This re-framing coincided with an overall conceptual shift marked by the notion of the European Research Area (ERA), which was underpinned by a move away from 'collaboration' towards 'integration' (Luukkonen and Nedeva 2010). It shifted policy attention from coordinating national research spaces to establishing a new, European, research space. It also precipitated the implementation of policy instruments that no longer simply sought to enable collaboration between researchers but further aimed to increase the level of integration in different aspects of European science and research. This lent political support to breaking away from the customary understanding of the role of the European level.[4]

What had to give way next was the belief that Europe was doing well in science but was not very good in its application. Many top-level scientists have claimed they have been aware of the folly of this assumption ever since the after-war period.[5] Nevertheless it dominated the political domain until the early twenty-first century. By the mid-1990s, however, there was growing evidence that Europe was not doing so well in science either.

The European Report on Science and Technology Indicators (2003) offered data showing that European countries, as a rule, invested poorly in science and research. It also showed that the increased investment in science that the USA and Japan made in the mid-1990s was not matched in Europe. A comparison between the USA and Europe also clearly put the USA in the lead, in terms of both number of publications and highly cited ones (Nedeva et al. 2003). The gap between Europe and the USA was clearly in science and its application rather than related to its application alone.

Accounting for this, Pavitt argued that the role of publicly funded academic research in Europe's future economic and social development had been largely ignored (Pavitt 2000). He attributed this to the adoption of mistaken and misleading models regarding the nature of knowledge and its role in society. One such model, according to Pavitt, was Mode 2 – and concentrating on it would lead both to 'cut price research motels' (David et al. 1999) and to the neglect of fundamental research. Yet another misleading view of academic research was that it had ceased to be useful to contribute to technological progress and had become a form of intellectual consumption for rich countries able to afford it to support from public funds. Pavitt (2000) also countered this by highlighting a US study which found that three-quarters of papers cited in US patents were results of publicly funded research, undertaken in academically prestigious universities, and published in academically prestigious journals. By 2000, the long-standing assumption of this 'European paradox' morphed into a full-blown 'gap' argument, that is, that Europe was clearly lagging behind the USA and Japan both in terms of science and its application. This was reflected in the documentation on the ERA (ERA 2000).

These changed rationales – from complementarity through cooperation and coordination to competition, and from defining the European paradox as a science implementation gap to seeing it as a gap in scientific performance – precipitated the change of target for policy intervention and provided a condition for the establishment, at European level, of a research funding organisation of a different kind.

Target of policy intervention

The remit of Europe supporting predominantly applied and strategic research could not hold for long. The need to develop a European knowledge base, and the mismatch between supporting applied and basic research, became more prominent in the research policy literature (Schatz 2003; EURAB 2003; EUROSCIENCE 2003; Spinney 2003; Schiermeier 2002; Philipson 2003). The apparent contradiction between the support for applied research and technology versus support for basic research was effectively resolved by introducing the notion of 'frontier' research in a report published in 2005 (HLEG 2005). The term 'frontier' implies a revised understanding of basic research; that basic research is linked, on the one hand, to economic and social progress and, on the other, to risky and uncertain search for knowledge at the forefront of understanding (ERC 2015).

Furthermore, while enabling research collaboration across the nation states of the EU has remained on the agenda, the European level has started to support more basic research through direct research support to prominent scientists, mainly directed through the funding schemes of the ERC, rather than simply coordinate the research efforts carried out in individual or collaborative projects based in the member states.

This change of focus of research policy intervention signalled the emergence of an organisational space for the support of research that is aligned, and in competition, with national-level research spaces.

Organisational architectonic

The change of policy rationales and the refocusing of policy intervention at the European level demanded the establishment of organisation(s) of a different kind. The ERC is an example of the kind of organisation that corresponds to, and stabilises, the transformation of the European research space.

The European Commission (EC) included the establishment of the ERC in its proposal for the Seventh Framework Programme (FP7); it was to implement 'the Community activities' in investigator-driven 'frontier' research at European level within a dedicated programme: the IDEAS Programme. The proposal was approved by the European Parliament in December 2006. The ERC was subsequently established with a Commission Decision of 2 February 2007 and the ERC Executive agency was set up with a Commission Decision of 14 February 2007. These documents outlined the rationale, activities, structure, operating principles, relationships with the EC and financial arrangements of this, the first pan-European organisation funding investigator-driven 'frontier' research in all fields of science.

The official documents approved by the Council and the EC framed the rationale for the IDEAS Programme in general, and for the ERC in particular, indicating that: a) investigator-driven research was a key driver of wealth creation and social progress; b) Europe was not making good use of its scientific potential and resources; and c) a Europe-wide funding structure for 'frontier' research was an essential part of the ERA.

Accordingly, the primary aim of the ERC and its funding schemes was to 'stimulate scientific excellence by supporting and encouraging the very best, truly creative scientists, scholars and engineers to be adventurous and take risks in their research. The scientists should go beyond established frontiers of knowledge and the boundaries of disciplines' (ERC website). Furthermore, the ERC aimed to 'create leverage towards structural improvements in the research system of Europe' (ERC website). In deference to the extant traditional research support organisations at European level, the ERC's sole criterion for selection was also emphasised as being 'scientific excellence' rather than political priorities or related considerations.

These objectives are to be achieved by developing and supporting European researchers (researchers based in European research organisations) and by supporting the research organisations of Europe (universities and research institutes) to develop their research strategies and priorities to become global players in research. The ERC's ambitions, however, reach beyond funding research to encompass strengthening and shaping the European research system and supporting research that can form the basis for new industries, markets and innovations.

The objectives of the ERC were initially pursued through two funding instruments. One of these, the ERC Starting Independent Researcher Grant scheme (StG), was targeted at researchers who are at a relatively early career stage. It aimed to enable them to transit into the highest

Table 2.1   *'Science in Europe' and 'European Science' at a glance*

	Science in Europe	European Science
Policy rationales for the support of science and research	(i) The 'added value' of European-level organisation achieved through co-ordination of national effort (ii) The way to maximise these effects was to enable the collaboration of scientists and researchers (iii) Europe very good in basic science but not good in its application (the 'gap' argument) (iv) The organisation of science at European level ought to focus on supporting applied and strategic rather than basic research	(i) European 'added value' shifted from coordination to competition (and emphasis on academic excellence) (ii) Move away from collaboration towards research integration (iii) Recognition that Europe is rather poor at both science and its application and that the 'gap' between it and the USA and Japan is likely to increase (iv) Bridging of distinction between applied and basic in new notion of 'frontier' research; re-framing of the role of the EC as a research funder
Target of policy intervention	(i) Focus on predominantly applied research and development (ii) Emphasis on enabling collaboration, networking and social inclusion	(i) Incorporating the funding of the science base and academic excellence (ii) Research excellence (and funding excellent research) becomes an objective independent of collaboration and networking
Organisational architectonic	(i) Large, transnational facilities in specific research fields and championed by powerful, organised but fragmented scientific elites emerged in the 1950s and 1960s	(ii) Establishment of the ERC in 2007 (iii) The organisations from Science in Europe persist but have been changing (e.g. the ESF's overhaul)

Table 2.1   (continued)

	Science in Europe	European Science
Organisational architectonic	(ii) 'Diffuse' organisations to coordinate national effort in the support of science and research (e.g. ESF, COST etc.) were established in the 1970s (iv) Framework Programme bringing together different research programmes in various technological fields. These were targeting research close to application and encouraging the collaboration between academic groups and industry. The Framework Programme was set up in 1983	

echelons of their respective knowledge communities.[6] The other funding instrument, the ERC Advanced Investigator Grant scheme (AdG),[7] was designed for already stellar scientists and scholars and aimed to provide support for highly innovative research ideas at the frontier of their respective research fields.

There have been arguments that the establishment of the ERC completed the long emergence of a European research space (Nijkamp 2003). We believe that the establishment of the ERC signalled the emergence of a different stage in the development of the European research space, a stage that is substantively different from the previous one.

To begin with, the ERC brought to European policy a clear focus on the support of science and research with particular properties – 'frontier' research – and on developing the social conditions for such science to occur. To this effect, it has established a peer review system based on clear and consistent selection criteria of excellence and provides generous grants. Furthermore, by focusing on competition rather than collaboration, the ERC is starting to shape a 'level playing field' for the top science talent in Europe. Last but not least, the ERC is shaping a European funding and policy space comparable to and competing with the already established national science systems.

The differences between 'Science in Europe' and 'European Science', and the transformations along the three dimensions that mark the transition from one to the other, are illustrated in Table 2.1 above.

INSTEAD OF CONCLUSION: IMPLICATIONS AND NEW AVENUES FOR RESEARCH

In this chapter we argue that the latest transformation of the science support system at European level can be usefully interpreted as a transition from one relatively stable stage of development, 'Science in Europe', to a different stage we refer to as 'European Science'. These we defined by their policy and governance rationales, the rules and arrangements around the funding of science and research, and the characteristics of the organisations framing the science and research space.

We demonstrated that core transformations, affecting all three dimensions mentioned above, have occurred and that support for science and research at European level is stabilising around: a) policy and governance rationales including not only complementarity and collaboration but also competition; b) funding rules for applied and close to application research as well as for developing and creating the European science base, with an emphasis on scientific excellence; and c) the reframing of the diffused organisations from the period of 'Science in Europe' and the establishment of the ERC as a powerful research funding organisational player.

This change could, and indeed has started to, generate a range of implications for policy that, in turn, are likely to shift considerably the research agenda relating to science and innovation policy, the internationalisation of research and, more generally, the study of science dynamics. The main effects of this transformation, we believe, are enacted through the emergence, at European level, of a research funding space aligned and commensurate with national research spaces.

One set of effects, for instance, can be expected to unfold at European level. While the science support system at European level has become congruent with the national arrangement for funding science, there are still not many research performing organisations; hence, one expected effect would be the emergence of European-level research and advanced education organisations (both research institutes and universities). Indeed, there appear to be some developments in this respect, most notably the establishment of the European Institute of Technology (EIT), which is used by Terttu Luukkonen in Chapter 3 of this volume as an example of new research performing organisational forms at European level (see also Gornitzka and Metz 2014 on the EIT). However, several chapters in this volume attempt to bring the organisational issues and problems of the European research space to centre stage, also highlighting the impediments to internationalisation, and its subset Europeanisation, of current research performing organisations. Most notably, Chapters 7 and 9 elaborate on the internationalisation of universities and research institutes, respectively, and provide a starting point for analysing the organisational dynamics of the evolving European research space.

In the context of changing organisational dynamics and processes of Europeanisation, a set of issues that has not yet been studied systematically has emerged. These include the ways in which the organisational funding space at European level may affect the 'Europeanisation' of knowledge communities that are still largely national (social sciences and humanities, for instance) and of composite research elites, in the form of networks, associations or academies. These issues, partly introduced in Chapters 6 and 7 and further developed in Chapter 8, suggest that more attention should be paid to how the organising of scholarly communities at the international, and particularly the European, level influence the shaping of elites, and how these in turn further influence the workings and procedures of science and of science policy at both the national and European levels.

Following in part from these organisational dynamics and changes, the establishment of 'European Science' is likely to have a range of micro-effects on such things as researchers' careers, their profiles and research practices. While there have been studies of the impact of institutional conditions on research practices (see for instance contributions in Whitley and Gläser 2014), the specific developments and European dynamics of change have not been particularly conceptualised, and the effects on academic practices are far from understood.

The emergence of a European-level research funding space comparable with national research spaces is precipitating two further effects: 1) it changes the nature of and enables further policy learning in the European context; and 2) it could enable Europe as a socio-political entity to compete more successfully in science, research and innovation with the US. In terms of policy learning, the effects are magnified by the European level providing a reference frame affording the basis for useful comparison.

Further, there is accumulating evidence that in the short time of its existence, the European Research Council has gained high visibility, acquired a considerable level of legitimacy and has become a symbol of and a measure for research excellence. Research shows that this is affecting the practices of national research councils (Nedeva et al. 2014) and the strategy of universities across EU member states (Edler et al. 2014). In this volume, Chapters 4 and 5 also explore the dynamics that the ERC creates between different actors and actor constellations in the European science space, opening – again – a new perspective on the European space, presenting it as a site for tensions and contradictions between the EC and other actors but also between different research and funding spaces.

'European Science', despite creating a level playing field in the support for science and research, thus carries forward some tensions between the European and the national level that are inherent to the current political arrangement. These include the tension between the national research councils and the ERC that are in a position of strong competition for resources, applicants, reviewers and legitimacy (see Chapter 4). There is also a set of tensions unfolding around the relative performance of national research systems at the European level. For instance, there are already voices bemoaning the relatively weak performance of Southern and Eastern European countries with the ERC, who see this as another route for depleting their science base. There seems to be a developing tension also between universities within nation states: being embroiled in competition for resources and obsessed with demonstrating their excellence, universities have begun competing to attract ERC grantees. Similarly, (some) scientists and scholars have gained relative power in relation to their organisations (universities) and have outgrown their national research spaces.

These transformations and challenges, we believe, have the potential to transform the research and policy agenda in Europe. 'European Science' is here to stay and the best we can do is attempt to understand the avalanche of further change it may engender.

ACKNOWLEDGEMENTS

This work is based on research undertaken within the EURECIA project (Understanding and Assessing the Outcomes of ERC Funding) sponsored by the ERC and funded by the Ideas Programme of the EU Seventh Framework Programme (grant number 229286).

NOTES

1. Although this instrument was largely dropped by the Seventh Framework Programme (FP7).
2. Here we use the notion of 'research space' to refer to the organisational space outlined by the essential relationships between research performers and funders of research setting the institutional context for science and research (Nedeva 2010).
3. The ESF has been undergoing further change recently, including change of statutes in 2014.
4. One clear implication of the notion of ERA was overcoming the 'harmful' fragmentation science in Europe and achieving a 'better organisation of the European research effort'

being conditional upon the development of a European research space (system) that went 'beyond the current static structure of "15+1" towards a more dynamic configuration' (COM (2000) 6, p.7).
5. Information from interviews with scientists.
6. There have been several changes to this since the establishment of the ERC; for instance a distinction between 'starters' and 'consolidators' has been introduced, thus distinguishing between early and mid-career stages.
7. Both types of grants are relatively generous whereby the StG is up to €2 million and the StG is up to €2.5 million over five years.

REFERENCES

Banchoff, T. (2002), 'Institutions, inertia and European Union research policy', *Journal of Common Market Studies*, 40(1), 1–21.
Boden, R., Cox, D., Nedeva, M. and Barker, K. (2004), *Scrutinising Science: the Changing UK Government of Science*, Basingstoke and New York: Palgrave Macmillan.
Borras, S. and Edler, J. (eds) (2014), *The Governance of Socio Technical Systems: Explaining Change*, Cheltenham, UK and Northampton, MA, USA: Edward Elgar.
Breschi, S. and Cusmano, L. (2004), 'Unveiling the texture of a European research area: Emergence of oligarchic networks under EU Framework Programmes', *International Journal of Technology Management*, 27(8), 747–72.
CERN Convention (1953), see http://council.web.cern.ch/council/en/Governance/ Convention.html, last accessed May 2015.
Chou, M-H. and Gornitzka, Å. (2014), *Building the Knowledge Economy in Europe. New Constellations in European Research and Higher Education Governance*, Cheltenham, UK and Northampton, MA, USA: Edward Elgar.
Corbett, A. (2005), *Universities and the Europe of Knowledge: Ideas, Institutions and Policy Entrepreneurship in European Community Higher Education Policy, 1955–2005*, Basingstoke, UK: Palgrave Macmillan.
David, P.A., Foray, D. and Steinmueller, W.E. (1999), 'The research network and the new economics of science: From metaphors to organizational behaviors' in Gambardella, A. and Malerba, F. (eds), *The Organization of Innovative Activities in Europe*, Cambridge, UK: Cambridge University Press.
Djelic, M-L. and Sahlin-Andersson, K. (eds) (2006), *Transnational Governance, Institutional Dynamics of Regulation*, Cambridge, UK: Cambridge University Press.
Djelic, M-L. and Quack, S. (eds) (2003), *Globalization and Institutions*, Cheltenham, UK and Northampton, MA, USA: Edward Elgar.
Dosi, G., Larena, P. and Labini, M.S. (2006), 'The relationships between science, technologies and their industrial exploitation: An illustration through the myths and realities of the so called European Paradox', *Research Policy*, 35(10), 1450–64.
Edler, J. (2003), 'Change in European R&D policy as a complex consensus building process', in Edler, J., Kuhlman, S. and Behrens, M. (eds), *The Changing Governance of Research and Technology: The European Research Area*, Cheltenham, UK and Northampton, MA, USA: Edward Elgar.
Edler, J., Kuhlman, S. and Behrens, M. (eds) (2003), *The Changing Governance of*

Research and Technology: The European Research Area, Cheltenham, UK and Northampton, MA, USA: Edward Elgar.

Edler, J., Frischer, D., Glanz, M. and Stampfer, M. (2014), 'Funding individuals – changing organisations: The impact of the ERC on universities', *Research in the Sociology of Organizations*, 42, 77–109.

Eklund, M. (2007), 'Adoption of the Innovation System Concept in Sweden, Acta Universitatis Upsaliensis', *Uppsala Studies in Economic History*, 81, Dissertation.

ERA Expert Group (2000), *Challenging Europe's Research: Rationales for the European Research Area (ERA)*, European Commission, Directorate-General for Research.

ERA Expert Group (2008), *Challenging Europe's Research: Rationales for the European Research Area (ERA)*, European Commission, Directorate-General for Research.

ERA Web (2015), available at: http://ec.europa.eu/research/era/index_en.htm (Accessed on 5 June 2015).

ERC (2015), available at: http://erc.europa.eu/glossary/term/267 (Accessed on 22 May 2015).

ERC website, http://erc.europa.eu/index.cfm?fuseaction=page. display&topicID=12, version 4 May 2011.

ERCEG (2003), The European Research Council: A Cornerstone in the European Research Area. Report from an expert group. Copenhagen, December 15, 2003.

ESF Mission Statement, http://www.esf.org/about-esf/what-is-the-european-science-foundation/mission-statement.html, as of 5 July 2011.

ESF website http://www.esf.org/, as of May 2011.

Etzkowitz, H. and Leydesdorff, L. (2000), 'The dynamics of innovation: from national systems and "Mode 2" to a triple helix of university–industry–government relations', *Research Policy*, 29: 109–23.

EURAB (2003), *European Research Council: EURAB input to the ongoing debates in Europe on the topic of a possible European Research Council*, EURAB 02.055 final (2003).

European Commission (2000), *Communication from the Commission to the Council, the European Parliament, the Economic and Social Committee and the Committee of the Regions: Towards a European research area*, COM (2000) 6, Brussels, 18 January 2000.

European Commission (2007), *Green Paper: The European Research Area: new perspectives*, COM (2007) 181, Brussels, 4 April 2007.

European Commission (2003), *Third European Report on Science & Technology Indicators*, Brussels.

EUROSCIENCE (2003), 'Towards a European Research Council', http://www. euroscience.org/WGROUPS/SCIENCE_POL/erc.htm.

Freeman, C. (1987), *Technology and Economic Performance: Lessons from Japan*, London: Pinter Publishers.

Georghiou, L. (1998), 'Global collaboration in research', *Research Policy*, 27(6), 611–26.

Gibbons, M., Limoges, C., Nowotny, H., Schwartzman, S., Scott, P. and Trow, M. (1994), *The New Production of Knowledge*. London: Sage.

Gornitzka, Å. (2014), 'How strong are the EU's soft modes of governance? The use of the open method of coordination in national policymaking in the knowledge policy domain', in Chou, M-H. and Gornitzka, Å. (eds), *Building the Knowledge Economy in Europe*, Cheltenham, UK and Northhampton, MA, USA: Edward Elgar, pp. 160–87.

Gornitzka, Å., Maassen, P., Olsen, J.P. and Stensaker, B. (2007), 'Europe of knowledge: search for a new pact', in Maassen, P. and Olsen, J.P., *University Dynamics and European Integration*, Dordrecht: Springer.

Gornitzka, Å. and Metz, (2014), 'European institution building under inhospitable conditions – the unlikely establishment of the European Institute of Innovation and Technology', in Chou, M-H. and Gornitzka, Å. (eds), *Building the Knowledge Economy in Europe*, Cheltenham, UK and Northampton, MA, USA: Edward Elgar, pp. 111–30.

Gronbaek, D.J.v.H. (2003), 'A European Research Council: an idea whose time has come?', *Science and Public Policy*, 30(6), 391–404.

Guzzetti, L. (ed.) (1995), *History of European Scientific and Technological Cooperation*, European Commission, Luxembourg.

Hedmo, T. and Wedlin, L. (2008), 'New modes of governance: the re-regulation of European higher education and research', in Mazza, C., Quattrone, P. and Riccaboni, A. (eds), *European Universities in Transition. Issues, Models and Cases*, Cheltenham, UK and Northampton, MA, USA: Edward Elgar, pp. 113–32.

HLEG (2005), *Frontier Research: the European Challenge, High-Level Expert Group Report, February 2005*, Brussels: European Commission, Directorate General for Research.

Keeling, R. (2006), 'The Bologna Process and the Lisbon Research Agenda: The European Commission's expanding role in higher education discourse', *European Journal of Education*, 41(2), 203–23.

Krige, J. (2006), *American Hegemony and the Postwar Reconstruction of Science in Europe*, Cambridge, MA, USA: MIT Press.

LERU (2007), The Future of the European Research Area, August.

Lisbon European Council (2000), 'Presidency conclusions: Lisbon European Council, 23–24 March, 2000', available at: http://consilium.europa.eu/ueDocs/cms_Data/docs/pressData/en/ec/00100-r1.en0.htm (Accessed on 27 September 2006).

Lundvall, B. A. (1992), *National Systems of Innovation; Towards a Theory of Innovation and Interactive Learning*, London: Pinter Publishers.

Luukkonen, T. (2002), 'Technology and market orientation in company participation in the EU Framework Programme', *Research Policy*, 31(3), 437–55.

Luukkonen, T. and Nedeva, M. (2010), 'Towards understanding integration in research and research policy', *Research Policy*, 39(5), 674–86.

Luukkonen, T., Nedeva, M. and Barré, R. (2006), 'Understanding the dynamics of networks of excellence', *Science and Public Policy*, 33(4), 239–52.

Maassen, P. and Olsen, J.P., (2007), *University Dynamics and European Integration*, Dordrecht: Springer.

Mazza, C., Quattrone, P. and Riccaboni, A. (eds) (2008), *European Universities in Transition. Issues, Models and Cases*, Cheltenham, UK and Northampton, MA, USA: Edward Elgar.

Morange, M. (1995), 'EMBO and EMBL', in Krige, J. and Guzzetti L. (eds), *History of European Scientific and Technological Cooperation*, European Commission: Luxembourg.

Nedeva, M. (2010), 'Public sciences and change: Science dynamics revisited', in Janusz Mucha and Katarzyna Leszczynska (eds) *Society, Culture and Technology at the Dawn of the 21st Century*, Cambridge, UK: Cambridge Scholars Publishing.

Nedeva, M. (2013), 'Between the Global and the national: organising European science', *Research Policy*, 42(1), 220–30.

Nedeva, M., Thomas, D., Caswill, C. and Nielsen, K. (2014), 'Study of research funding trends and practices of research funding organisations', *Report to the Swiss Science and Technology Council*.

Nedeva, M. and Jacob M. (2012), 'Comparative research funding landscapes: typology of public research systems and funding mechanisms', unpublished manuscript.

Nedeva, M. and Boden, R. (2006), 'Changing Science: The Advent of Neo-liberalism', *Prometheus* 24(3), 269–81.

Nedeva, M., van der Meulen, B. and Barré, R. (2003), 'Towards a European Research Council: A structured review of the evidence', report to the ERCEG, October 2003.

Nelson, R. (ed.) (1993), *National Innovation Systems: A Comparative Analysis*, Oxford, UK: Oxford University Press.

Nijkamp, P. (2003), 'The European Research Council – a Point of No Return', *Innovation*, 16 (1).

Nowotny, H., Scott, P. and Gibbons, M. (2001), *Re-Thinking Science: Knowledge and the Public in an Age of Uncertainty*, Cambridge, UK: Polity Press.

Olsen, J.P. (2002), 'The Many Faces of Europeanization', ARENA working paper, No. 2 <http://www.sv.uio.no/arena/publications/wp02_2.htm>

Pavitt, K. (2000), 'Why European Union funding of academic research should be increased: a radical proposal', *Science and Public Policy*, 27(6), 455–60.

Peterson, J. and Sharp, M. (1998), *Technology Policy in the European Union*, Houndmills and London: Macmillan Press.

Philipson, L. (2003), 'A European Research Council for basic research', *Nature Medicine*, 9, 637; http://www.nature.com/nm/journal/v9/n6/full/nm0603-637. html (Accessed 01 August 2011).

Rip, A. and van der Meulen, B. (1995), 'The post-modern research system', *Science and Public Policy*, 23(6), 343–52.

Sandholz, W. and Stone Sweet, A. (1998), *European integration and supranational governance*, Oxford, UK: Oxford University Press.

Schatz, G. (2003), 'Do we need a European Research Council? A scientist's View', *ERC Conference*, Dublin, 13 March 2003; http://www.ria.ie/events/papers.html.

Schiermeier, Q. (2002), 'European Research Council: A window of opportunity', *Nature*, 419, 108–09; http://www.nature.com/cgi-taf/.

Sharp, M. (1997), 'Towards a federal system of science in Europe', in Barre, R. Gibbons, M., Maddox, J., Martin B., and Papon P., (eds), *Science in Tomorrow's Europe*, Paris: Economica International.

Spinney, L. (2003), 'European Research Council gets thumbs up: Scientists support idea of new pan-European research body', *The Scientist;* www.the-scientist.com, February 20, 2003.

Stampfer, M. (2008), 'European Added Value of Community Research Activities: expert analysis in support of ex post evaluation of FP6', WWTF Vienna Official Report, October 2008.

Stone Sweet, A., Sandholtz, W. and Fligstein, N. (eds) (2001), *The Institutionalisation of Europe*, Oxford, UK: Oxford University Press.

Trondal, J. (2002), 'The Europeanisation of research and higher education policies: some reflections', *Scandinavian Political Studies*, 25(4), 333–55.

Van der Meulen, B. (2002), 'Europeanization of Research and the Role of Universities: an Organizational-Cultural Perspective', *Innovation: The European Journal of Social Sciences*, 15(4), 341–55.

Wagner, C. and Leydesdorff, L. (2005), 'Network Structure, Self-organization and the Growth of International Collaboration in Science', *Research Policy*, 34(10), 1608–18.
Whitley, R. and Gläser, J. (2014), 'Organizational Transformation and Scientific Change: The impact of institutional restructuring on universities and intellectual innovation', *Research in the Sociology of Organizations*, vol. 42.

3. European Research Area: an evolving policy agenda

Terttu Luukkonen

In reality, the history of the European research policy could almost be described as that of the gradual development of a small pool of ideas formulated thirty years ago, that, broadly speaking, we continue to exploit today.
(Michel André 2007)

INTRODUCTION

The European Research Area (ERA) was launched in the year 2000 through a Commission Communication "Towards a European Research Area" (European Commission 2000), and given a new impetus by the 2007 Green Paper on ERA (European Commission 2007a). The ERA is an inclusive concept covering the whole of the EU research policy and it was launched in parallel with the Lisbon Strategy objectives. Its overall aim is to help coordinate the EU and Member State policies towards common objectives. The European Research Area is mentioned in the Treaty of Lisbon, which gives it a strong legal backing and raises this policy area within the mandate of the EU. The definition of what the ERA stands for has evolved during the ten-year period of its existence. The Commissioner of Research, Innovation, and Science, Máire Geoghegan-Quinn (2010), encapsulated it as "a single, unified research area in Europe, within which researchers and knowledge can move around freely."

The main focus of this chapter is on the interpretations and reinterpretations of the ERA concept and agenda, as evidenced by the documentation related to it. Central to the ERA and its development is a move towards a more Europeanised research policy field where the ERA agenda provides justification for the adoption of new institutions and funding tools. These new tools are an indication of a more integrated policy approach.

Edler (2003) analysed changes in the European Community research policy and the adoption of the ERA by paying attention to three aspects as drivers of change, namely, 1) new policy ideas, 2) functional interaction

37

at different levels of different stakeholder groups, and 3) the role of the European Commission as a change agent. These processes were all invoked in the adoption of the ERA and its further development. The focus of this chapter will be at *the level of new policy ideas*, but it will also refer to *functional interaction among different stakeholder groups* and *the role of the Commission* in the further development of the ERA.

Here we suggest that early on the ERA agenda concentrated on factors related to restructuring the European research base and on making this work as one 'internal market' – in other words, to factors of the nature of 'policy for science' (see, e.g., Science, Growth and Society, 1971: 37). Towards the end of the decade, attention was increasingly devoted to solving pressing societal problems of European and global reach and utilising scientific research in this process, that is, 'science for policy' or utilising science for society and policy (ibid.).

Another import of the chapter is the suggestion that when new support forms are introduced, there will be a co-evolution of the ERA agenda and the new support forms. The debate on a European Research Council (ERC) is a prime example of this kind of development, and the chapter will explore this example. The ERC was legitimised by the invoking of some early discussions and concepts, that is, those related to excellence and quality in the original ERA concept, while the debate transformed excellence from a marginal issue into an essential part of the ERA agenda. The establishment of the ERC also necessitated a modification in the definition of the European value-added to include, besides cross-country collaboration, competition at the European level.

There is another example, that of the European Institute of Innovation and Technology (EIT), which is, to some extent, similar in terms of changing the ERA agenda to accommodate the new programme features. This example is also referred to, though not analysed with equal attention.

With the evolution of the ERA concept, the Sixth and Seventh Framework Programmes (FP6 and FP7) have increasingly delegated the formulation and implementation of strategy (JTIs, ERC, EIT) and new programme types have emerged which are mixed community and intergovernmental programmes (JTIs, Art. 169/185 Joint Programmes, ERA-nets, see Appendix, this chapter) highlighting an increased attention to coordination of Member State policies.

The chapter considers the period of the first ten years of ERA policy, which is covered by the Sixth and Seventh Framework Programmes and will not deal with the changes as evident in the 8th, Horizon 2020, which has laid greater stress on innovation, and thus, utilisation of science in the economy.

The chapter is mainly based on documentary analysis of the various documents handling and communicating Community policy. It also draws upon the interviews carried out for the EURECIA project on the ERC in the European research funding landscape (see Luukkonen 2014).

THE EUROPEAN RESEARCH AREA AND THE LISBON AGENDA

The notion of the European Research Area (ERA) was adopted in 2000 in parallel with the adoption of the Lisbon Agenda targets and can be regarded as one of the means to achieve it. The notion of what the Lisbon Agenda stands for has changed since its adoption. At the heart of it is, nevertheless, the definition of scientific research, technological development and innovation as key factors in growth, the competitiveness of companies, and employment in the knowledge-based economy (European Commission 2004a). The major target was to make European economies knowledge-based, completing the internal modernising of the European social model, and sustaining favourable growth prospects by applying an appropriate macro-economic policy mix (Rodrigues 2002). The objective adopted by the Lisbon European Council of March 2000 was for Europe "to become the most competitive and dynamic knowledge-based economy in the world capable of sustainable economic growth with more and better jobs and greater social cohesion".[1] This Lisbon objective was complemented in 2002 by the Barcelona target of 3 per cent R&D intensity and during the 2000s further attention was paid to growth and jobs (2005) and social objectives, like those related to environment and citizens (2008). Overall, the objectives required changes that not only involved technological innovations, but also deep-going institutional transformation in knowledge production, diffusion, and utilisation (Rodrigues 2002).

After the realisation that the original Lisbon Agenda targets would not be achieved by 2010, the EU launched the 2020 Strategy, presented by the Commission in March 2010 to replace the Lisbon Agenda.[2] It highlights a vision of Europe's social market economy: "smart, sustainable and inclusive economy delivering high levels of employment, productivity and social cohesion" (European Commission 2010a: 3). It includes policy objectives related to structural reforms in seven policy areas, called 'flagships'. Research and innovation play an important role in the flagship initiative called "Innovation Union", which poses targets for both the Union and the Member States. It includes the completion of the ERA – though gives no specific explanation of what this means. As an indication of increased emphasis on innovation, the Commission suggestion for the new framework programme for research, the 8th, is a Common Strategic Framework,

Horizon 2020, including both innovation and research programmes under the same framework for 2014–2020.

Innovation systems and evolutionary economics thinking is underlying the close association of the ERA concept with the knowledge-based economy strategy – and now in the Innovation Union flagship. This thinking pays attention to education, research, knowledge transfer, entrepreneurship and finance as important prerequisites for fostering the growth of the economic system (see, e.g., Edquist 2005). It also emphasises learning, knowledge transfers, and connectivity between the various actors, and the resulting system is a complex 'socially distributed' structure of knowledge production activities, involving now a much greater diversity of organisations (Soete 2002).

The fact that the Treaty of Lisbon mentions the ERA gives it a strong legal backing and raises this policy area within the mandate of the EU. The Treaty of Lisbon defines the ERA in article 179 paying attention to the aspect of internal market in research as well as to addressing the other policy areas and needs of the Union (European Commission 2008a).

ERA GOALS – INCREASING FOCUS ON COORDINATION

The ERA includes ideas about coordination of policies that were quite radical at the time when the ERA was adopted. Edler (2010) has defined international *policy coordination* as adjusting and combining activities in an area in order that they better *interact* and *create synergies* with activities of other countries in the same area. He contrasts coordination with integration, which would entail a "complete merger of research capacities" (like a merger of organisations into a new virtual or real entity, or the merger of programmes into a new joint programme). In this chapter, coordination of policies is used in a way similar to Edler (2010). Alignment of policies is part of the notion of coordination. Alignment and coordination can take place both through top–down processes and through spontaneous and self-directed activities. When referring to integration in research policy objectives and tools, it is used to denote the process of formation of a new entity that uses joint principles and procedures in its operations.[3] Thus, a joint programme does not represent integration, but coordination, if in implementation the partners putting in money follow their own priorities and/or procedures.

Ideas of research policy coordination have a long history in the European Community. For example, Research Commissioner Ralf Dahrendorf in 1974 coined a 'European Scientific Area' as a term to describe the situation with greater cooperation and coordination among the Member States (Guzetti 2009). In fact, Dahrendorf enlisted several objectives that were not so far from the objectives later to appear within the 'European Research Area' project, though the latter is much more ambitious. There were further attempts at coordination of research policy in the European Community,[4] but these did not advance before the launch of the ERA.

Before the adoption of the ERA, the coordination that existed was mainly based on cooperative research programmes that require that the partners additionally use their own institutional and other national resources ('de facto coordination'). These programmes were grouped under the umbrella of the Framework Programme, preceded first by the ESPRIT pilot phase, approved in 1982, and functioned on a regular basis since the First Framework Programme running in 1984–87.[5]

One of the major changes ERA policy introduced was an attempt to coordinate the research activities in the Member States through research funding and coordination (like Open Method of Coordination) tools, most of which were now mixed tools between Community-based and intergovernmental (see Appendix, this chapter, Tables A1 and A2). Earlier the research funding tools had all been Community-based. At first, most of the tools in FP6 were also Community-based, but the situation changed in FP7 and the European Research Council (ERC) is the only Community-based funding tool introduced in FP7 and is very different from any other tool since it is fully integrated and pan-European.

The fact that ERA funding tools increasingly combined features of Community-based and pure intergovernmental tools provides evidence of a change in ambition. In these new tools Commission money or procedures act as a catalyst, but the continuation of the activities is dependent on the concerted action of the Member State level stakeholders who are expected to commit their own resources (see for instance the Joint Technology Initiative (JTI), Art. 169[6] Undertakings, and European Institute of Technology (EIT) in Table 3.A2). This development entails a delegation of strategy definition and implementation to new Community bodies. The new ERA tools have blurred the distinction between 'research policy' and 'research funding' instruments, since both purposes are intertwined in a set of instruments having ambitious overall objectives to promote the coordination of efforts. Nevertheless, Member State level stakeholders have turned out to be reluctant to cede national-level decision-making powers to Community-level undertakings, thus making these tools quite weak coordination devices (European Commission 2010b).

To summarise, ERA policy introduced coordination in a stronger form than 'de facto coordination' as represented by the traditional framework programme. In order to implement this coordination, new tools were introduced, increasingly attempting to align and coordinate Member State level policies through mobilising their funding instruments for joint action.

The idea of coordination implied by the concept of the ERA was radical at the time of its introduction. What led to its acceptance is an interesting question. Banchoff (2003) attributed the acceptance of the concept and policy of the ERA to a combination of factors, for example, the fact that it coincided with reforms of national research policies and attempts to improve the competitiveness of their national research bases in the three scientifically leading countries, Germany, Great Britain and France, and that the Commission, which was proactive in launching it, showed political entrepreneurship in advancing its acceptance (Banchoff 2003). We further highlight that the ideas of the ERA initiative are strongly supportive of the Lisbon knowledge-based economy agenda, and thus the interplay between the policy ideas between these two new visions is an important explaining factor for the acceptance of the ERA.

ERA AGENDA – FROM RESTRUCTURING SCIENCE TO SOCIETAL UTILISATION

It is important to note that the ERA concept has evolved during its first decade. The ERA concept has been interpreted and reinterpreted several times, and each time, its targets have been expanded to some extent and regrouped in a slightly different manner. The ERA was launched when Philippe Busquin was the Commissioner for research, and like the previous initiatives to change EU policy in research it is strongly associated with the Commissioner.[7]

The original Commission paper "Towards a European Research Area" (European Commission 2000) did not give a simple and neat definition of the ERA. This paper talked first about the problems, low investment in R&D by both public and private investors and the lack of a European policy for research (causal ideas), and then listed targets (normative ideas). The distinction is based on Edler (2003: 102–103): causal ideas "help define the current situation and explain what action leads to what outcome", normative ideas "suggest where one should head and what is perceived as legitimate". The launch of the ERA was related to the observation (causal ideas) that public and private investment in research in Europe was too low as compared with the USA and Japan.[8] Improvement was needed in the organisation of research, especially because European research effort evidenced systemic failures: "fragmentation, isolation and compartmentalization of national research efforts and systems and disparity of regulatory and administrative systems" compounding the "impact of lower global investment in knowledge" (European Commission 2000: 7).

The original ERA-related objectives (normative ideas) included a long list (in all ten, of which some had subgroups). The questions included, first, objectives related to better networking and more coherent implementation of national and European research activities to overcome the above-mentioned fragmentation and compartmentalisation of research efforts and to achieve a "European internal market" for research. Then there were objectives related to a wider innovation policy (patents, risk capital), which have lately been coined as being part of a broad-based innovation strategy (see Edler 2009). A third group of objectives was related to human resources (of which greater mobility was one, though it is also part of the European internal market for research; further, *inter alia*, there was the aspect of the attractiveness of Europe for the researchers from the rest of the world), and a fourth, the promotion of social and ethical values in scientific and technological matters. The above ideas of more coherent implementation of national and European research activities entailed a weak idea of coordination. Virtual centres of excellence entailed an idea of integration, but overall, the idea of coordination gained strength over time.

A Commission communication, "The European Research Area: Providing a New Momentum" (European Commission 2002), summarised the objectives of the ERA in three groups and this list has often been used in communicating the ERA objectives, since it is simpler and clearer. It included: 1) the creation of an "internal market" in research, an area of free movement of knowledge, researchers and technology; 2) a restructuring of the European research fabric, in particular by improved coordination of national research activities and policies; and 3) the development of a European research policy, not just addressing funding but all relevant aspects of EU and national policies.

The 2007 Green Paper on the ERA (European Commission 2007b) restructured the ERA objectives into six groups. It highlighted excellence and competence with regard to researchers, research infrastructures and research institutions, emphasised coordination of programmes and priorities and knowledge-sharing between public research and industry, and introduced 'world-class' infrastructures and 'excellent' research institutions, further, putting more emphasis to opening up to the world.

In the 'revival' of the ERA through the so-called 'Ljubljana Process', a better governance of the ERA was discussed and agreed upon at the informal ministerial meeting held in Ljubljana and Brdo (Slovenia) on 14–15 April 2008. Attention was also paid to research excellence and the creation of a "researcher- and enterprise-friendly research environment".[9] This process was based on the ERA Vision 2020, which discussed the concept

of 'knowledge triangle',[10] the major import of which was the introduction of education as part of the essential prerequisites for the creation of
a knowledge-based society, the societal dimension, and tackling 'grand'
societal challenges, such as climate change and environmentally friendly
energy technology (European Commission 2010a). The Lund Conference,
"New Worlds – New Solutions", during the Swedish Presidency in July
2009 strongly endorsed a focus on the Grand Challenges. This preceded the
emphasis to be adopted in Horizon 2020, the 8th Framework Programme.

The range of questions the ERA concept has come to include has thus
become wider. Since 2007, excellence has been in a visible position on the
agenda. For instance, the Lund Declaration from July 2009 linked excellence with the achievement of major objectives, such as knowledge diversity, and an ability to meet with Grand Challenges and 'shocks'. Towards
the end of the decade, environmental and social issues gained importance.
The so-called 'Grand Challenges' represent areas such as global warming,
tightening supplies of energy, water and food, ageing societies, public
health, pandemics and security (European Commission 2009a).

Table 3.1 summarises the issues highlighted in the different versions of
the ERA concept over the decade using the three-group classification of
the 2002 document (European Commission 2002). As is seen in Table 3.1,
a number of the specific objectives relate to the restructuring of the
European research fabric. Coordination of activities plays an important
role in this process, though other structural issues are important as well
(such as improving cohesion between east and the west, promotion of
women and young people's interest in science, attraction of Europe for
researchers from the rest of the world, and sustaining common social and
ethical values in science and technology).

Excellent research base is one of the prerequisites for the achievement of
the objectives. However, towards the end of the decade – as is also seen in the
Europe 2020 Strategy – more and more attention is devotedto the pressing
societal issues. The ERA is no longer important just for restructuring the
European research base in an effort to make it more effective, but also for
helping to solve societal problems of European and global reach.

It is obvious that the ERA has become a central concept embracing
both the overall research policy goals but also all the funding tools of the
Framework Programme since its adoption (in FP6 and FP7) – the more
traditional and new measures. Since the ERA has come to denote the
overall EU research policies, it seems apparent that whenever new issues
are adopted on the agenda, it is included in the newest definition of the
ERA. According to a working document by the Commission, "ERA has
proven itself to be a powerful mobilising concept" (European Commission
2007b: 11). This highlights its role as a flexible label which signals common

Table 3.1   Issues included in the ERA concept in consecutive versions

	Creation of 'internal market' in research	Restructuring the European research fabric, especially through co-ordination of national research activities and policies	Addressing relevant aspects of EU and national policies
Towards a European Research Area COM(2000) 6 final	Greater mobility of researchers; European scientific careers	1) Better networking and coherent implementation of national and European research activities 2) Promotion of women researchers plus stimulation of young people's interest in careers in science 3) Greater European cohesion in research (bringing together scientific communities and companies from the east and west) 4) Improving attraction of Europe for researchers from the rest of the world 5) Promotion of common social and ethical values in S&T	Better use of instruments encouraging investment in research and innovation: tools of wider innovation policy
2007 Green Paper	1) High levels of mobility of competent researchers between institutions, disciplines, sectors and countries	1) Excellent research institutions engaged in effective public-private cooperation; forming research and innovation clusters; attracting a critical mass of resources	A wide opening of the ERA to the world, addressing global challenges with Europe's partners

Table 3.1   (continued)

	Creation of 'internal market' in research	Restructuring the European research fabric, especially through co-ordination of national research activities and policies	Addressing relevant aspects of EU and national policies
2007 Green Paper	2) World-class research infrastructures, integrated, networked and accessible to research teams from across Europe and the world	2) Effective knowledge sharing between public research and industry 3) Well-coordinated research programmes and priorities, including a significant volume of jointly-programmed public research investment at a European level	
ERA Vision 2020	Fifth freedom: intra and extra-EU openness and circulation	1) Knowledge activities: volume and quality. European way to excellence 2) Knowledge triangle: education, research and innovation	1) The societal dimension 2) Sustainable development and grand challenges

policy and acts as a cognitive integrative mechanism mobilising support for specific policies (Luukkonen and Nedeva 2010). The ERA concept is also flexible and allows different working groups to interpret and rearrange the ERA dimensions according to their preferences.

ADOPTION OF NEW TOPICS INTO THE ERA AGENDA

Excellence as a 'Causal' Idea

The Lisbon Agenda objective about 'the most competitive and dynamic knowledge-based economy in the world' had from the start an underlying assumption that European organisations, involved in knowledge production and transfer, needed to be excellent and of high quality. This was referred to in, for example, "The role of the universities in the Europe of knowledge" (European Commission 2003a). However, the first listing of the ERA objectives did not specifically mention 'excellence', except in the context of existing (virtual) centres of excellence in Europe, paying special attention to their networking with each other in an effort to overcome 'fragmentation' (European Commission 2000: 7). Thus, though excellence was highlighted in the name of one of the major ERA instruments (Network of Excellence) in the Sixth Framework Programme, it did not figure prominently on the agenda.

Gradually excellence started to emerge on the agenda. First, the 2002 Barcelona Council, which presented the target of raising R&D intensity to 3 per cent by 2010, set the objective of making the European "education and training systems a world quality reference by 2010" (European Commission 2003: 18). Further, the action plan "Investing in research" (European Commission 2003a), intended to summarise the policies to implement the Lisbon Agenda and ERA objectives, maintained that "abundant and excellent researchers and research personnel and a vibrant, world-class public research base" were among the factors that firms considered when deciding whether and where to invest in research (European Commission 2003b: 11). It also referred to excellence and integration of research as some of the central principles that FP6 needed to foster and referred a few times to the new instrument "networks of excellence" (ibid: 14).

However, it was not until the Communication from the Commission on "The role of the universities in the Europe of knowledge" from 5 February 2003 (European Commission 2003a) that the issues of excellence and world-class universities were explicitly put on to the agenda. This communication invoked the Lisbon Agenda and the above-mentioned Barcelona Council reference to high-quality education and training systems as a justification for devoting attention to these matters. Subsequently, on the initiative of the French Presidency, the Competitiveness Council in September 2003 adopted a resolution on "Investing in Research for European Growth and Competitiveness" recognising that "basic research and scholarship are crucial for the sustainable development" and asked the European Commission to bring forward a communication covering the entire issue of basic research and the role of the European Union in this area (Europe's Search for Excellence in Basic Research 2004). The outcome was the Communication "Europe and Basic Research" (European Commission 2004b). This communication recognised the discussion that had been going on about a need for a "Basic Research Fund" and a "European Research Council" (ibid.: 3).

The discussion of an ERC had begun earlier within the scientific community, and especially the life scientists were active in its promotion (van Dyck and Peerenboom 2003; Nedeva 2013). The project on the ERC was related to the broader concern about the reconstruction of European science and science institutions after the Second World War,[11] thus highlighting the role of excellence as a 'causal' idea in Edler's sense (2003). There was a concern about funding being too low for basic research and about quality of science and its institutions in Europe and, as in European research policy in general, the USA provided a benchmark with which comparisons were made, in this instance, especially with the National Science Foundation, but also with foundations like the US Howard Hughes Institutes (Gronbaek 2003; van Dyck and Peerenboom 2003; Nedeva 2013). Several meetings were organised by the scientific community to promote the idea, among others, a meeting in February 2003 in Paris, organised by ELSF, EMBO, FEBS,[12] and Unesco.

This discussion was put on the European Union agenda during the Swedish EU Presidency in 2001 (Gronbaek 2003). It gained momentum during the Danish Presidency in the second half of 2002, when an ERC Expert Group (ERCEG) was set up in November 2002 under the chair of Professor Frederico Mayor, former Director-General of Unesco. This group submitted its report in December 2003 (ERCEG 2003).[13]

Excellence as a 'Normative' Idea

The debate on the ERC prompted the before-mentioned Commission communications, and the communication on "Europe and Basic research" (European Commission 2004b) was a direct justification for the establishment of the Council. Thus, it ended up recognising "a need to introduce a European level support mechanism for individual teams' research projects, modeled on the 'individual grants' given by the NSF" (ibid.: 12). Further, the Communication saw this initiative to be "quite natural in the context of the European Research Area", and perceived its importance "to combat the effects produced by the compartmentalized nature of the national systems", and stimulating *"creativity, excellence and innovation by exploiting a form of European value added other than that produced by cooperation and networking: the added value which comes from competition at EU level."* (ibid.: 3; emphasis added). Within a short period of time there was a complete change in the views of the Commission on the matter of a European Research Council and on its justification, illustrated by the fact that at the meeting on an ERC, organised by the leading life sciences organisations in Paris in February 2003, Commission representative Peter Kind expressed reservations with regard to the ERC project (van Dyck and Peerenboom

2003). Reasons why this change of views took place is a matter to be further explored and one which goes beyond the purpose of this chapter. It is assumed here that the change was largely related to the wide support of an ERC among the stakeholder groups, which was an outcome of the successful promotion of the idea by the scientific and scholarly communities.

In February 2004, the Irish Presidency organised a symposium in Dublin entitled "Europe's Search for Excellence in Basic Research", with participants representing "the highest levels of Member States, Acceding States and Associated Countries, senior industrialists, leading academics, representatives of national funding organizations and other representative bodies" to discuss the importance of investment in basic research. The participant list highlights the importance of enlisting the support of all major stakeholder groups[14] for the ERC endeavour. The meeting reached a consensus on "a need to enhance the excellence of European research" and agreed that "industry needs excellent research, and excellent people, . . . including implementation of the knowledge generated through basic research, as a basis for competitiveness". The consensus statement further maintained that the national initiatives were not sufficient for enhancing the excellence of European research, but that a European initiative was required. "The objectives of this European initiative would be to promote excellence in basic research by promoting international competition among individual research teams. The sole criterion should be excellence, identified by international peer review" (Europe's Search for Excellence in Basic Research 2004: 3). Commissioner for Research Philippe Busquin attended the conference and strongly endorsed the suggested "support mechanism for research projects by individual research teams competing at European level, particularly in the field of basic research, along the lines of the US National Science Foundation" and promising detailed measures before the summer (ibid.: 33). He had been supportive of the idea as early as October 2002, but had made its foundation conditional on the strong commitment of the national research organisations, including "pooling a certain amount of national resources" (Gronbaek 2003). The considerable growth of funds in the Seventh Framework Programme eventually enabled the setting up of the new body fully on the basis of European money.

The process culminated in the summer of 2004 in the conclusion of the Spring Council in seeing "merit in enhanced support for basic research of highest quality" and the informal Competitiveness Council of 1–3 July 2004, which welcomed the creation of "a mechanism to support research conducted by individual teams in a competition at European level and expressed its will to conclude before the end of 2004 on the principles for such a funding mechanism" (European Commission 2004c).

It is obvious that, first, in the debate on an ERC, support of basic research became legitimate for the EU by reference to the underlying assumptions about the need to build up excellent research organisations, which were part of the ERA vision and entailed in the broader knowledge-based society objectives. At the same time, however, this debate changed the way European research policy was framed. It put forward the question of basic research and excellence of European research on the EU research and innovation policy agenda. While this debate continued, it highlighted the importance of excellence for the whole ERA initiative. It thus got fuel from the ERA but also changed the way in which the ERA and the achievement of its targets were perceived. A lack of excellence became part of the way in which both the 'causal' and 'normative' ideas were framed (Edler 2003).

Henceforward, promotion of excellence has featured as an important target among the ERA objectives. For example, the before-mentioned Green Paper on the ERA (European Commission 2007a) highlighted excellence of researchers and research institutions as well as world-class infrastructures as ERA targets. Further, as exemplified by the earlier quote from the Lund Declaration (European Commission 2009a) about the fact that meeting the Grand Challenges requires, among other things, "strengthening frontier research initiated by the research community itself" and "excellence and well-networked knowledge institutions". A report by the European Research Area Board (EURAB) of 2009, enti-tled "Preparing Europe for a new Renaissance", advocated "an ERA to deliver excellence ... where risk-taking in research, regardless of its public or private origin, will be the guiding principle for ERA policy" as one of the six areas of action the Board outlined (European Commission 2009b). These quotes seem directly to point to the principles of the ERC to promote excellence, frontier research and risk-taking.[15]

It is to be noted, nevertheless, that the ERC is not the only inspiration of this concern on excellence. An interest in the ERC and excellence reflects an acknowledgement of the importance of excellence for the construction of a knowledge-based society and a concern over the quality of research performing organisations and research in general in Europe. It became both a 'causal' and 'normative' idea.

'Frontier research' is another concept evoked to justify the support of excellence and the establishment of the ERC. The concept of frontier research was suggested by an expert group which had a task to provide a convincing argument that ERC-funded research can at the same time support both fundamental research and useful knowledge (European Commission 2005a: 18). The concept was adopted to highlight that emerging research areas embrace substantial elements of both basic and applied research. The ERC has used the report's claims and on its webpage it "expects that its grants will help to bring about new and unpredictable scientific and technological discoveries – the kind that can form the basis of new industries, markets, and broader social innovations of the future,"[16] thus providing a strong argument that the ERC is justified from the point of view of technological and economic competitiveness, not just of scientific competitiveness. The term frontier research has also found its way to ERA declarations and debates as exemplified by the Lund Declaration (European Commission 2009a) as well as the aforementioned EURAB report (European Commission 2009b).

A New Definition of European Value Added

As referred to, the foundation of the ERC required a change in necessitating a new interpretation of European value added. The European Community has adopted a general principle of subsidiarity, which is expressed in the consolidated Treaty of Lisbon (art. 5) as follows:

> Under the principle of subsidiarity, in areas which do not fall within its exclusive competence, the Union shall act only if and in so far as the objectives of the proposed action cannot be sufficiently achieved by the Member States, either at central level or at regional and local level, but can rather, by reason of the scale or effects of the proposed action, be better achieved at Union level.

In research policy, this principle has traditionally been interpreted to justify the funding of research collaboration through transnational consortia (Muldur et al. 2006: 186). The Communication from the Commission, "Europe and Basic Research" (European Commission 2004b), already expressed a new definition of European added value justifying the establishment of the ERC, namely "the added value which comes from competition at EU level" (ibid.: 13). At the Dublin Conference on the ERC entitled "Europe's Search for Excellence in Basic Research" on 16–17 February 2004, Dr. Achilleas Mitsos, the then Director-General for Science, Research and Development, presented this new interpretation of European value added, and referred to the fact that "competition is to be on a European scale, drawing on an enlarged pool of researchers" (p. 36).

The momentum of the ERC emergence thus influenced the re-interpretation of an important principle of action. The book on the Seventh Framework Programme by Muldur et al. (2006) enlists several further objectives "giving rise to European added value," including better integration of European R&D and dealing with pan-European policy challenges (ibid.). This exemplifies that the concept of value added has become flexible and has further developed to encompass the various dimensions of the ERA concept.

Education on the Agenda

The debate on the ERC put forward, not just excellence and basic research, but also – to some extent – the universities, one of the reasons being that the majority of the grant recipients are active in European universities. Since universities are the major seats for basic research, the question of what could and should be European research and innovation policies with regard to the universities was raised in the Communication from the Commission on "The role of the universities in the Europe of knowledge" from 5 February 2003 (European Commission 2003a). The European Institute of Innovation and Technology, originally the European Institute of Technology[17] (EIT) is, however, the first ERA initiative that has directly addressed education and the universities.

Education is another example of a domain that was suggested on to the agenda decades ago, as early as the 1950s (den Bak 2008). Even though higher education is a policy domain that is outside the mandate of the European Union, the Communication to the Spring European Council in 2005, "Working together for growth and jobs: A new start for the Lisbon Strategy" (European Commission 2005b), brought universities to the agenda as an important part of the Union policy. The original idea of an EIT is said to have come from European Commission President José Manuel Barroso and based on the model of the US MIT (den Bak 2008). The document that was prepared for the Spring European Council in February 2005 (European Commission 2005b) re-launched the Lisbon Strategy and suggested the idea of the EIT as part of a revised Lisbon Agenda and stated that high-quality education was the best way to guarantee the long-term competitiveness of the Union. Thus, the idea of an EIT became yet another 'normative' idea which suggested "where one should head and what is perceived as legitimate" (Edler 2003).

The idea of an EIT first met with a lot of resistance from the stakeholders (den Bak 2008), and in the debate and negotiations concerning its establishment, the idea was watered down; for example, instead of an institute with a specific location, the EIT became a distributed institute, the EIT degrees became only labels, and the budgetary allocation during FP7 was much lower than originally envisaged. The point here is, however, that the process of legitimation of the new instrument again modified the ERA agenda by bringing there a new element, that of education and the concept of the 'knowledge triangle'. The Regulation[18] establishing the European Institute of Innovation and Technology specifically mentions "the integration of the knowledge triangle – higher education, research and innovation – across the European Union" as the core idea of the EIT. The institute was formally established in 2008, became operational in 2009 and began its first practical activities in 2010.

CONCLUSIONS

This chapter has described the policy of the European Research Area (ERA), which has come to denote the European Union's research policy and is part of a broader Lisbon Agenda promoting the overall competitiveness of the EU economies. This umbrella concept has proved to be flexible in embracing new elements and mobilising support to the adoption of new features and tools in policy. The ERA concept has provided explanations for the state of affairs in Europe ('causal' ideas) and suggested policy measures to improve them ('normative' ideas) (Edler 2003).

The Treaty of Lisbon mentions the ERA, which gives it a strong legal backing and raises this policy area within the mandate of the EU. In effect, the ERA stands for the whole of the Union research policy and reflects changes occasioned by the adoption of new issues on the political agenda. We can see some trends in the overall understanding of what the ERA stands for. While at first more attention was devoted to restructuring the European research base ('policy for science'), towards the end of the decade attention has increasingly been devoted also to solving pressing societal problems of European and global reach ('science for policy'). The concept also reflects the increasing trend to promote the coordination of Member State research policies. Further, in the evolution of the ERA agenda and in connection with the adoption of new institutions, it has adopted new dimensions, the prime example of which is the promotion of excellence.

The idea of coordination of research policies entailed in the ERA concept was quite radical at its inception. The adoption of this policy can be attributed to a number of factors, among which the proactive role of the Commission has been highlighted. Over the ten years there have, however, been changes in the emphasis given to the various dimensions, and new dimensions have been included in the ERA concept. Why this has happened has not been addressed in research, and attempting to answer it goes beyond the resources of this review. The acceptance of the ERC has, however, been commented upon in more length.

The idea of an ERC emerged outside the Commission as a project of the scientific community,[19] and the life scientists were especially active in this process, probably because they had quite early formed European-level organisations (EMBO, EMBL, FEBS), which helped them formulate joint goals and provided them with more resources and influence (Nedeva 2013). The process of the adoption of the ERC included a lot of networking, conferences, and debates organised by the members of the scientific community and their associations. While the scientists succeeded in convincing the Member State and European policy-makers and industry of the justification of their project, the Commission papers addressing ERA policies underwent a change in which the question of excellence gained more prominence. The ERC was justified by invoking the scant references to excellence and quality in the original ERA concept. As it turned out, during the project to establish an ERC, the scant references to excellence gained force and became an important part of the whole ERA notion. These references were directly related to the debate on an ERC, but also reflected overall concerns about the quality of science and scientific institutions in Europe, especially as compared with the USA. The emergence of the ERC thus influenced the ERA agenda and reinforced the weight of the question of excellence. The establishment of the ERC also necessitated the transformation of the definition of the European value-added to include, besides cross-country collaboration, competition at the European level.

The adoption of the European Institute of Innovation and Technology in 2008 provides a somewhat different example: the Commission and its President were active from the start in advocating the new institute. While originally received with scepticism among the stakeholders (den Bak 2008), the idea became watered down in the process of emergence and in the end, did not have so many novel features as the ERC. Its resources were also quite limited during FP7; it was in a kind of probation period, which did not provide it with a strong start. However, this is yet another example highlighting how the introduction and acceptance of this new institute made necessary to introduce a new element in the ERA agenda, namely, education in connection with innovation and research, that is, the knowledge triangle.

The Eighth Framework Programme, Horizon 2020, represents a yet new shift in policy focus, namely, that towards emphasising utilisation of science and introducing innovation within the same funding frame. An analysis of this shift is, however, beyond the scope of this chapter.

To summarise, the ERA agenda has proved to be a powerful instrument in integrating different policy objectives under one umbrella and has provided a useful tool to mobilise support for the adoption of new institutions and funding tools. These new tools on the whole represent an ambitious policy approach and aim to promote coordination of Member State activities and in specific cases, such as the ERC, a fully integrated pan-European funding approach.

ACKNOWLEDGEMENT

This chapter draws on the research carried out for EURECIA, "Understanding and assessing the impact and outcomes of the ERC funding schemes", a collaborative project no 229286, funded from the FP7 IDEAS programme, 1 February 2009 – 30 April 2012.

NOTES

1. Lisbon European Council 23 and 24 March, 2000.
2. The target year of the Lisbon Agenda is 2010, and the targets both in terms of R&D intensity or employment have not been achieved. The 2005 target for employment rate was set for 70 per cent, while it was 65.9 per cent in 2008, and has probably decreased as a consequence of the financial and economic crisis. The R&D intensity in the Union in 2008 was 1.9 per cent, well below the 3 per cent objective.
3. Luukkonen and Nedeva (2010) define 'integration' as the process of forming a new entity from different parts where the result is something 'composite' or 'integral'. They emphasise that integration is a dynamic process framed by a continuum from fragmentation to uniformity.
4. Research Commissioner Antonio Ruberti in 1993–94 had a vision of a "European scientific and technological space" (Banchoff 2003). Even though research ministers adopted a stand to advance such efforts, these were thwarted by the economic situation and political crisis accompanying the ratification of the Maastricht Treaty (ibid.: 87).
5. The Framework Programme emerged as an outcome of concerns about a 'technology gap' and Europe falling behind the United States and Japan in the major fields of science and technology (Caracostas 2003). The first programmes were set up in the information and communications sciences where Japan's emerging leadership in particular raised concerns.
6. According to the Lisbon Treaty, the article number is 185.
7. E.g., Caswill (2003: 67) states that the original Commission paper on the ERA was "the work of a single hand within or close to the Busquin Cabinet".
8. Later India, China, South Korea, Brazil and others have been added on the list of competitors (see Rodrigues 2002).
9. http://www.eu2008.si/en/News_and_Documents/Press_Releases/April/0415MVZT_CO MPET.html, accessed on 1 April 2014.
10. This usually means interaction between education, research and innovation, and has been emphasised by EU leaders since 2006, and a concrete manifestation of which was the European Institute of Innovation and Technology (EIT) (see section on Education on the Agenda).
11. Based on a stakeholder interview.
12. ELSF is the European Life Sciences Forum, EMBO the European Molecular Biology Organization, FEBS the Federation of Biochemical Societies.
13. There were other reports from the scientists' organisation, such as the ESF (2003), ELSF (2003) and EUROHORCS (2004, together with the European Commission), which discussed and detailed the justification and basic principles of a European Research Council.
14. EURAB, European Research Advisory Board in 2001–2004, twice took a positive stand concerning the ERC: the first issued in November 2002 was about the guiding principles of the new funding body, the second, issued in October 2003 was about its possible implementation model (EURAB 2004). EURAB is a high-level, independent, advisory committee created by the Commission to provide advice on the design and

implementation of EU research policy and whose members are nominated in a personal capacity and come from a wide range of academic and industrial backgrounds, as well as representing other societal interests.

15. http://erc.europa.eu/index.cfm?fuseaction=page.display&topicID=12, accessed on 1 April, 2014.

16. http://erc.europa.eu/index.cfm?fuseaction=page.display&topicID=12, accessed on 1 April, 2014.

17. At that time, it was the European Institute of Technology, which was later called the European Institute of Innovation and Technology by the European Parliament in 2008.

18. Regulation (EC) No 294/2008 of the European Parliament and of the Council of 11 March 2008.

19. Cf., that the ETPs and JTIs emerged as projects of European industries while the EIT first emerged as s project of the Commission.

REFERENCES

André, Michel (2007), 'The 7th Framework Programme in the history of European research', Interview in the *Magazine on European Research*, Special Edition, June 2007. http://ec.europa.eu/research/rtdinfo/special_fp7/fp7/01/article_fp709_en.html, accessed August 2015.

Banchoff, Thomas (2003), 'Political Dynamics of the ERA', in: Edler, Jakob, Stefan Kuhlmann and Maria Behrens (eds), *Changing Governance of Research and Technology Policy: The European Research Area*, Cheltenham, UK and Northampton, MA, USA: Edward Elgar, pp. 81–97.

Caracostas, Paraskevas (2003), 'Shared Governance through Mutual Policy Learning: Some Implications of the ERA Strategy for the "Open Co-ordination" of Research Policies in Europe', in Edler, Jakob, Stefan Kuhlmann and Maria Behrens (eds), *Changing Governance of Research and Technology Policy: The European Research Area*, Cheltenham, UK and Northampton MA, USA: Edward Elgar, pp. 33–63.

Caswill, Chris (2003), 'Old Games, Old Players – New Rules, New Results', in Edler, Jakob, Stefan Kuhlmann and Maria Behrens (eds), *Changing Governance of Research and Technology Policy: The European Research Area*, Cheltenham, UK and Northampton MA, USA: Edward Elgar, pp. 54–80.

den Bak, S.W. (2008), 'The Flagship Sets Sail: An Analysis of the Agenda Setting Process of the European Institute of Technology', Bachelor Thesis, Centre for Higher Education and Policy Studies, School of Management and Governance, University of Twente, The Netherlands.

Edler, Jakob (2003), 'Change in European R&D Policy as a Complex Consensus-building Process', in Edler, Jakob, Stefan Kuhlmann and Maria Behrens (eds), *Changing Governance of Research and Technology Policy: The European Research Area*, Cheltenham, UK and Northampton, MA, USA: Edward Elgar, pp. 98–132.

Edler, Jakob (2009), 'Demand Policies for Innovation in EU CEE Countries', Paper presented at the workshop Innovation for Competitiveness INCOM Prague / 22–23 January 2009.

Edler, Jakob (2010), 'International Policy Coordination for Collaboration in S&T', Manchester Business School Working Paper No 590.

Edquist, Charles (2005), 'Systems of Innovation: Perspectives and Challenges',

The Oxford Handbook of Innovation, Oxford: Oxford University Press Chapter 7, pp. 181–208.

ELSF (2003), 'European Research Council – the Life Scientist's View', *European Life Sciences Forum*, October 2003.

ERCEG (2003), 'The European Research Council – A Cornerstone in the European Research Area. Report from an Expert Group (The 'Mayor report')', *Ministry of Science, Technology and Innovation*, Denmark, December 2003.

ESF (2003), 'New Structures for the Support of High-Quality Research in Europe', A report from a High Level Working Group constituted by the European Science Foundation to review the option of creating a European Research Council, An ESF position paper, April 2003.

EURAB (2004), 'European Research Advisory Board', *Report of Activities (2001–2004)*, Brussels: European Commission.

EUROHORCS (2004), 'European Commission – EUROHORCs High Level Working Group on a European Funding Mechanism for Basic Research,' Report of the Working Group, 28 July 2004.

European Commission (2000), 'Towards a European Research Area', *Communication from the Commission to the Council, the European Parliament, the Economic and Social Committee and the Committee of the Regions, COM(2000) 6 final*, Brussels, 18 January 2000.

European Commission (2002), 'The European Research Area: Providing New Momentum – Strengthening – Reorienting – Opening up New Perspectives', *Communication from the Commission, COM(2002) 565 final*, Brussels, 16 October 2002.

European Commission (2003a), 'The Role of the Universities in the Europe of Knowledge', *Communication from the Commission, COM(2003) 58 final*, Brussels, 5 February 2003.

European Commission (2003b), 'Investing in Research: An Action Plan for Europe', *Communication from the Commission (COM(2003) 226 final/2*, Brussels 4 June 2003.

European Commission (2004a), 'Science and Technology, the Key to Europe's Future, Guidelines for Future European Union Policy to Support Research,' *Communication from the Commission COM(2004)353 final*, Brussels, 16 June 2004.

European Commission (2004b), 'Europe and Basic Research.' *Communication from the Commission, COM(2004) 9 final*, Brussels, 14 January 2004.

European Commission (2004c), *Interim Working Document on the Implementation of a Funding Mechanism for Basic Research*, from the Commission, 29 September 2004.

European Commission (2005a), Frontier Research: The European Challenge. 2005. High-Level Expert Group Report, European Commission, Brussels, February 2005.

European Commission (2005b), 'Working Together for Growth and Jobs. A New Start for the Lisbon Strategy', *Communication to the Spring European Council, COM(2995) 24 final*, Brussels, 2 February 2005.

European Commission (2007a), 'The European Research Area: New Perspectives', *Commission Staff Working Document: Accompanying the Green Paper*, COM(2007)161, Brussels, 4 April 2007, SEC(2007)412/2.

European Commission (2007b), 'Inventing our Future Together. The European Research Area: New Perspectives', *Green Paper* 04 April 2007. European Commission, EUR 22840. Luxembourg: Office for Official Publications of the European Communities, 2007.

European Commission (2008a), 'The Lisbon Treaty', *OJ/C115*, 9 May 2008.

European Commission (2008b), 'Conclusions on the Definition of a "2020 Vision for the European Research Area", Council of the European Union, Brussels, 1 and 2 December 2008.

European Commission (2009a), *The Lund Declaration: Europe Must Focus on the Grand Challenges of our Time*, July 2009.

European Commission (2009b), 'Preparing Europe for a New Renaissance, A Strategic View of the European Research Area', *First Report of the European Research Area Board – 2009*, Directorate-General for Research, EUR 23905 EN, Brussels, 2009.

European Commission (2010a), 'Europe 2020: A European Strategy for Smart, Sustainable and Inclusive Growth', *Communication from the Commission. COM(2010)2020*, Brussels, 3 March 2010.

European Commission (2010b), 'First Interim Evaluation of the ARTEMIS and ENIAC Joint Technology Initiatives', *European Commission*, 30 July 2010.

"Europe's Search for Excellence in Basic Research", *Symposium Report*, 16 February – 17 February 2004, Dublin Castle, Ireland 2004 Presidency of the European Union.

Geoghegan-Quinn, Máire (2010), 'The 2010 Guglielmo Marconi lecture at the Lisbon Council's innovation summit', 5 March 2010 http://europa.eu/rapid/pressReleasesAction.do?reference=SPEECH/10/68&format=HTML&aged=0&language=EN&guiLanguage=en, accessed 12 April 2014.

Gronbaek, David JvH. (2003), 'A European Research Council: An Idea Whose Time Has Come?', *Science and Public Policy*, 30(6): 391–404.

Guzetti, Luca (2009), 'The "European Research Area" Idea in the History of Community Policy-making', in Delanghe, Henri, Ugur Muldur and Luc Soete (eds), *European Science and Technology Policy: Towards Integration or Fragmentation?*, Cheltenham, UK and Northampton MA, USA: Edward Elgar, pp. 64–77.

Luukkonen, Terttu and Maria Nedeva (2010), 'Towards Understanding Integration in Research and Research Policy', *Research Policy*, 39(5): 674–86.

Luukkonen, Terttu (2014), 'The European Research Council and the European Research Funding Landscape', *Science and Public Policy*, 41(1): 29–43.

Mitsos, Achilleas (2004), European Commission Presentation, in 'Europe's Search for Excellence in Basic Research', Symposium, 16–17 February 2004, Dublin Castle, Ireland 2004 Presidency of the European Union.

Muldur, Ugur, Fabienne Corvers, Henru Delanghe, Jim Dratwa, Daniela Heimberger, Brian Sloan, and Sandrijn Vanslembrouck (2006), *A New Deal for an Effective European Research Policy: The Design and Impacts of the 7th Framework Programme.* Dordrecht, The Netherlands: Springer.

Nedeva, Maria (2013), 'Between the Global and the National: Organising European Science and the Establishment of the European Research Council', *Research Policy*, 42: 220–30.

Regulation (EC) No 294/2008 of the European Parliament and of the Council of 11 March 2008.

Rodrigues, Maria João (2002), 'Introduction: For a European Strategy at the Turn of the Century', in Rodrigues, Maria João (ed.), *The New Knowledge Economy in Europe: A Strategy for International Competitiveness and Social Cohesion*, Cheltenham, UK and Northampton MA, USA: Edward Elgar, pp. 1–27.

Science, Growth and Society: A new perspective. 1971. Paris, OECD (the so-called Brooks report).

Soete, Luc (2002), 'The Challenges and the Potential of the Knowledge-based Economy in a Globalised World', in Rodrigues, Maria João (ed.), *The New Knowledge Economy in Europe: A Strategy for International Competitiveness and Social Cohesion*, Cheltenham, UK and Northampton MA, USA: Edward Elgar, pp. 28–53.

Telò, Mario (2002), 'Governance and Government in the European Union: The Open Method of Coordination', in Rodrigues, Maria João (ed.), *The New Knowledge Economy in Europe: A Strategy for International Competitiveness and Social Cohesion*, Cheltenham, UK and Northampton MA, USA: Edward Elgar, pp. 242–72.

Telò, Mario (2009), 'Assessing the Implications of the Lisbon Treaty for the Lisbon Agenda', in Rodrigues, Maria João (ed.), *Europe, Globalization and the Lisbon Agenda*, Cheltenham, UK and Northampton MA, USA: Edward Elgar, pp. 272–82.

Van Dyck, Luc, and Ellen Peerenboom (2003), 'Life Sciences in the European Research Council', *Euro/Biotech/News*, No. 1, Vol. 2003.

Veillard, Patrick, 'Public-Private Partnerships to Boost Efficiency', *Europolitics/ Research*, 9 September 2009. www.europolitics.info/sectorial-policies/public-private-partnerships-to-boost-efficiency-art247288-18.html, accessed August 2011.

APPENDIX

Table 3.A1   Community-based tools and mechanisms to promote the ERA

Community-based tools	Launched before FP6	Launched in or during FP6	Launched in FP7
Collaborative research projects	STREPs	IPs, NoEs	
Mobility, training	Marie-Curie, Erasmus		
Collaboration among funding agencies		ERA-nets	
Benchmarking to promote alignment of policies towards common goals		ERAWATCH, InnoPolicy Trendchart	
Promotion of frontier research			The European Research Council

The Commission has outsourced the creation and updating of two online platforms which collect data on the Member States' progress in research and innovation policy (InnoPolicy Trendchart since 2000 and ERAWATCH since 2007). ERAWATCH pays special attention to the implementation of the ERA, the Lisbon Strategy, including the implementation of structural reforms.

Table 3.A2   Lisbon Agenda and ERA promoting tools that are in between Community-based and inter-governmental

Tools in between Community-based and inter-governmental	Launched before FP6	Launched in or during FP6	Launched in FP7
Collaboration among funding agencies			ERA-Net-Plus
Agenda-building		ETPs	
Public-private partnerships for funding large-scale research and education activities			JTIs EIT, KICs
Public-public partnerships towards integration of national-level programmes into European programmes		Art. 169 (185) Joint Programmes	
Alignment of national policies towards common goals	OMC*		ERA Joint Programming and other ERA Initiatives

* According to Rodrigues (2002) OMC is a mixture between community-based and intergovernmental tools. I have similarly classified the JTIs, Art. 169 (185) and EIT as being in between the two extremes. OMC here refers to the OMC processes related to investment in research and as practised by the Scientific and Technical Research Committee (CREST), which introduced its first OMC cycle in 2003.

4. Actor constellations in the European Funding Area

Dietmar Braun

INTRODUCTION

While the making of the European Research Area (ERA) has caused a lot of scientific debates since its inauguration in 2000, the construction of the European Funding Area (EFA) has caught less attention. This is surprising as both "areas" are intricately connected while they remain functionally differentiated: research needs financial resources continuously in order to produce new knowledge, and funding would be void without producers of knowledge. The promotion of a "world-class", competitive research area that the EU strives for must therefore go hand-in-hand with a well-functioning and supportive funding area.

In contrast to its main economic competitors – the United States, Japan and China – the European Union has, however, specific difficulties in making the most of its funding potential (Muldur, et al. 2006; Bonaccorsi 2007). While the former countries have either a unitary research and funding space (Japan) or a centralised funding structure within a federal environment (USA, China), the European Union comprises 28 different national research systems (plus a number of associated members like Switzerland, Norway and Israel), quite a few among them with an individual (successful) long-standing research and funding tradition. While in the competitor countries major funding resources for research are distributed at the national level by nationally organised funding agencies (and ministries), in Europe we find a *"multi-level funding system"* where different types of funding agencies on different territorial levels are active (Kuhlmann 2001). The "actor matrix" of the funding system in Europe is more complex than in most countries as it entails horizontal *and* vertical relationships between funding agencies. In contrast to the United States, Japan, or China, therefore, Europe must harmonise the interests of a multitude of funding actors, and overcome large asymmetries in research quality and equipment as well as in funding activities between the member countries (and associated

61

countries). The challenge is not only to find a "modus vivendi" in order to cooperate but also to overcome considerable transaction costs that are involved in the process of harmonisation and of finding a functional division of labour. Without such a balance of interests, the EFA will be subject to constant conflicts and questioning of funding claims from different agencies with obvious negative results for the promotion of the ERA.

The chapter tries to shed light on actor dynamics and conflicts in the EFA by treating it as a "multi-level governance system". The research focus is, however, limited to one sub-area of the EFA and that is research funding directed to basic research or, in other words, is "science-driven". Though the overwhelming part of research funding in the EFA is directed to strategic and applied research and "policy-driven", basic research funding has received more attention and recognition during the last ten years or so, which has led to a number of changes in funding instruments, actor constellations, and institutions. These changes are of interest in this chapter. The development of actor constellations in basic research funding will be described and actor dynamics today are analysed with the intention to understand to what extent the actor constellation can overcome fragmentation of the European funding landscape while continuing to support national funding systems.

In the following sections, we discuss funding actors and their "logic of action" and then present the governance structure in the EFA. Both dimensions together explain the actor constellation in the EFA. Next, we give an overview of the institutional development and the evolution of actor constellations in the EFA and analyse the present actor constellation. Conclusions follow.

LOGICS OF ACTION IN THE EFA

The EFA can be seen as part of the European "research space" (Nedeva 2013) being constituted by all "corporate actors" (Coleman 1990) that are involved in one way or the other in funding activities. We focus on those corporate actors that are directly responsible for the formulation and implementation of research funding policies, that is, funding agencies or funding programmes, which have obtained the status of an organisation, and in particular on those funding agencies or programmes that are involved in the support of basic research. In addition, there are other actors, from the political or the scientific system, which can influence relations between funding agencies but which will not be considered in our analysis.

With this restriction in mind we consider four types of corporate actors as relevant for actor dynamics in basic research funding in the EFA: *"first-order" actors*, that is, national funding agencies and the Commission of the European Union represented by the "Directorate General for Research and Innovation", and *"second-order" actors*, which are constituted on the basis of representation or delegation of first-order actors. One example of such second-order actors are organisations that are based on collective action of individual national actors, that is, on "transnational cooperation". An example, we will discuss later, is the European Science Foundation. A second type of the second-order actor are "agents" like the European Research Council, which has been created by the European Union in order to fulfil certain tasks in basic research funding.

In order to understand the possible "actor dynamics" – for example, tensions, conflicts, competition, cooperation – one needs to sketch the assumptions about the basic interests of funding actors.

One can start with the assumption that funding agencies in general are corporate actors with a profound interest in *maximising their budgets* (Niskanen 1971) and in *maintaining a maximum of discretion* in the determination of their funding policies (Epstein and O'Halloran 1999). In order to increase their budgets, they must impress their political "principals" in two ways: on the one hand by attempting to acquire a maximum of funding applications and on the other hand by demonstrating successful investments with their funding money, which actually means to find the best researchers and projects that offer a high probability of scientific discoveries and knowledge progress. Increasing funding applications and successful funding are the legitimate bases for asking for further increases of the budget.

If this is accepted, one can sketch possible tensions in the EFA in the following way:

The establishment of an additional, supranational level of funding to national level funding can jeopardise the basic interests of national funding agencies (NFAs), especially when it comes to the direct support of funding projects and scientists.[1] *Budget-maximising capacities* of NFAs, for example, can suffer from competition with the supranational level in two ways:

By *"crowding out"* or *"brain drain"*: This means that EU funding activities can, if they are accepted by scientists in Europe, draw away researchers from the national level and integrate them in EU projects. Though there is a certain flexibility of researchers to share their time resources between several funding projects, increasing success of EU funding may nevertheless lead researchers to focus more and more on the supranational level in order to get their funds instead of on the national level. This can happen either if the EU offers more generous resources than one can find at the national level or if the "reputation gain" of EU projects would be much higher than scientists could gain at the national level.

By *"substitution of the budget"*: National research budgets usually entail a part for support of EU funding and a part that sustains its national funding agencies. Because these shares are paid out of the same portfolio, conflicts in the distribution of research money can arise. This is the case if political actors start to compare funding activities of the EU and NFAs and would reduce funding money for NFAs because the EU is doing similar activities. Or if they would consider investments into EU funding as more promising in terms of research output than one can expect from the NFAs. Both decisions indicate rational behaviour of political actors: in the first case they aim for a reduction of research expenditures and in the second case they create better conditions to legitimise their spending in research funding. In both cases NFAs lose part of their budget and one can expect strategies of NFAs to prevent such a situation.

The *discretion* of NFAs could be endangered by claims of the EU authority rights in the same activity fields the NFAs are working in. This can lead to an open competence struggle within the EFA.

The EU, on the other hand, can suffer of course in a similar way from crowding out and brain drain effects if it competes directly in the same research fields and research modes (basic or strategic/applied) with the NFAs. Researchers can decide to not accept the offers by the EU and stay at the national level for funding applications, especially if transaction costs of obtaining funds at the EU level are very high, resources are not outbidding what NFAs have to offer, and reputation gain would be in doubt.

The NFAs and the EU have therefore latent competitive relationships with each other, though this does not mean that competition must dominate the interaction between both corporate actors. Governance structures are an important intervening variable here and can mitigate such latent tensions, for example by distributing authority rights in such a way that funding activities become more complementary or cooperative than competitive (see below).

The NFAs and the EU are, as already mentioned, the first-order actors in the basic science part of the EFA. They are, however, not the only actors. While these actors are confronted with each other in *"vertical"* relations, simply by executing their funding activities on the national level on the one hand and on the supranational level on the other hand, they also meet on the *"horizontal"*, supranational level.

NFAs can appear as individual actors on the supranational level, for example, by concluding bilateral or multilateral contracts with other NFAs, but they can also combine forces and organise collective action in *"transnational organisations"*. The EU, on the other hand, can have its own activities of funding in basic science, for example, within the Framework Programmes or in the "Marie-Curie"-Programme, or it can delegate part of this funding activity to an "agent", in this case the European Research Council. How can we briefly describe the "logics of action" of these two "second-order" actors?

Collective action by NFAs on the supranational level in the form of networks, programmes, or organisations is a rational strategy of NFAs, as it allows them to achieve some of the advantages of supranational funding without, however, being obliged to lose discretion by delegating such action to the EU. Transnational organisation allows "voice" in decision-making on the supranational level and "exit" from cooperation and is as such the preferred strategy of any NFA. Such advantages are for example the reduction of transaction costs in organising cross-border research, cost pooling in setting up research infrastructure, and "capacity-building" in the EFA by exchange of information and coordination of funding strategies. Transnational cooperation can also be used to organise funding in research areas that are not taken into account by other organisations on the horizontal level. Moreover, transnational cooperation of NFAs has the obvious advantage of being able to integrate the knowledge about national circumstances and problems when setting up funding schemes and instruments. And last but not least there are additional funding resources that are flowing in favour of transnational cooperative research projects of scientists.

The advantage in terms of corporate actor interests of NFAs is, as said, that they maintain a substantial veto-position in decisions of the transnational network, programme, or organisation and that they have the possibility to "exit" if they see their interests jeopardised by collective decisions.[2] This is, however, at the same time also a weakness for the sustainability and effectiveness of such forms of cooperation: transnational cooperation in funding must face a considerable uncertainty with regard to the continuing support of its members. The amounts of money flowing to the supranational level may moreover be restricted: NFAs may not be willing – or are restricted by domestic budget rules defined by national governments – to spend too much money in an enterprise that competes with funding activities on the national level and which is characterised by uncertainties about the "return" for the reputation of the NFA.

Intermediary agencies, the last type of actor we find in the EFA, are usually created by one corporate actor in order to delegate some activities that can be better done by such an "agent" than by the actor himself (Braun 1993, 2003). The organisational form of an intermediary agency allows for relative freedom to define action (operational autonomy) and also in many cases to formulate policies, though it depends to what extent the principal is willing to grant this right.

Intermediary agencies in research funding are standing in between science and the principal and are obliged to both of them (Braun 1993). In fact, scientists often have a decisive voice within such an organisation. However, they depend, as do the NFAs, which are intermediary agencies themselves, on finding legitimacy with their principal and must therefore, in a similar way as do NFAs and the EU, focus on strategies of budget maximising and autonomy seeking. They must demonstrate to their principal that their creation has been worthwhile and that it contributes to the "well-being" of the principal, that they use money in an efficient way, and that they are successful.

In sum, actor constellations in the EFA have a potential for conflict. They have a complex structure because they entail a vertical and a horizontal level and – in the case of basic research funding – because four different types of actors with partly competing interests constitute the EFA. It remains to be seen what actor dynamics unfold in the EFA under such actor constellation, whether it leads to confrontation or to more integration. An intervening variable here are governance structures.

GOVERNANCE STRUCTURES

Governance structures are an intervening factor in the struggle for interests by attributing authority rights to actors. Authority rights mean the right to act and decide in certain policy matters (see also Whitley et al. 2010). They distribute therefore the legitimacy for actors to decide how to act in such policy matters. In principle, one can distinguish between three ways to govern the vertical and horizontal relations in the EFA, that is, in a competitive, complementary, or cooperative way.

In the case of *competitive governance*, the EU and the NFA have authority to fund in the same research fields, use the same instruments and apply the same criteria of funding. This has obvious advantages for researchers, as they profit from plural sources of funding and increased funding resources. It may also contribute to more efficiency and effectiveness in funding in general as both corporate actors have an incentive to improve their funding instruments and procedures in order to demonstrate the superiority of own funding in the EFA. Competitiveness also introduces, however, incentives to marginalise the other side and expand their own sphere of influence at the cost of the other side. Tensions and frictions between the NFAs and the EU and even between NFAs themselves are a corollary of competitive relationships. NFAs have few interests in such competitive relationships, because as isolated individual organisations they have difficulty competing with the supranational organisation EU and as a "transnational actor", that is, in collective action together with other NFAs, it may be difficult to establish the necessary consensus to act in a united way vis-à-vis the EU.

Complementary governance, by contrast, is a governance form which avoids duplication of authority rights and insists on labour division within the EFA: authority rights are distributed in such a way that activity fields are distinguished from one another in order to avoid confrontation and friction. The delimitation of such fields is, however, often difficult and blurring boundaries belong to such a type of authority distribution. The advantage for researchers is that funding activities are multiplied across different kinds of activities and it becomes easier to find support for specific research activities. An example is the support for cross-border research cooperation financed by the EU, which was a new element in the nationally fragmented landscape of the EFA. Complementary governance is conceived to avoid duplication, overlapping and inefficient spending, and unnecessary conflicts between funding actors, and to protect the "lower" territorial levels and their funding activities ("subsidiarity" is the term used in order to describe this form of governance). It does not, however, give incentives for improvement of funding procedures and it may lead to higher transaction costs linked to struggles about the delimitation of funding activities.

Cooperative governance, finally, attempts to join forces between the NFAs and the EU and coordinate funding activities in such a way that synergetic effects become possible, for example by putting resources and knowledge together in order to organise funding on the European level (take as an example the European Space Agency). It can be a way to overcome negative effects of competitive relations or avoid conflicts in the case of blurring boundaries of authority in complementary governance. Joint action also promotes mutual learning and increases the collective potential to act. Tensions between funding actors can be better avoided. An obvious problem of cooperative governance is to find a consensus between the two sides, especially if funding instruments come into conflict with national funding interests. Transaction costs may be high.

These governance forms can play a role both in vertical and horizontal relations and lead to different dynamics of conflict and consensus and to different implications for the funding of research in the EFA. It is not excluded that they exist together as different funding instruments may be based on different governance relationships, which adds to the already existent complexity of horizontal and vertical relations between large numbers of actors.

In the following sections we analyse the actor dynamics in the basic science part of the EFA on the base of a description of actors, interests, and governance structures, provide the historical development of actor constellations in the basic science part of the EFA, and discuss the relationships in the EFA today.

EVOLUTION OF BASIC RESEARCH FUNDING IN THE EFA

The historical development in actor constellations within the basic science part of the EFA can be seen as consisting of two main periods: a) a period with a monopoly of one transnational organisation, whereby basic research funding becomes more advanced but competition remains on a low level; and b) a period that started with the creation of the ERC.

Science-driven or basic research on the supranational level of the EFA has for a long time been exclusively a matter of one transnational organisation, the *European Science Foundation* (ESF), founded in 1974 (for a general and more extensive overview of historical developments in the EFA, see Georghiou 2001; Kuhlmann and Edler 2003; Nedeva 2013). Its establishment can be seen as a reaction to funding initiatives of national governments in policy-driven or applied research funding (Georghiou 2001). Founding members of the ESF were scientific organisations (scientific academies, public research organisations) and national funding agencies. Seventy-eight such organisations have signed as members, each one paying a contribution that finances the activities of the ESF. The "Assembly", in which all members are represented, decides on activities. The "Governing Council" sets, approves, directs and monitors the strategic direction and is composed of one representative from each national group of member organisations. The intention to found such an organisation was similar to other transnational initiatives: the cooperation in research on the European level became a concern because national boundaries were increasingly felt as a restriction of scientific developments by researchers. Lack of critical mass in many disciplines, partly insufficient funding resources, and developing cross-border networks of scientists all contributed to the interest of scientists in European countries to have a supranational funding level.

Since the beginning, the intention of the founding members of the EFA was, however, also to establish a concern for the interests of basic research on the European level at all, something which no other agency had taken into account in the beginning days of the EFA. The ESF filled a gap in this respect.

Funding was considered to be a bottom-up activity, though the ESF later introduced framework programmes with general topics of interest. Research that was funded by the ESF was clearly fundamental with no application in mind. Transnational networks in research were seen, like in the case of EU funding, as an added value to national funding. The ESF did not, however, finance research on the base of own funding budgets – this would have meant the creation of a relatively autonomous European funding agency. Funding agencies in individual countries had, each time a funding project was selected, to decide whether they wanted to support the research projects. The authority of funding decisions remained therefore at the country level. Thus, the ESF only took the responsibility of organising the funding process. Researchers, then, were obliged to undergo the usual funding procedures in each participating country. This meant uncertainty for researchers about the funding of cooperation projects and considerable transaction costs, though over the course of time some of the national funding agencies accepted the decision of the ESF about suitable research projects as a final decision and accorded money without further inspection. This was, however, by no means always the case and therefore the planned composition of collaborative projects could be seriously curtailed in the aftermath of national funding decisions.

The ESF had developed a couple of funding instruments directed to collaborative research but also to "foresight activities", an activity which filled a gap on the supranational level.

One notices that the construction of the ESF corresponds to what one can expect with regard to a transnational form of cooperation: members of the ESF were not prepared – or only after some time and only to a certain degree – to abandon their decision-making rights in funding matters. Membership was voluntary and could be cancelled. The sums of money at the disposition of the ESF for organisation and support for coordination activities of scientists remained modest (about €40 million before the decision to wind down the ESF was taken in December 2014).

Science-driven research on the European level was strengthened in the 1990s by the creation of EUROHORCS ("European Heads of Research Councils") by basic science-oriented funding agencies. It should have a complementary mission to ESF activities. In fact, its creation demonstrated that the ESF did not fulfil all expectations of its members. The main mission of EUROHORCS was to lobby for a stronger role of science-oriented funding on the European level. Later on, it also started to invest in funding – together with the ESF – by setting up one research instrument, the EURYI ("European Young Investigator Award"), which was supposed to support young and excellent researchers. This project was quickly abandoned when the ERC was founded in 2007 and based its funding activities in part on this target group. The funding instrument was chosen to complement existing funding activities of the ESF. It neverthe-less demonstrates that the ESF was no longer the only organisation that should be responsible for all funding activities of interest to the NFAs.

EUROHORCS was dissolved in 2011 and became – together with a large number of basic science research organisations – *"Science Europe"*. The main intentions of EUROHORCS remain virulent in this new organ-isation: the strengthening of the role of basic research on the European level and the development of funding and research capacities through-out the ERA. Funding activities are not foreseen anymore, however. The creation of Science Europe was the outcome of conflicts between members within the ESF about funding strategies and general activities for the promotion of basic science research on the supranational level. It led finally, in 2014, to the decision to wind down the ESF by abandon-ing its research and policy activities and only to continue to work with a number of expert boards and committees, which are supposed to give scientific expertise in different areas. In fact, the ESF has ceased to exist as a funding agency.

The position of the ESF as a monopolist was already weakened to some extent by the activities of other agencies on the supranational level since the 1990s. Funding in the framework of the COST programme, for example, demonstrated increasing openness to "exploratory research", though its basic mission is policy-driven and intends to contribute to Europe's competitiveness and socio-economic development. The EU had started its funding activities with the intention to strengthen the "scientific and technological bases of Community industry and encouraging it to become more competitive at the international level" (quoted in Gronbaek 2003: 394) and bases its legitimacy in research funding until today mainly on the fulfilment of this objective, though general problems of society have in the 1990s become an additional focus of interest. It is especially in the framework of such problems that basic research topics could become part of funded projects. Basic science projects were also part of the mobility enhancement programme "Marie Curie" of the EU for younger scientists.

Because of the expansion of the EU funding to the basic science part, there was now a potential danger for "crowding out", that is, the loss of interested scientists for ESF programmes, but such dangers did not lead to any confrontation or unwanted dynamics in the basic science part of the EFA. First, both the EU and COST did not consider their funding as an integral part of basic science funding and did not intend to compete with such programmes for reputation with the ESF. Second, neither of the amounts of funding of ESF or COST and the EU for basic science projects were so large that a crowding out effect could have taken place. In addition, the ESF started, as did COST and the EU, to define Framework Programmes (the EUROCORES programmes), which gave room to distinguish also thematically the funding of the three agencies. Participation of the EU in assemblies of the ESF and COST and of the ESF in COST helped to present and discuss funding programmes and, if need be, to adjust the contents to some extent. EU funding had, however, the advantages, in comparison to the two transnational organisations, that it granted itself the money and that curtailing of parts of the cooperative projects could be avoided. Transaction costs existed, however, because of cumbersome and bureaucratic application procedures. Overall, one can state that the actor constellation in the second period, which lasted from the beginning of the 1990s to 2007, was relatively peaceful because no actor contested the position of the other and competition, though potentially there, remained on a low level, both vertically and horizontally.

The creation of the ERC in 2007 signifies a third period in actor dynamics in the EFA, which still exists. The next section analyses in detail actor dynamics during this, the current, period.

ACTOR CONSTELLATION IN THE EFA TODAY

What are the relations between actors today? How can we describe the governance structure? In order to answer these questions we will look at the "actor triangle" that is constituted by the three agencies and discuss each of the different relationships in this triangle: the relationship between the NFAs and the EU, the relationship between the EU and the ERC, and the relationship between the ERC and the NFAs.

The Relationship between NFAs and Their Organisations on the One Hand and the EU on the Other

With the adoption of the "Ideas Programme" as part of the Seventh Framework Programme, the EU acknowledged for the first time its willingness to fund basic research, or, in the terms of the programme, "frontier research".[3] The Ideas Programme is therefore the institutionalisation of EU funding in the basic science part of the EFA. But even then the EU insists on research funding that contributes to "wealth and social progress" (EU 2006, Annex 1). The mental step the EU has taken is to recognise that fundamental or frontier research can be a "key driver" (ibid.) in achieving this.[4] Frontier research, it is said, is at the base of "new opportunities for scientific and technological advance" and "is instrumental in producing new knowledge leading to future applications and markets" (ibid.). The basic philosophy of the EU concerning research funding has therefore not changed but has enlarged the spectrum of instruments one can use to achieve the basic objectives.

At the same time, the EU has declared its willingness to not use such funding to "replace national funding". The funding in the framework of the Ideas Programme should be *in addition to* national funding. It is supposed to above all create a *competitive European-wide funding structure* but not enter into competition with the NFAs. Competition is seen – as the ERC Scientific Council states (ERC 2011) – as an excellency mechanism that would enhance creativity of researchers and, hence, effectiveness. It is the primary step in developing a prospering ERA followed later on by "coordinated, mission-orientated initiatives" (p. 2). The advantage of European-level funding in this respect is supposed to "be able to draw on a wider pool of talents and ideas than would be possible for any national scheme" (ibid.).

ERC activities do not indeed replace funding activities on the national level but there can be disturbing aspects for the NFAs as we have already noted, that is, the competition for reputation and for the best researchers. The EU brings in additional funding[5] for researchers but it puts pressure on the NFAs by its intentions to set benchmarks for funding, its growing prestige in funding and by its search for the best researchers in the EU. This can be a potential for future conflicts.

Despite these developments the Commission, in particular the Directorate General of Research and Innovation, has never lost its reputation as a funding actor that remains "political" and hence applied-oriented. This is why the NFAs have a profound distrust of the EU and its intentions with regard to the future status of the ERC and to the development of basic research in general. This explains the attempts – despite declarations of the EU and its "turn" concerning the value of basic science – to create a strong "political organisation" like EUROHORCS and then "Science Europe", which can directly defend the interests of the basic science community in the EFA against possible encroachments of the EU or against a degradation of the status of basic research funding compared to other funding activities.

The relationship between the NFAs and the EU is potentially full of tensions. This does not exclude that they find an agreement on the way to set up the EFA. The creation of the ERC can perhaps already count as such an implicit agreement that can satisfy both interests. We will return to this point below.

The Relationship between the EU and the European Research Council

The ERC – organised in the form of a "Scientific Council" and a "European Research Council Executive Agency" as the executing administration – is the organisation which is supposed to manage the "Ideas" programme of the EU. Theoretically, the EU can decide every six years to change its agenda in this respect. Until now, however, it has confirmed its intention to continue the financing of the ERC at least until the end of the Eighth Framework Programme in 2020. The "Horizon 2020" budget signifies a 77 per cent increase of the ERC budget. It seems unlikely that such an enterprise would be reversed in the future because:

- being a budget maximiser, the EU has an interest to remain a "full-fledged funder" in Europe and even to further widen its portfolio. Basic science serves this aim;
- the EU has recognised the importance – at least this is the narrative – of basic research for welfare and growth;
- one can trust the effects of path dependency and of possible "sunk costs" that are involved in the dismantling of the ERC: the longer the ERC exists, the more difficult it will become – above all if it is successful – to dismantle this organisation. Many actors who profit from the ERC today will rise as defenders of the organisation.

We are here only interested in the relationship between the Directorate General for Research and Innovation of the EU, responsible for research funding, and the newly set-up agency. As already indicated, this relationship is most important for understanding the actor dynamics in the "actor triangle". Given that the relations between the EU and the NFAs are burdened by certain mistrust, the ERC could obtain the status of an agency that can possibly mediate between all sides and contribute to "pacification" in relationships.

The ERC is an intermediary agency, as are most national funding agencies (Luukkonen 2011). This means that it must bridge political interests and scientific interests. With the recognition of the Commission, represented by the Directorate General of Research and Innovation, of the inherent advantages of the funding of frontier research for the general welfare of the EU, it seems that the bridging is not too difficult a task. Possible encroachments by the Commission seem to be limited. The EU stance of *"policy at a distance"* is expressed in the formal construction of the ERC:

> The ERC is a delegated agency according to EU Law (Art. 55) with the right to implement "all or part" of Community programmes or projects "on behalf

of the Commission and under its responsibility" (EU 2008: 3). The delegation entails explicitly that the "Scientific Council" acts in an independent way "according to the principle of scientific excellence, autonomy, efficiency, transparency, and accountability" (EU 2006). The Commission has the task to guarantee the "autonomy and integrity" of the ERC.

All administrative executive tasks are taken over by the Executive Agency. The role of the Commission is to pay attention that the ERC respects in its work the "principles of scientific excellence, autonomy, efficiency, and transparency"; it must adopt the work programmes and the financing decisions that are prepared by the ERC; take care of the interim evaluation and represent the Commission in a "Programme Committee" which is set up to support the Commission before it adopts the annual work programme of the ERC. It is composed of "representatives from all EU Member States". The Programme Committee is also a kind of mediation committee that helps to solve differences "in substance between the Commission and the position of the Scientific Council" (see ERC Glossary, "Programme Committee"; http://erc.europa.eu/glossary/8/letterp).

The Commission has therefore the role of a "principal" of the ERC as it remains responsible for the use of EU money, has to assess and defend the political implications of ERC funding, and makes sure that the ERC respects the agreed-upon principles of "good conduct" and the objectives of funding. It does not interfere with the development of the ERC funding programme nor with the funding decisions but, being the responsible agency before the European Council, it must adopt the general work programme and the funding decisions ex post. This gives some leverage to intervene but not on the grounds of political objectives. Even if there are disagreements, the Commission cannot just interfere and decide otherwise but it needs again an intermediating Programme Committee to accommodate differences. In this sense the Programme Committee functions like a "political board" in the "control arena" of funding agencies, as an "interface between the funding agencies and its environment" (Braun 1998: 815). All in all, this makes for a relatively autonomous position of the ERC in its funding policy.

Possible tensions between the ERC and the Commission are moreover not very likely, as the ERC does not decide on "programmatic funding". It does not fund specific research programmes, which could lead to confrontations in priority setting between the Commission and the ERC. The funding instruments are directed to a type of funding (frontier research), which does not allow for political interpretation once the principle as such is accepted.

This explains why political interests are not yet communicated in a stronger way in the "control arena": instruments are until now accepted as they are and are not contested. These instruments do not, however, lend themselves to manipulation in terms of policy preferences. This, however, can change and the Commission can of course insist on other types of instruments to be developed. Demands for the development of project funding can be brought in. The exercise of influence of the Commission is therefore, on the basis of the existing organisation structure, possible but at the moment not opportune.

In sum, the ERC seems to be well protected until 2020 to develop an independent science-driven funding of basic research.

Uncertainties about a possible "capture" of the ERC by political considerations do, however, remain because of:

- the still temporary status of the ERC as part of the Framework Programmes, which needs to be re-instated every six years, though it is not very likely that this will change, as we stated above;
- the formal possibility of the Commission to contest the funding instruments and to demand other instruments;
- possible financing problems, which could lead to selection and choices other than scientific ones;
- capture by "policy-driven" intentions, which remains an option because of the formal proximity of the ERC to the EU.

On the other hand there are only few principal-agent problems, for example "moral hazard", which indicates that the "agent", that is, the ERC, would not work in the interest of the "principal", because the Commission has no clearly defined action programme for the management of basic science funding. The criteria to be respected by the ERC correspond partly to scientific values (excellence) or are part of "good government" (transparency, accountability). Both do not disturb the possibilities of the ERC to function as a scientifically recognised funding agency – which is an essential condition to obtain high reputation among scientists. In fact, this recognition serves the EU well because only by recognition of scientists can all further objectives of "capacity-building" be achieved. The discretion of the ERC in funding decisions is therefore instrumental for the EU. This must be understood in order to see why the Commission can accept this arrangement and abstain from its traditional interventionism. This also creates some optimism for scientists.

The Relationship between NFAs and the ERC

The ERC is part of the European Union but does not represent it. It disposes of "delegated authority" and discretion. Its main focus is on the promotion of excellence in science and the development of the European Research Area, with positive spillovers for all countries and for all NFAs. Its distance to the Commission makes the ERC a credible part of the "science-driven" funding community and creates affinities with the interests of the NFAs.

In order to understand the relationship between the NFAs and the ERC, one should consider the distinction of vertical and horizontal relationships. Relationships differ in this respect. Horizontal relations are relatively harmonious in one respect and that is that both the NFAs and their transnational organisations and the ERC stand for a "science-driven" way of funding in the EFA. Here, both are possible allies. There are other arguments for a rather peaceful co-existence on this level: the ERC can reduce transaction costs in the setting up of coordination and can avoid collective action problems that arise when the NFAs have to group together and find a consensus on the setting of strategies on the European level. The disadvantage is that the NFAs do not have any direct influence in the decisions of the ERC. It is the scientific community which runs the ERC. This may protect the interests of basic science – and the NFAs support this – but it does not take into account the corporate interests of funding agencies that have to compete in the EFA.

The ERC has a specific programme of funding instruments that has been developed without official voice by the NFAs. Partly, it has taken into account ideas from the NFAs, when for example they copied the EURYI programme in the form of the "Starter Grants". All instruments are developed within the ERC and are discussed in the Programme Committee with the Commission (and other representatives from European countries). The NFAs do not officially participate here. They are lacking therefore the possibility to influence the way the EFA in basic science is set up.

The only alternative for the NFAs is then to use their own means if they want to influence the development of the EFA. Until recently such a way has been the use of the ESF and its various funding programmes. This option has been abandoned and no alternative has yet been presented. The remaining way to organise transnational cooperation is in the fashion of "variable geometry" (for example cooperation in the framework of the EU programme "ERA-NET" or by setting up regionally limited transnational programmes of cooperation like the German-Austrian-Swiss "DACH" programme). "Regional cooperation" built for special occasions (for example, for certain disciplines) and with a small group of NFAs is an option that guarantees discretion[6] to the NFA and raises the chances to increase the individual budgets. Moreover, it can reduce some of the transaction costs of cross-border cooperation and can have some importance for capacity-building in the EFA, for example by setting good practices and benchmarks for other funding agencies. Its scope is, however, still limited, as only few of such cooperation forms exist in the EFA.

CONCLUSIONS

The analysis of the current actor constellation reveals that there are dynamics in force that strengthen supranational funding in the basic science part of the EFA. The interesting point is that this does not automatically mean a stronger role for the EU Commission. The construction of an intermediary agency like the ERC, which is typical for basic science funding systems, brings in a different governance element that does not fit easily into the dividing line of supranational and national funding.

In order to grasp at the dynamics of such an actor constellation, one can distinguish between two conflict dimensions that characterise the European Funding Area: vertical relations entail a national and a supranational funding dimension, and on the horizontal, supranational level exists a distinction between the policy-driven and the science-driven part of funding.

In Figure 4.1 we have sketched these two conflict dimensions and situated the kind of funding that is taking place in the EFA:

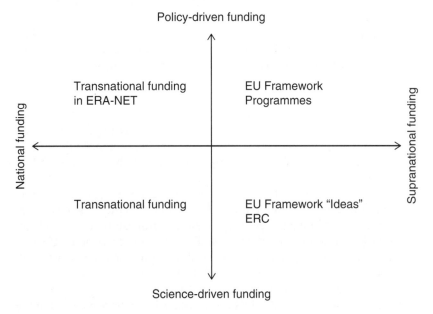

Figure 4.1   Conflict dimensions in the EFA

If we look at the *vertical* dimension, the ERC is both an ally and a competitor for NFAs. They both have an interest in the development and strengthening of the ERA. Despite these ideological affinities, there are continuing latent tensions because of possible crowding out and substitution mechanisms. The point is that the ERC is a "corporate actor", that is, an actor which has to defend its interests of organisational survival and its position within an actor constellation where a large number of actors fight for advantages. A natural tendency under these conditions is not only to maintain its position but also to enlarge the scope of action and resources as well as reputation. If this is the case it should affect the interests of NFAs.

It would, for example, come as a surprise if the ERC obtained gradually increasing resources to invest (which is already the case) and if a permanent expansion of its instrument set took place. The more successful the ERC becomes, the more leeway there is to develop further action. The first signs of such tendencies are the expansion from two to four funding instruments in the Eighth Framework Programme. The main point "of no return" would be the acquisition of the right to do project funding instead of "people funding" which the ERC favours at the moment. This would enlarge the scope of action exponentially, open up all doors to a differentiation into many more instruments, and intensify the competition with NFAs for researchers and resources considerably.

This might not yet be an important or salient point of discussion, but the more resources the ERC will have at its disposal and the more instruments will be implemented, the more competition will play a role. This can lead to serious tensions. The ERC is clearly a supranational actor and not a national actor. The role of an intermediary agency does not matter on the vertical dimension confronting national and supranational actors. On the contrary, the similarity in the organisational set-up and the anchoring in the ideology of basic research funding make the ERC a serious competitor because it is recognised in a similar way as the NFAs by scientists.

If we then take a look at the *horizontal* funding dimension, one can state that here the ERC is both an ally of NFAs and a "buffer" against forces in the EU that defend a policy-driven view in European funding. Both are promoting basic science funding in the EFA. In this sense the ERC is not playing against but with the NFAs while also accommodating the EU with the funding of the basic science part of the EFA.

Funding relations on the horizontal dimension between the EU and the ERC on the one hand, and NFAs on the other hand, have changed in the new actor constellation.

Transnational funding in the form of an organisation like the ESF, however, seems to belong to the past. "Science Europe" is at the moment a pure "political organisation" not intending to set up its own funding programmes but to contribute to "capacity-building" by its own analysis and also by acting as a forum among NFAs about funding policies, instruments, and strategies. The remaining part of the ESF goes in the same direction. This constellation at the moment means that the occasional, often temporary and geographically limited type of funding becomes the only option for the NFAs to undertake their own transnational funding activities.

Such a system still gives sufficient legitimacy for NFAs to continue their work at home – the EU claims not to "replace national funding" – but the role of the NFAs in funding activities in the EFA is seriously reduced. The EFA can still be considered to be a mix of transnational and supranational funding, but the transnational funding part is becoming more limited. It is the ERC which becomes the centre of funding actions in the basic science part of the EFA, which also signifies a tendency towards centralisation and monopolisation, accompanied by limited and occasional "regional cooperation".

This system gives the ERC a large burden to carry. If the existing delegated authority is undermined and capture by the EU takes place, the basic science part of the EFA would become more and more dominated by policy-driven intentions as the NFAs and their allies would then lack organisational forms that could set a counterweight to such developments.

A final question is why we see these centripetal tendencies in funding, the abandoning of transnational funding intentions by NFAs. A large part of this must be explained by a constellation, which is typical in "territorially divided systems", that is, by the heterogeneity of member states in a federal country or here of different national funding agencies.

The "science-driven funding alliance" is not only heterogeneous in the types of actors that are participating (scientific disciplines, scientific academies, research organisations, NFAs) but also in the types of funding agencies. Research and funding systems differ widely in Eastern, Southern, and Northern Europe. So do funding cultures. The still developing East European countries in the EU depend to a larger extent on EU support than do the Northern ones. The "state-led" funding systems in Southern Europe often follow different funding philosophies than those in Northern Europe. One can therefore not speak of a united front of NFAs that defends "its" position against the supranational level. Some NFAs, the more successful ones, insist on their autonomy and capacity to self-organise funding on the transnational level, while others count on the EU to ameliorate their funding and research systems. This heterogeneity in interest may very well have been at the heart of the discussion about the functioning and role of the ESF. Finally, it seems that fragmentation of interests has led to a rupture in the science-driven alliance of NFAs.

In sum, both tendencies – the increasing competition in vertical relations with a more prominent share in funding activities by the ERC and the trend towards monopolisation in horizontal relations – suggest that the EFA is heading for a "normalisation" compared to its main competitors: with a dominant role of a major intermediary funding agency at the central level in basic research funding. These dynamics imply medium- and long-term changes for the role of NFAs in the EFA, as these centripetal forces challenge the role and significance of national level of funding. It remains to be seen how the NFAs will react to this challenge, either individually or collectively.

NOTES

1. While other funding instruments like the support of research infrastructure offer mutual advantages in the form of "cost pooling".
2. The strife for maximum discretion can also limit the possible forms of transnational cooperation. The creation of an intermediary agency, an "agent", will probably be seen more as a liability than an asset because such agencies profit from relative autonomy in operational decision-making and need a firm and guaranteed financial support. Both features jeopardise the discretion of NFAs.
3. Frontier research is defined as excellent basic research, which is conducted at the frontiers of existing knowledge. It is supposed to open up new avenues for future research and therefore contribute to further innovation.
4. Nedeva (2013) makes clear that the EU Commission did not strive for occupying the basic science funding space. Obviously, it was not part of the "identity" of the EU. After intense lobbying above all from the life sciences a "conceptual shift" seems to have taken place and basic research was recognised as an essential precondition for the welfare of the EU and for the competitiveness of the European region (see also Banchoff 2003; Edler 2003; Gronbaek 2003, for the early discussions on the origins of the ERC).
5. Up to €80 billion planned for the budget period 2014–2020, in which €25 billion are only for the "strengthening of the EU's position in science" (http://ec.europa.eu/research/horizon2020/index_en.cfm?pg=h2020).
6. Though some discretion usually must be sacrificed in order to reduce transaction costs, for example by giving priority to one agency in one country to decide on the cooperation. However, this is not a necessary condition.

REFERENCES

Banchoff, Thomas (2003), "Political Dynamics of the ERA", in Edler, Jakob, Stefan Kuhlmann and Maria Behrens (eds), *Changing Governance of Research and Technology Policy: The European Research Area*, Cheltenham, UK and Northampton, MA, USA: Edward Elgar, pp. 81–97.

Bonaccorsi, Andrea (2007), "Explaining Poor Performance of European Science: Institutions versus Policies", *Science and Public Policy* 34(5), 303–16.

Braun, Dietmar (1993), "Who Governs Intermediary Agencies? Principal-Agent Relations in Research Policy-Making", *Journal of Public Policy* 13(2), 135–62.

Braun, D. (1998), 'The Role of Funding Agencies in the Cognitive Development of Science' *Research Policy* 27:807–21.

Braun, Dietmar (2003), "Lasting Tensions in Research Policy-Making – A Delegation Problem", *Science and Public Policy* 30(5), 309–21.

Coleman, James S. (1990), *Foundations of Social Theory*, Cambridge, MA, and London: Belknap Press of Harvard University Press.

Edler, Jakob (2003), "Change in European R&D Policy as a Complex Consensus-building Process", in Edler, Jakob, Stefan Kuhlmann and Maria Behrens, *Changing Governance of Research and Technology Policy: The European Research Area*, Cheltenham, UK and Northampton MA, USA: Edward Elgar, pp. 98–132.

Epstein, David and Sharyn O'Halloran (1999), *Delegating Powers. A Transaction Cost Politics Approach to Policy Making under Separate Powers*, Cambridge: Cambridge University Press.

ERC (2011), "Statement by the ERC Scientific Council to the Consultation on the European Research Area Framework. European Research Council", Brussels, European Research Council. http://erc.europa.eu/sites/default/files/document/file/111130_draft_ERA_Framework_ERC_-Scientific_Council.pdf.

EU (2006), Council Decision of 19 December 2006 concerning the specific programme: "Ideas" implementing the Seventh Framework Programme of the European Community for research, technological development and demonstration activities (2007 to 2013). (2006/972/EC). European Union. Brussels, Official Journal of the European Union. http://eur-lex.europa.eu/LexUriServ/LexUriServ.do?uri=OJ:L:2006:400:0243:0271:EN:PDF.

EU (2008), Commission Decision of 8/X/2008 delegating powers to the European Research Council Executive Agency with a view to performance of tasks linked to implementation of the specific programme Ideas in the field of research comprising in particular implementation of appropriations entered in the Community budget. Brussels, 8/X/2008 C(2008) 5694 final. European Union. Brussels, http://erc.europa.eu/sites/default/files/document/file/comm_c_2008_5694_f_en.doc.

Georghiou, L. (2001), "Evolving Frameworks for European Collaboration in Research and Technology", *Research Policy* 30(6), 891–903.

Gronbaek, David JvH. (2003), "A European Research Council: An Idea Whose Time has Come?", *Science and Public Policy* 30(6), 391–404.

Kuhlmann, Stefan (2001), "Future Governance of Innovation Policy in Europe – Three Scenarios", *Research Policy* 30, 953–76.

Kuhlmann, Stefan and Jakob Edler (2003), "Changing Governance in European Research and Technology", in Edler, Jakob, Stefan Kuhlmann and Maria Behrens (eds), *Changing Governance of Research and Technology Policy. The European Research Area*, Cheltenham, UK and Northampton, MA, USA: Edward Elgar, pp. 3–32.

Luukkonen, Terttu (2011), "The ERC and the European Research Funding Landscape", *EURECIA Funding Project (Understanding and Assessing the Impact and Outcomes of the ERC FundingSchemes), 18-10-2011*, Helsinki, Research Institute of the Finnish Economy: 43.

Muldur, Ugur, Fabienne Corvers, Henri Delanghe, Jim Dratwa, Daniela Heimberger,

Brian Sloan and Sandrijn Vanslembrouck (2006), *A New Deal for an Effective European Research Policy*, Dordrecht: Springer.

Nedeva, Maria (2013), "Between the Global and the National: Organising European Science", *Research Policy* 42(1), 220–30.

Niskanen, William A. (1971), *Bureaucracy and Representative Government*, Chicago: Aldine.

Whitley, Richard, Jochen Gläser and Lars Engwall (2010), *Reconfiguring Knowledge Production: Changing Authority Relationships in the Sciences and their Consequences for Intellectual Innovation*, Oxford, UK: Oxford University Press.

5. Executive governance of European science – technocratic, segmented, and path dependent?

Åse Gornitzka

INTRODUCTION

Realising the political visions for a common European science space depends on building a robust governance system. This in turn requires executive capacity supporting the initiation and preparation of policy, as well as for implementing and translating political decisions into concrete results. Consequently, understanding the dynamics of integration in European science also implies grasping the nature of the European executive branch in this policy domain. Historically, it has played an essential role in setting the path that a policy for European science has taken. Moreover, with increased ambitions for European area building enshrined in the Treaty of Lisbon, the evolving governance framework is likely to have implications for the future direction of European science. This chapter argues that any research policy ambition on the part of the EU, be it for realising the 'European Research Area', 'Innovation Union' or 'the fifth freedom', relies on organising executive capacity. The rationale of this chapter is to start unpacking this aspect of European science: What kind of executive governance can be observed in this policy domain? How has it evolved over time and how can it be accounted for? How does it compare to executive governance in other policy domains and what can this tell us about the policy dynamics of a European scientific space?

This exploration does not start from a clean slate. Key studies of EU research and technology policy have directly and indirectly addressed central issues relevant to executive governance. Moreover, this scholarship has made strong claims about the nature of research policy that should lead us to expect policy-making in this area to be particularly *technocratic* as policy-making takes place insulated from political steer, *segmented* where policy-making is conducted within 'sector-silos', and where the institutionalisation of one type of supranational policy approach has created a *path dependency* that impedes change and further coordination of EU member states' policies. This chapter revisits each of these arguments in light of developments in EU research policy since the turn of the millennium. The analysis rests on documentary evidence, reviews of the literature, and quantitative data on patterns of participation in EU executive governance (data base on Commission expert groups from 2007).

The first section of this chapter sketches two main theoretical perspectives on executive governance: First a set of arguments based on organisation theory is put forward. In short this perspective argues that *organisational and institutional characteristics* of a government bureaucracy intervene in the policy process and affect its output (Egeberg 2012). A second perspective highlights how the *nature of a policy* creates particular patterns of participation, conflict and cooperation in the policy process, that is, 'policies can determine politics'. The following section outlines how executive governance has developed in EU research policy, reviewing the studies that form the basis for claims of technocratic dominance, segmentation and path dependence. Finally, an overview is given of some main developments in the executive governance of research policy in the last decade, looking first into change and stability at the European level and then at patterns of executive governance in committees and networks as evidenced in the data on the Commission's expert group system.

THE THEORETICAL ARGUMENTS

Organisational and Institutional Factors in Executive Governance

Organisational structure

An organisation theory perspective gives privilege to organisational factors as explanations for political life. Organisational structures have implications for policy-making and implementation in the following main ways. Firstly, establishing formal executive organisations creates capacity for action. Secondly, formal organisations structure the attention of decision-makers, they filter in and filter out information, and regulate the access of participants to decision-making situations (Egeberg 1999, Simon 1976[1945]). In this way organisational structures have behavioural implications. Especially, the principle of *specialisation* according to which executive organisations are structured makes some behavioural patterns more likely than others. *Vertical* specialisation increases and elaborates the number of executive levels within an executive system, for instance through establishing relatively independent agencies. This has implications for the exercise of political leadership of the executive branch and how autonomously administrative levels can operate from the political helm of the executive. *Horisontal* specialisation can follow different principles – executive organisations that are arranged according to territory will activate a spatial perspective among policy-makers, for example, as is the case in intergovernmental organisations or secretariats of international organisations that have 'country desks'. A sectorally arranged organisation will emphasise sectoral concerns over territorial ones in its decision-making, that is, it will operate according to a sectoral logic. The Commission, for instance, is mainly specialised according to a sectoral-functional principle, contributing to making the EU a segmented/ compartmentalised multi-level system (Cram 1994, Kohler-Koch 1997). The Commission's sectorially arranged departments also become natural access points for (transnational) interest-groups that have sector-specific expertise as well as stakes in the policy outcome (Mazey and Richardson 2001). The Commission's formal structure thus undergirds a sector-internal orientation in policy-making.

Bureaucratic path dependency

Building on institutional theory, we can also expect that formal organisations develop informal, taken-for-granted practices and routines, as well as a set of norms and beliefs that are perpetuated in organisational cultures. They, in turn, can be seen as sources of *path dependency* where bureaucratic behaviour is subject to 'thick' institutionalisation and increasing commitment to established values, ideas and practices (Selznick 1966). Institutionalisation is likely to take place within the formal organisational boundaries of a bureaucracy, as well as through a bureaucracy's interaction with its environment. Bureaucratic cultures and practices are developed and sustained by intimate relationships with its outside constituents. Such processes of institutionalisation in turn can be conditioned by the *organisational demography* (Pfeffer 1983) of bureaucracies where department cultures are supported by value sets and worldviews members of organisations bring with them into the bureaucratic setting. Shared professional/educational background and department tenure of staff can reinforce the cultural path dependency of executive organisations. The main point of relevance here is that policy development and execution becomes embedded in systems of norms and administrative practices and therefore policy change and reform strategies are shaped more by what already exists than by what actors want to accomplish for the future (Peters and Pierre 1998).

Policy Specific Conditions – Does 'Policy Determine Politics'?

Although we can expect the organisational structures and path dependencies to heavily influence the nature of executive governance of a sector, a
more policy specific approach is potentially relevant for understanding
policy-making processes in the EU (Héritier 1999). It might be that type of
policy affects policy-making and interest mediation in the policy process,
that is, the nature of a policy determines the characteristics of the policy
process. This idea can be traced back to the theoretical argument made
by Lowi (1972), who distinguished between different policy types according to the kinds of (expected) impact on society. He argued that policy
types caused the politics associated with them. For instance, *redistributive*
policy triggers a polarised pattern of conflict between those broad groups
of society who will benefit and those who will bear the cost of a public
policy, as in the case of social policy and taxation. *Distributive* policies on
the other hand can be decided upon without identifying who will carry the
costs in the short term, that is, without there being clear 'losers' that are
activated in policy-making. Moreover, distributive policies cause a patron-
age relationship between the state and those to whom resources are distributed. Although this categorisation is not easily transferable to the context
of EU decision-making, the main idea can be relevant for understanding
policy-making at this level and in specifying the policy specific conditions.
If research policy can be seen as a type of distributive policy, we can expect
that the policy process is dominated by close relationships between the
administrative apparatus of the EU and the actors that benefit directly
from the distribution of EU funds. There will be low levels of political
conflict and research policy processes will not trigger engagement from
broad societal interests.

Radaelli (1999) advances a related type of argument as he distinguishes
between different prevailing logics of policy-making looking specifically at
policy *uncertainty* and *salience*. The dominant policy logic will be political if policy issues are highly salient and information is readily available,
and policy problems and solutions are easy to identify (low uncertainty).
In areas that are radically uncertain yet politically visible he expects the
policy process to be dominated by an epistemic logic and supranational
policy entrepreneurs. For policies with low political salience, he identifies
two types of politics of expertise – a technocratic versus bureaucratic logic.
Radaelli argues that a logic of technocracy is likely to prevail when there is
a lack of public attention to the policy issue (low saliency) and a high level
of policy uncertainty that places high demands on specialised expertise
and knowledge. The bureaucratic logic of policy-making is likely to dominate in areas where policies have 'no public' and policy uncertainty is low.

This leaves little room for external experts to contribute to policy-making. Policy-making is introvert as a bureaucracy responsible for the policy domain will be self-sustained. From this perspective identifying the specific *policy* characteristics of EU research policy is the key to understanding the executive governance of European science.

EXECUTIVE GOVERNANCE AND EU RESEARCH POLICY: BACKGROUND AND BUILD-UP

Building Executive Capacity for European Science

In the post-World War II period science policy has become a distinct area of public policy (Drori et al. 2003). Worldwide, governments in the post-World War II period developed state bureaucracies to coordinate scientific research. The norm that states should direct science spread regardless of whether these states had any science to coordinate (Finnemore 1993). At the same time this policy area was marked by little party-political salience, low level of contestation, as well as little general public and media attention (Banchoff 2005). At the European level scientific cooperation was early on coupled to the European integration project. However, European involvement in research governance did not happen overnight or without kindling controversy. The issue was not only *whether* to develop a European-level involvement or not, but *what kind of* involvement this should be: supranational versus intergovernmental, science policy as an instrument for industrial policy or as a domain of its own, and what kind of sectoral research and technologies that should be prioritised (Héritier 1999). Hence both the vertical and horizontal principles for how to organise executive capacity in this area were at stake.

Tensions in defining the role of Europe as a governance level in scientific research were also running high within the Commission. In the 1970s some pushed for a common R&D policy explicitly linked to the industrial policy of the European Community and they wanted to keep the European Community out of intergovernmental scientific research cooperation (Schredardus and Telkamp 2001: 12–13). Others did acknowledge the link between science, economic growth and industrial development, but sought to put research also into a context of cultural development, calling for a 'European Scientific Area'. In particular, European Commissioner Ralph Dahrendorf envisioned a European research policy that was based on national policies – the Community effort should be to coordinate these policies. Indeed, the basic organisational model for research cooperation in the 1970s was intergovernmental rather than supranational, and this period saw the establishment of several intergovernmental pan-European, publicly funded big-science cooperation measures (Borrás 2003: 45–7).

With the general reorganisation of the Commission in the wake of the 1973 enlargement of the European Community, a new DG for research (and education) was established that severed the organisational connection between industrial and R&D policy at the European level. This was a formative event in the development of an executive capacity for a European research policy. Establishing sector-specific, full-time administration in the Commission services gave European research policy an organisational memory and policy-making capacity. Other DGs also continued to have stakes in developing R&D policy for their sectors, yet this DG became the lead administrative body in this sector.

The second quantum leap in EU research policy instrumentation came ten years later with the introduction of the multiannual Framework Programme (FP). EU expenditure on research started to take off. The FP became institutionalised as the epitome of European research policy in the latter half of the 1980s and the 1990s. It provided the European level with a basis for developing a generic research policy as the FP expanded in disciplinary scope and funding. The FP machinery grew to encompass a complex web of organisational structures to support the development and implementation of the consecutive programmes. DG XII (research) was at the heart of the decision-making and implementing machinery at the supranational level, by the beginning of the twenty-first century totalling more than 1,000 officers (Spence and Edwards 2006: 176).

The administrative rules of the FPs were based on the principle of *direct management* by the Commission, a principle that stands in contrast to the indirect implementation that has been the hallmark of EU legislation. This implied that FP governance could bypass the national executives by addressing its activities directly towards the research performing level and viceversa. The member states' authorities responsible for R&D at the domestic level could through FP 'Programme Committees' oversee how the Commission put the FPs into effect. However, the principle of direct management placed the DG Research at the hub of transnational networks in the implementation of the FPs, which included the running of a vast system of experts involved in assessing/peer reviewing project applications.

In terms of policy initiation and preparation, DG Research also took a leading role and developed strong relationships to a growing number of transnational actors. These associations developed interests in and capacity for taking part in shaping European research policy. The establishment of European academic associations and interests group organisations within the sector peaked in the 1990s (Beerkens 2008). They were partly a bottom-up reaction to the intensified supranational research policy, and partly a result of the Commission actively promoting the build-up of organised interests to support Community-level activities against the member states. Yet in their study of these transnational groups, Grande and Peschke (1999) conclude that by the end of the 1990s this pattern had resulted in strong horizontal segmentation rather than links between science, industry and politics. This shows how sectoral differentiation is evident not only in the development of political-administrative capabilities and policy instruments, but also in the creation of European-level interest groups/associations specific to the sector.

Political-administrative Relations and the 'Politics of Expertise'

By the mid-1990s European involvement in research policy had taken on the key characteristics of a complex system of multilevel executive governance. Peterson (1995) analyses the link between type of policy and patterns of participation, interaction and conflict in policy-making in his study of EU research policy in this period. Here he argues that the basic logic of EU research policy was 'the politics of expertise'. At the political level, the shaping of policy was characterised by considerable political contention along the territorial conflict line: small member states were pitched against the big ones over the FP decisions when the *overall volume of the research budget* was to be decided. The political contention revolved around the overall relative level of spending much more than the content, strategy and direction of the FP. This kind of politicised bargaining among actors and between the EU's formal decision-making institutions took place as 'bursts' in the budget negotiations. These were exceptions at political peak-hours that veiled the fundamental technocratic nature of EU research policy-making. Technocracy was more paramount in this area than in other policy domains of the EU, Peterson (1995) argues.

This claim rests on three main observations. First, Peterson identifies a particularly strong role of the Commission. Member states in the Council of Ministers were less intrusive vis-à-vis the Commission in research policy matters than elsewhere. Although the overall budget increases for the FPs in the 1990s that the Commission had proposed were slashed by the Council, the Commission's proposals for funding priorities and thematic orientation of the FPs met few Council amendments. Moreover, the major conflicts over the FPs were triggered *within* the Commission and along sectorial lines, that is, as bureaucratic politics more than as conflict over the distributional effects of the FPs on member states. Also, the minimal intervention from the political level of the Commission (especially the Commissioners' Cabinet) left the Commission's administrative level with considerable autonomy in priority setting and in shaping the operative content of the FPs, which is in line with Radaelli's concept of bureaucratic logic of policy-making. This, Peterson (1995: 402) argues, has to do with the experience that the DGs had acquired in handling research funding. At the operational level the technical complexity and specialisation discouraged the invention from the Commission's political leadership.

The second basis for the technocracy claim is the significant body of committees of experts that constituted a key resource for the Commission. These committees included key stakeholders in EU research policy, such as scientists and industry. They were part of the DG's technocratic 'fiefdom'. Consultation with experts was a way of building a common position that was presented to the member states as a *fait accompli*.

A third basis for the special technocratic nature of EU research policy in the 1990s can also be traced back to the diverging organisational demography of the DG Research (then XII Science, later DG RTD): this DG's officers tended to have a degree in science and technology rather than in law/social sciences, the dominant overall educational background of Commission officials. This made DG Research more prone to a technocratic logic.

Relating Peterson's analysis to Radaelli's analytical scheme, we see that he portrays a politics of expertise that combines the bureaucratic and the technocratic logics of policy-making. On the one hand, the know-how, specialised experience and organisational demography of the DG Research shielded its operational policy-making from political intervention, both from member states and the political level of the Commission (Commissioner and his/her Cabinet). On the other hand, this logic operated in tandem with the chain that DG Research had forged with its issue-specific constituency in committees and networks with men/women of science/academia and stakeholders from industry. Consequently, we can argue that EU research policy developed a particularly strong pattern of interaction between interest groups and the EU's executive body in this sector. Grande and Peschke's (1999) study of the pattern of transnational interest mediation and interaction between interests groups and EU institutions supports this claim. Moreover, their survey of 18 transnational organisations representing national research organisations showed a highly segmented pattern of interaction between these organisations and the EU institutions. The range of established and new transnational organisations for universities, publicly funded research organisations, national research funding agencies/national administrations, and industrial R&D did indeed have access to EU policy-making, but they accessed separate venues. Few bodies linked politics, industry and science.

So we have evidence to support the idea that the nature of research policy toward the end of the 1990s (low salience – highly dependent on sector-specific information and expertise) and the type of executive specialisation and interest group formation particular to this sector contributed to making research policy technocratic and bureaucratic, a policy sector that followed its internal logic, to a large extent shielded from direct political steer and less dependent on national administrations for implementing policies than most other areas.

Furthermore, Banchoff (2002) argues that this pattern of policy-making became institutionalised by the end of the 1990s to the extent that it created a situation of inertia. This undercut the politically articulated goals of moving towards a stronger integration of policies beyond FP-style distributive programmes. The sources of inertia he identifies lie in the very organisation of DG Research. In this executive apparatus the bureaucratic expertise and attention was developed around running increasingly voluminous FPs, a highly complex set of formal rules of FP formulation and implementation, coupled to increasing policy autonomy of the DG. He argues that sector internal policy networks encompassing beneficiaries and administrators across levels of governance developed joint stakes in keeping the status quo (Banchoff 2002). When the FP was established it was thus such a key defining moment that it froze European science governance to distributive politics where executive dominance was underpinned by strong, sector-internal policy networks.

THE ORGANISATION AND LOGIC OF EXECUTIVE GOVERNANCE IN EU RESEARCH POLICY IN THE 2000s

Based on these observations, what can we expect to see as the key characteristics of executive governance in the 2000s? We are likely to observe the following: (1) The pattern established in the 1990s will also be predominant in the following decade as long as the organisation of the executive capacity remains intact, the FP instrument remains at the heart of EU research policy, and the policy saliency and uncertainty of research policy have not changed. (2) A sectorial introvert type of policy-making, with little coordination between policy-making of sub-systems (segmented pattern of interaction). (3) The pattern of participation in EU research policy is still less dominated by member states, governments and authorities than in other policy areas.

Research Policy of the 2000s: More Attention – Same Political Saliency?

Drawing on data from the Nordic countries, Kallerud et al. (2011) argue that there has been an increase in the research policy debates in the mid-2000s, but that it is the researchers themselves that drive and engage in these publicly mediated debates. This indicates that research policy is still a domain left to a small core of research policy experts and stakeholders, with a highly technical content that impedes the general politician and public from engaging in research policy debates. While controversy over science has engaged the electorate in cases such as climate change and bio-technology (Jasanoff 2005), research policy is rarely a key item in national electoral politics in Europe. Other types of knowledge policies, especially education, are for instance much more salient issues in national elections. In comparisons research policy is not even mentioned in studies of electoral issue agendas (Singer 2011).

Against this background the developments at the European level since the 2000s are somewhat paradoxical. Many events at the European level in the 2000s have intensified the political rhetoric of the knowledge economy. The knowledge sectors are increasingly seen as a kind of 'transversal problem-solver'. Consequently, most sectors of society directly or indirectly have stakes in knowledge production and dissemination. The attention attached to knowledge policy areas is unprecedented in the history of the EU. In the framework of the Lisbon strategy, the heads of state in the European Council had research and innovation repeatedly on their agenda. Attention to Europe's innovative capacity, economic and scientific competitiveness, and universities seems to have been at an all-time high, especially in the mid-2000s. This attention also included the apex of the Commission, such as when Commission President Barroso personally got involved in proposing new initiatives, most notably the establishment of the European Institute of Innovation and Technology. Also the FP7 decision (2006)[1] was more politically salient than its predecessor (FP6), sparking considerable contestation (Metz 2011). Yet, it was more the specific issues *within* the FP7 that fuelled some media attention rather than the overall profile and volume of EU research funding or the direction of the EU research policy. In the end it was the question of stem cell research that made a minority of member states cast a negative vote in the FP7 decision (Muldur et al. 2006).

Furthermore, there is not much evidence to suggest that EU research policy in the same period experienced increased saliency among European citizens. We do not know whether general insight into what constitutes EU research has changed as the activities in this policy domain have intensified in the 2000s. However, the EUROBAROMETER's opinion polls do not indicate much change in citizen's attitudes to EU level involvement in research policy[2] (see Table 5.1). These data suggest that research is a policy area where transfer of competences to the EU is not contested. Among European citizens there is much less national sensitivity attached

Table 5.1   *Support among European citizens for joint decision-making at the EU level in scientific and technological research and in education*

Decisions should be made jointly within the EU within the area of:	2001 (EU 15)	2006 (EU 25)	2006 (EU 15)	2006 (New member states 10)	2011 (EU 27)
Scientific and technological research	68%	70%	68%	80%	73%
The education system	36%	29%	28%	35%	34%

Question: 'In the following areas, do you think that decisions should be made by the (NATIONALITY) Government, or made jointly within the European Union?'

Sources: Standard EUROBAROMETER 2001, 2006, 2011.

to research than to the education system. It might also indicate that the general public does not take much interest in and attach much 'sentiment' to this area. These opinions are fairly stable over a ten-year period, although the EU averages conceal national variations.

Stability in Executive Governance

The formal rules and practices of policy-making at the EU level for the FPs have been fairly stable after the turn of the century. The two-layered decision-making processes determining the core of the EU research policy (the FPs) have continued, as was evident in the case of FP7 decision. The size of the research budget for FP7, for instance, was a highly politicised, contentious issue (Muldur et al. 2006, Schild 2008). At administrative level decision-making over the FPs have followed a familiar path: the Commission's role has been central in initiating and preparing the overall FP guidelines, proposals for the FPs' specific programmes, rules of partici-pation, as well the annual 'work programmes' of the FPs. Representatives from member states' *administrations* have been involved in shaping the thematic emphases and development of new instruments in the FPs (espe-cially through CREST[3]/ERAC) and in overseeing the implementation, through the FP programme committees (Muldur et al. 2006). In preparing for the FP6 and FP7 bureaucratic politics *within* the Commission (between different 'research family' DGs) have been dominant in forming the Commission's position, alongside a more technocratic approach involving extensive use of external expertise (Metz 2011). In this respect executive governance shows the same signs of bureaucratic and technocratic logic that Peterson (1995) pointed to. This combination of logics is rooted in the basic set of rules for how to shape and implement the FPs and in the organisation of the main executive centre of EU research policy.

Attempts at creating another form of executive governance were made after the turn of the century. Coordination of member states' policy gained a renewed emphasis through the application of the Open Method of Coordination (OMC). This would involve national administrations and potentially also other levels of authority together with stakeholders and experts. OMC became the working methodology for increasing the R&D investment within the EU area to 3 per cent of GDP. To some extent this did create new, but fragile, venues at the European level. However, the concept was subject to multiple interpretations and in the end did not represent a centre-stage, radical break with the ways of cooperating inherited from the past (De Ruiter 2010, Expert Group OMC Research 2009, Gornitzka 2007, Kaiser and Prange 2004), even though its application did make a decisive impact in some sub-areas (see McGuinness and O'Carroll (2010), for an analysis of the application of the OMC for researcher mobility strategy). The research policy domain's experience with the OMC-template shows some degree of change resistance along the lines argued by Banchoff (2002).

Change in Executive Governance: Increasing Complexity

What happened simultaneously within DG Research as the executive core? EU research policy has remained one of the most administratively endowed areas in terms of Commission officers. A recent survey of the Commission also shows that DG Research continued to be among the DGs with the highest concentration of scientists, that is, its educational profile deviates from most of the other DGs (Kassim et al. 2013). Both of these traits can be assumed to perpetuate a particular logic of executive governance and administrative culture in this policy domain at the European level.

Yet we do see changes. Overall, a growing administrative complexity of executive governance is observed. The 2000s brought consecutive calls for stronger vertical and horizontal coordination in EU research policy. The launch of the European Research Area (ERA) in combination with the Lisbon strategy (later Europe 2020) directly addressed the purported need for horizontal coordination of research policies in Europe. We can also observe an increased attention to making the overall executive governance of European science more effective. For instance, a broader initiative to strengthen the management of the ERA by instigating the so-called Ljubljana process (Kajnč 2009) did come towards the end of the 2000s.

Yet, the impact of this initiative and whether this has implied a shift in the logic of executive governance remains unstudied.

Several innovations inside and at the rim of the FPs have had implications for the executive governance of the ERA, among them ERA-NETs[4] (FP6) and Joint Programming Initiatives (JPIs[5] – first launched 2010). These did not *replace* the existing organisational structure of the European executive branch in this policy domain, but should be seen as smaller new elements that were *layered* onto it. This layering process has implied more specialisation and complexity. One clear sign of increasing *vertical* specialisation of Union administration is the 'outsourcing' (vertical differentiation) of FP management in a new Research Executive Agency (REA), which was set up in 2008 in Brussels to manage large parts of the FP7, and from 2014 a large part of Horizon 2020, the biggest EU Research and Innovation programme ever (see below). This was argued to 'free up' staff capacity within DG Research in order for it to take on a 'more ministerial type approach'.[6] This echoes a common argument made for agencification in the public sector in general. It builds on the assumption that the technical versus the policy-relevant aspects of administration can be organised separately. Giving executive agencies the tasks of managing EU programmes was intended to create efficiency gains and unleash capacity within the DG to take on a more active policy-making role. This stands in stark contrast to the rational for establishing another Executive Agency under DG Research, the European Research Council's Executive Agency (ERCEA) (Gornitzka and Metz 2014a). The establishment of this agency was more the result of compromise in institutional design when the European Research Council as a new path-breaking institution was realised as an FP7 programme and not established as a formally autonomous EU institution (Vike-Freiberga et al. 2009). Yet, in sum these changes increased both the vertical and horizontal complexity in the executive governance of EU research policy.

Recent developments have also entailed changes in the basic distribution of portfolios between the 'knowledge DGs'. When the Barroso II Commission took office, the Commission president asked the new Commissioner, Geoghegan-Quinn, to 'lead a cross-cutting approach to innovation',[7] giving her the responsibility for the renamed DG Research and *Innovation*. This can be seen as an attempt to organisationally anchor the link between research and innovation in tune with the knowledge triangle idea and create greater crosscutting coordination between hitherto separately organised administrative portfolios. The implications of these changes for the logic of executive governance remain to be studied. The same goes for potential executive coordination in the new funding framework, Horizon 2020, a programme that can be read as an EU research policy attempt at exercising 'joined-up governance', as well as the attempt to create stronger links between EU regional policy and research/innovation policy through for instance 'smart specialisation'.

Commission Expert Groups in EU Research Policy

The expert group system of the Commission serves several purposes that are central to the functioning of a multi-level executive system. It feeds the Commission with information and technical expertise, but it also functions as a sounding board testing the reactions of Commission proposals. If research policy has continued to be more technocratic than other policy areas, we should expect this to be reflected in the lead DG's use of expert groups and in the configuration of participants in these organised research policy networks.

The first observation drawn from the evidence clearly supports the idea that executive governance of EU Research policy is more extrovert than most other areas. In 2007 DG Research organised more expert groups than any other DG.[8] Together with DG Environment and DG Enterprise, this DG made up the overall top three expert group users in 2007 (Gornitzka and Sverdrup 2008). Since then the number of groups has dropped but this DG still remains among the top users (Gornitzka and Sverdrup 2015).

The second observation is equally striking: unlike most other policy areas, national administrations do not dominate these policy networks. Only a small fraction of the expert group system in research policy is 'pure government'; in 2007 11 out of the 129 committees convened only representatives of national administrations. The pattern of participation in this policy area is thus considerably more transnational and less purely intergovernmental than the pattern for the Commission as a whole (47 per cent of Commission expert groups had only participants from national government offices).

Table 5.2 specifies the pattern of participation in expert groups. We see from these data that *mixed* participation is the paramount characteristic of EU research policy networks. Academics/scientists were present in an overwhelming majority of the groups. This is not surprising given the dual role they have in research policy: as the primary stakeholder in EU research policy and as scientific experts. As expected from a policy-oriented perspective, the technical complexity of preparing and implementing research policy is in this way reflected in the patterns of participation specific to this DG. Yet, technical complexity and uncertainty of research policy might not be the only explanation to this pattern of participation. The norms of who constitutes particularly legitimate participants might equally well regulate the access of scientists/academics into the policy process.

Table 5.2   *Types of participants present in expert groups under DG*
Research, DG Enterprise, DG Education and Culture and all
expert groups (per cent of total number of expert groups under
each DG)

Type of participant present in expert group	RTD EGs	ENTR EGs	EAC EGs	All EGs
Academics/scientists	79	18	65	33
National ministries	45	88	56	70
Competent national authorities/agencies	23	41	62	34
Regional administrations	5	10	9	8
Consumers	4	19	–	8
Enterprises/industry	54	63	16	29
Social partners/unions	7	17	42	12
Professionals/practitioners	13	15	14	13
Non-governmental organisations	6	16	23	17
International organisations	9	–	–	2
N	*129*	*120*	*71*	*1236*

Source: Own data (data base on Commission Expert Groups 2007 (Gornitzka and Sverdrup 2008, 2011a)

Developing and implementing a science policy without the involvement of scientists and academics might not only be technically ineffective but also lack legitimacy.

However, it is relatively rare that scientists/academics are the only members of a group: only 17 per cent of the expert groups are 'purely' scientific. Members from enterprise and industry are present in more than half of DG Research's groups. The kind of segregation between science versus industry suggested in earlier studies we do not retrieve here.

We also note that even though the national dominance is a less pronounced trait in the organised research policy networks, representatives from national *ministries* constitute the third most frequent type of participant in DG Research expert groups. They are present in 45 per cent of DG Research expert groups. Relatively speaking, national *agencies* are not a frequent participant in this setting. Non-governmental actors besides industry and academics/scientists are less present than in other policy areas. There is, for instance, a striking difference between DG Research and DG Education in this respect. The expert groups system is clearly not the place for civil society organisations to take part in shaping research policy. They may have other access points, such as public consultations or consensus conferences,[9] but in this venue they are marginal. The same goes

Table 5.3   Task assigned to expert groups under DG Research, DG Enterprise, DG Education and Culture, and all expert groups (2007) (per cent of total number of expert groups under each DG)

Share of expert groups that:	RTD EGs	ENTR EGs	EAC EGs	All EGs
1) Assist in preparation	49	38	40	43
2) Coordinate	45	64	64	61
3) Draft implementation	18	20	4	16
4) Monitor	3	17	29	11
N	*129*	*120*	*71*	*1236*

Source: Own data (data base on Commission Expert Groups 2007 (Gornitzka and Sverdrup 2008, 2011))

for regional administrations, but this is also the case for the Commission in general.

What do these patterns of participation tell us about EU research policy-making modes? First, they indicate that EU research policy entails a co-production and co-implementation of policy across multiple governance levels. We also see that compared to neighbouring policy areas (enterprise/education and culture) and the Commission DGs in general, the research policy domain is different in several respects. The prevalence of scientists and academics is found nowhere else – a fact that arguably is linked to the nature of research policy. In this sense there is support for the idea that distributive policy (still the core of EU research policy) with high technical complexity has indeed generated a particular pattern of executive governance. This, and the fact that the expert group system under DG Research is vast, demonstrate how densely tied this DG is to its closest policy constituency.

We have already argued that executive governance of EU research policy is less single-mindedly oriented towards national administrations than other policy areas. Is this also reflected in the types of functions that expert groups have in this sector? And in what stages of the policy process do they play a role? We distinguish between the following tasks: groups that (1) assist the Commission in the preparation of legislation or in policy definition ('Preparation'); (2) coordinate with member states and promote the exchange of views between actors ('Coordinate'); (3) provide expertise to the Commission when drafting or implementing measures, that is, before the Commission submits these draft measures to a comitology committee ('Draft implementation'); (4) monitor the development of national policies and the enforcement of EU policies ('Monitoring').

*Table 5.4   Institutionalisation of expert groups (2007) (per cent of expert
groups that are informal and temporary under each DG)*

Share of expert groups that are:	RTD EGs	ENTR EGs	EAC EGs	All EGs
Informal	77	68	79	76
Temporary	75	49	64	51
N	*129*	*120*	*71*	*1236*

Source: Own data (data base on Commission Expert Groups 2007 (Gornitzka and
Sverdrup 2008, 2011a))

The findings show that the task structure of the research expert groups
is not that deviant from the overall picture. They are more engaged in the
policy shaping stage (task 1 and 2) than in the implementation stage (task 3
and 4). The role of monitoring national policies and the enforcement of EU
policy at the national level is virtually absent in research policy committees.
This we assume is related to the FPs' principle of *direct management*. We
also note that the use of expert groups to coordinate research policies with
member states is somewhat less prevalent than in other policy areas.

Governance by committees/networks was in the 2000s as prevalent as it
was in the 1990s. It is likely that a department culture and sector-specific
norms of appropriate behaviour have supported such a network-based
system of executive governance. Data on the types of expert group can
in addition tell us something about the degree of institutionalisation of
DG Research's expert group system. Overall, expert groups vary in formalisation and permanence. As we see from Table 5.4, most of the research
policy groups are both informal and temporary. Consequently, this aspect
of executive governance in this area is less anchored in formal rules of
procedure and this might be more flexible. Furthermore, the sectorally
segmented approach to governance is upheld more through a mechanism
of habituation and practice than via formalisation.

CONCLUSIONS

Executive governance of EU research policy is far from being a simple
two-level system. The system that has developed spans levels of governance and EU level administrative bodies, national ministries/agencies and
non-governmental actors. Previous studies of EU research and technology
policy have portrayed this field as the pinnacle of 'the politics of expertise',
where policies are shaped far away from the political leadership, elected

office holders, and the public eye. In short, the operational decision-making in EU research policy has been dominated by an established technocracy (Peterson 1995). Partly this is still the case in the 2000s. However, political attention has increased considerably in this domain, but without activating traditional party-political conflicts. Increasing visibility for research policy issues seems partly based on increasing consensus on a 'knowledge policy paradigm' and less on contestation in the public and political sphere. Among the general public the role of the EU in this area has not been contested – citizens attach little national sensitivity to research policy. According to a 'policy determines politics' perspective this should be conducive to a technocratic logic of executive governance. Technocratic and sector-specific logics we find in the everyday implementation and policy shaping taking place within the Commission and in its vast expert group system. Yet, the overall decisions on the size of EU programmes are still taken at the apex of political leadership in the EU and it involves scrutiny from the European Parliament. In addition, Commission leadership (the President and the designated Commissioner) have directly engaged in key research policy initiatives. Considerable contestation within the Commission is involved when the main FP sub-programmes have been formulated, between the DG Research and other DGs with stakes in research (Metz 2011). Technocratic governance is not unfettered but takes place within the larger political setting.

A second observation made by prior studies is that research policy shaping is *segmented*, that is, policy-making takes place within policy networks that are internal to sub-sectors within the policy domain (Grande and Peschke 1999) and are too opaque for actors outside the closed circles to scrutinise (Peterson and Sharp 1998: 177–84). The executive complexity of EU research policy has certainly not been reduced – it has rather become even more compartmentalised. There are clear signs of increasing vertical and horizontal specialisation associated with a string of new initiatives. This complexity contributes to making the EU's research governance less transparent and could be an impediment for the exercise of political control and scrutiny and for the public to engage in research policy debates. Specialised segments of policy-making and implementation define the set of actors that command the terminology and rule-setting specific to the policy domain. More than most other policy areas the DG Research is *extrovert* towards its sector-specific constituency. The data on the networks of executive governance demonstrates technocratic rather than bureaucratic, introvert logic.

And finally, a strong claim has been made with respect to the *dynamics* of EU research policy-making in the transition to the 2000s. Actor constellations and administrative path dependencies that crystallised around the EU's main research policy instrument, the FPs, had created *inertia* in EU research policy. We have identified the creation of a separate specialised DG and administrative capacity for EU research as a fork in the road. The build-up of executive capacity for action (first) and the adding of an eventually strongly institutionalised FP (ten years later) have resulted in a tight web of interactions with strong historical roots, specialised along sectoral lines. Interaction patterns that were established in the 1990s created a path-dependency that also lasted into the 2000s. Some of these interactions *bypass* the national executive level and engage the EU administration with sub-national actors directly. However, continuity runs parallel to change as several changes in executive governance came in the wake of new FP instruments and when new research policy instruments were added outside and in the fringe of the FPs.

Some tentative lessons for building a European scientific space can be sketched. Under these sector-specific conditions the scope for rational *design* of common European space is limited. The policy uncertainty in this area is considerable and the link between politically agreed objectives and the instruments available for achieving them are tenuous and not well-understood. Under such conditions also the formulation and execution of EU policy is more likely to follow an evolving path than a pre-planned roadmap, be it towards excellence, innovation or addressing grand challenges. Certainly, a scientific space cannot be constructed by political-administrative fiat, and in the current political and financial climate member states and EU institutions might have less tolerance for investing in policy instruments and capacity whose direct economic benefits appear uncertain and at best long-term. Also, policy innovation and change that has taken place in this policy domain in the past ten years has happened for a large part through *layering* – the establishment of the European Research Council is the case in point. In times of scarcity and acute battles over political priorities – between sectors, and between supranational and national solutions – the room for change through layering is narrower. This might profoundly change the dynamics of policy change also in this domain. The massive call for coordination across and within sectors as well as between levels of governance might well be seen as a sign of the research policy 'silo' being challenged. The current attempts of inserting a policy for innovation into the political-administrative research portfolio of the EU is a test as to what changes redesign of executive structures entails. Finally, executive governance cannot be reduced to a question of political effectiveness and administrative efficiency. It also concerns how to find a *legitimate* balance between change and continuity; between political steer, administrative leeway for action, stakeholder involvement, and scientific self-governance; and between different values and justifications that underpin a European scientific space.

NOTES

1. Decision no 1982/2006/EC of the European Parliament and of the Council of 18 December 2006 concerning the Seventh Framework Programme of the European Community for research, technological development and demonstration activities (2007–2013).
2. http://ec.europa.eu/public_opinion/archives/eb/eb56/eb56_en.pdf; http://ec.europa.eu/public_opinion/archives/eb/eb66/eb66_en.pdf; http://ec.europa.eu/public_opinion/arch ives/eb/eb74/eb74_publ_en.pdf.
3. CREST was the strategic policy advisory body assisting the Commission and the Council in policies for research and technological development. In 2009 this committee was renamed ERAC (European Research Area Committee) and given a new mandate.
4. In recent years the expert group system has changed – research on the general causes and implication of these changes is currently being undertaken (see http://www.sv.uio.no/arena/). The data analysed in this chapter are valid for the period 2000 to 2009.
5. JPIs for instance each have a small but relative independent executive organisation of their own (see http://ec.europa.eu/research/era/areas/programming/joint_programming_en.htm).
6. Interview with former Commissioner for Research Potočnik, Cordis news 2008-01-25.
7. Mission letter from President Barroso to the Commissioner designate, 27 November 2009.
8. The number of recorded expert groups in the research portfolio has dropped significantly since 2007. Yet DG RTD, with its 64 groups, was in 2013 still among the five DGs with the highest number of active expert groups in the Commission (Gornitzka 2015: 107).
9. FPs have also devoted special programmes for promoting science and society link.

REFERENCES

Banchoff, Thomas (2002) 'Institutions, Inertia and European Union Research Policy', *Journal of Common Market Studies* 40(1): 1–21.

Beerkens, Eric (2008) 'The Emergence and Institutionalisation of the European Higher Education and Research Area', *European Journal of Education* 43(4): 407–24.

Borrás, Susana (2003) *The Innovation Policy of the European Union: From Government to Governance*. Cheltenham: Edward Elgar.

Cram, Laura (1994) 'The European Commission as a Multi-organization: Social Policy and IT Policy in the EU', *Journal of European Public Policy* 1(2): 195–217.

De Ruiter, Rik (2010) 'Variations on a Theme. Governing the Knowledge-based Society in the EU through Methods of Open Coordination in Education and R&D', *Journal of European Integration* 32(2): 157–73.

Drori, Gili S., John W. Meyer, Francisco O. Ramirez and Evan Schofer (2003) *Science in the Modern World Polity: Institutionalization and Globalization*. Stanford: Stanford University Press.

Egeberg, Morten (1999) 'The Impact of Bureaucratic Structure on Policy Making', *Public Administration* 77(1): 155–70.

Egeberg, Morten (2012) 'How Bureaucratic Structure Matters: An Organizational Perspective', in Peters, B. Guy and Jon Pierre (eds) *The SAGE Handbook of Public Administration*. Sage Publications, pp. 157–68.

Expert Group OMC Research (Expert Group for the follow-up of the research aspects of the revised Lisbon strategy) (2009) *The Open Method of Coordination in Research Policy: Assessments and Recommendations.* Brussels: European Commission, Directorate-General for Research.

Finnemore, Martha (1993) 'International Organizations as Teachers of Norms – The United Nations' Educational Scientific and Cultural Organization and Science Policy, *International Organization* 47(4): 565–97.

Gornitzka, Åse (2007) 'The Lisbon Process: A Supranational Policy Perspective', in Maassen, Peter and Johan P. Olsen (eds) *University Dynamics and European Integration.* Dordrecht: Springer, pp. 155–78.

Gornitzka, Åse (2015) '"All in"? Patterns of Participation in EU Education Policy', in Souto-Otero, Manuel (ed.) *Evaluating European Education Policy-Making.* Houndmills: Palgrave Macmillan, pp. 92–123.

Gornitzka, Åse and Julia Metz (2014a) 'Dynamics of Institution Building in the Europe of Knowledge: The Birth of the European Research Council', in *Building the Knowledge Economy in Europe: New Constellations in European Research and Higher Education Governance.* Cheltenham: Edward Elgar, p. 252.

Gornitzka, Åse and Julia Metz (2014b) 'European Institution Building under Inhospitable Conditions: The Unlikely Establishment of the European Institute of Innovation and Technology', in *Building the Knowledge Economy in Europe: New Constellations in European Research and Higher Education Governance.* Cheltenham: Edward Elgar, p. 252.

Gornitzka, Åse and Ulf Sverdrup (2008) 'Who Consults? The Configuration of Expert Groups in the European Union', *West European Politics* 31(4): 725–50.

Gornitzka, Åse and Ulf Sverdrup (2015) 'The Expert-Executive Nexus in the European Administrative System: Expert Groups and the European Commission,' in Bauer, Michael and Jarle Trondal (eds) *The Palgrave Handbook of the European Administrative System.* Basingstoke: Palgrave Macmillan.

Gornitzka, Åse and Ulf Sverdrup (2011), "Access of Experts: Information and EU Decision-Making', *West European Politics* 34 (1): 48–70.

Grande, E. and A. Peschke (1999) 'Transnational Cooperation and Policy Networks in European Science Policy-making', *Research Policy* 28(1): 43–61.

Héritier, Adrienne (1999) *Policy-Making and Diversity in Europe. Escape from Deadlock.* Cambridge: Cambridge University Press.

Jasanoff, Sheila (2005) *Designs on Nature – Science and Democracy in Europe and the United States.* Princeton: Princeton University Press.

Kaiser, Robert and Heiko Prange (2004) 'Managing Diversity in a System of Multi-Level Governance: The Open Method of Co-ordination in Innovation Policy', *Journal of European Public Policy* 11(2): 249–66.

Kallerud, Egil, Thorvald Finnbjørnsson, Lars Geschwind, Marja Häyrinen-Alestalo, Inge Ramberg, Karen Siune and Terhi Tuorninen (2011) *Public Debate on Research Policy in the Nordic Countries.* Oslo: NIFU.

Kanjc (2009), 'The Slovenian Presidency: Meeting Symbolic and Substantive Challenges', *Journal of Common Market Studies* 47(s1): 89–98.

Kassim, H., J. Peterson, M.W. Bauer, S.J. Connolly, R. Dehousse, L. Hooghe and A. Thompson (2013) *The European Commission of the Twenty-first Century.* Oxford: Oxford University Press.

Kohler-Koch, Beate (1997) 'Organized Interests in the EC and the European Parliament', *European Integration Online Papers* (EIoP) 1(9): 1–14.

Lowi, Theodore J. (1972) 'Four Systems of Policy, Politics, and Choice', *Public Administration Review* 32(4): 298–310.

Mazey, Sonia and Jeremy Richardson (2001) 'Institutionalizing Promiscuity: Commission-Interest Group Relations in the European Union', in Stone Sweet, Alec, Wayne Sandholtz and Neil Fligstein (eds) *The Institutionalization of Europe*. Oxford: Oxford University Press, pp. 71–93.

McGuinness, Nina and Conor O'Carroll (2010) 'Benchmarking Europe's Lab Benches: How Successful has the OMC been in Research Policy?', *JCMS: Journal of Common Market Studies* 48(2): 293–318.

Metz, Julia (2011) *The European Commission's Expert Groups and Their Use in Policy Making*, Doctoral Dissertation, Fachbereich Politik- und Sozialwissenschaften, Freie Universität Berlin.

Muldur, Ugur, Fabienne Corvers, Henri Delanghe, Jim Dratwa, Daniela Heimberger, Brian Sloan and Sandrijn Venslembrouck (2006) *A New Deal for an Effective European Research Policy: The Design and Impacts of the 7th Framework Programme*. Dordrecht: Springer.

Peters, B. Guy and John Pierre (1998) 'Governance Without Government? Rethinking Public Administration', *Journal of Public Administration Research and Theory* 8(2): 223–43.

Peterson, John (1995) 'EU Research Policy: The Politics of Expertise', in Rhodes, Carolyn and Sonia Mazey (eds) *The State of the European Union, Vol 3: Building a European Polity*. Boulder, CO: Lynne Rienner, pp. 391–412.

Peterson, John and Margaret Sharp (1998) *Technology Policy in the European Union*. London: Macmillan.

Pfeffer, Jeffrey (1983) 'Organizational Demography', *Research in Organizational Behavior* 5: 299–357.

Radaelli, Claudio M. (1999) 'The Public Policy of the European Union: Whither Politics of Expertise?', *Journal of European Public Policy* 6(5): 757–74.

Schild, Joachim (2008) 'How to Shift the EU's Spending Priorities? The Multi-Annual Financial Framework 2007–13 in Perspective', *Journal of European Public Policy* 15(4): 531–49.

Schredardus, Peter and Gerard J. Telkamp (2001) *Van coöperatie via coördinatie tot integratie. Van Spinelli tot Busquin: Onderzoeksbeleid van de Europese Unie in perspectief*. Den Haag: Nederlands Instituut voor Internationale Betrekkingen 'Clingendael'.

Selznick, Philip (1966) *Leadership in Administration: A Sociological Interpretation*. New York: Harper & Row.

Simon, Herbert A. (1976[1945]) *Administrative Behavior: A Study of Decision-Making Processes in Administrative Organization*. New York: Free Press.

Singer, M. (2009), 'When do Voters Actually Think "It's the Economy"? Evidence from the 2008 Presidential Campaign', *Electoral Studies* 30(4): 621–32.

Spence, David and Geoffrey Edwards (2006) *The European Commission*. London: John Harper.

Vike-Freiberga, Varia et al. (2009) *Towards a World-class Frontier Research Organisation. Review of the European Research Council's Structures and Mechanisms. Following the Commission's decision of March 2009 (C(2009) 1871) to create "panel of independent experts for the review of the structures and mechanisms of the ERC"*. 23 July 2009.

6. Transnational organisations defining quality and excellence

Linda Wedlin and Tina Hedmo

INTRODUCTION

Excellence is a keyword in contemporary debates about higher education and research. The creation of excellence and the achievement of excellence in research as well as in higher education have been explicit goals in much of the policy work done across Europe in the past decade. As expressed in the 'Aarhus Declaration 2012', developed during the Danish presidency of the European Union in 2010, excellence in research is 'essential to *the future of Europe*', and 'is the *essential foundation* that secures the development and availability of *human capital* to meet the needs of the future' (Aarhus Declaration 2012: 4). This declaration was an agreement on a set of guidelines for future policy work on higher education and research within the European Union. At about the same time, the European Network for Quality Assurance (ENQA) initiated a working group on 'excellence', aiming to increase knowledge on the concept of excellence, particularly in relation to higher education, and to discuss the potential role for quality assurance agencies in the development and fostering of excellence (ENQA 2014). With this, the notion of excellence has, if not replaced, then at least supplemented the rather strong focus on quality and quality assurance that has dominated higher education governance debates since the 1980s (Bleiklie 2011; Hedmo 2012).

Why is the concern for excellence so important and so prominent in the policy debate? In this chapter, we explore the role of this policy rhetoric, and the general discourse on excellence and quality, in shaping a European governance field for higher education and research. How and why have European systems of assessment and evaluation of quality and excellence developed, and what does that development mean?

Our argument is twofold. First, excellence discourses guide the development of new forms of assessments, evaluations and quality assurance mechanisms, which, in turn, set standards and establish principles for how to control the behaviour of actors in academic systems. For instance, as evident from studies of national reforms in countries such as Germany, France and the UK, this policy discourse on excellence has guided the transformation of higher education and research systems leading to, among other things, the development of new funding systems, assessment principles, and evaluation systems (Rostan and Vaira 2011). These have significantly influenced the conditions for higher education and research organisation in these contexts (see for example, Whitley et al. 2010). The development of excellence as a guiding principle for reform is thus inter-linked with an expansion and elaboration of external evaluations and quality assessment tools (Bleiklie 2011), such as accreditation, rankings, and other means to measure and assure quality (see for example, Hedmo 2004; Wedlin 2006).

Second, the debates and negotiations involved in setting up these systems are part of the formation of a transnational governance field – in our case at the European level. Policies for excellence are promoted, supported and organised largely by transnational non-governmental organisations, but they interact with both formal and informal policy and governance processes at both governmental and supranational levels. They are developed in conjunction with other agendas, policy processes and mechanisms, such as the Bologna Process and the Lisbon Agenda (Rostan and Vaira 2011). Through this interaction, the policy discourse is both strengthened and serves to support and legitimate these processes. Taking control of debates on what constitutes quality and excellence, and creating means to assess this, are thus ways to govern and to strengthen the role of other govern-ance efforts and actors in this field.

We develop our arguments using two recent European processes. The first is the development of a European dimension of quality assurance, a dimension being translated into a set of European-specific quality stand-ards for what characterises appropriate and good-quality assurance and a European Quality Assurance Register for Higher Education (EQAR). This register was constructed as a tool for certifying those national quality assurance agencies that comply with the European standards. This case relates most clearly to discussions and developments taking place within the higher education community, especially the Bologna Process, which is fundamental to the creation of a harmonised European Higher Education Area (EHEA). It starts in the quality debates of the 1990s, which largely preceded the current debates on excellence in higher education.

The second case illustrates efforts to establish a new funding mechanism for basic research at the European level, the European Research Council (ERC). The launch of the ERC has – besides its funding mission – served a particularly important role in shaping notions of excellence in research at the European level. In this chapter we are thus not primarily interested in the role or characteristics of the ERC as a funding organisation (cf. Chapter 4), but rather in the discourse supporting and legitimating the organisation during its early stages. This process illustrates most clearly how the excellence framework and rhetoric were used by organisations and actors to link concerns about basic research to contemporary policy ideals and principles.

These examples highlight how transnational systems of governance have developed gradually over time, and how new organisations are beginning to populate the academic landscape and gain authority to establish criteria and set standards for what constitutes quality and excellence in this field. Before turning to the empirical examples, however, we will briefly provide a theoretical background to our argument.

CONCEPTUAL FRAMEWORK

Transnational Soft Regulation

Our theoretical framework takes as its departure point the assumption that there has been a governance turn in contemporary society. In literature, it is argued that a 'new paradigm' (Nicolaidis and Egan 2001) has brought about a shift in governance, replacing the traditional, bureaucratically organised, command and control systems with networks of relationships in which cooperation and coordination with non-state actors such as firms, epistemic communities, value-based advocacy networks, international non-governmental organisations (INGOs) and cross-border social movements must be constantly negotiated and managed (see for example, Kohler-Koch and Eising 1999). Governance may also include 'partial organisations' (Ahrne and Brunsson 2010), operating outside the boundaries of formal organisations.

In the governance literature, the new steering approach is described as encompassing soft and informal rules and compliance mechanisms (that is, economic and social) (Djelic and Sahlin-Andersson 2006). The new mechanisms are particularly appropriate in transnational settings; they facilitate coordination of social and functional action (Tamm-Hallström 2004), cooperation, the transfer of information, compatibility, communication and comparison (Brunsson and Jacobsson 2000) across national boundaries. In addition, these mechanisms are regarded as more flexible and open than formal command and control systems, leaving room for interpretation and diversity. They are not legally binding but rely on principles of voluntariness (at least formally) and they are not directly coupled to systems of sanction or resource allocation (Mörth 2004). Rather, they are assumed to rely on non-hierarchical and decentralised methods of steering that are combined with incentive-based compliance mechanisms such as mutual recognition, comparison, certification, licensing and naming and shaming (Brunsson and Jacobsson 2000; Knill and Lehmkuhl 2002).

These shifts towards soft forms of regulation are associated with a more dynamic and agency-oriented research agenda in transnational governance (see for example, Djelic and Sahlin-Andersson 2006; Risse 2007) stating the substantial impact of 'rationalised others' (Meyer 1994), such as non-governmental actors (Boli and Thomas 1999), in the issuing, diffusion, making and monitoring of norms and rules in contemporary society. These organisations function in a sense as 'teachers of norms' (Finnemore 1993), formulating or specifying what is appropriate and legitimate for actors in the field.

Transnational Governance of Higher Education and Research

Empirical studies distinguish how an increasing number of actors operating outside the jurisdiction of nation states, such as accreditation organisations, professional associations, funding agencies and media organisations, take a keen interest in quality assurance, evaluation and measurement of higher education and research (Hedmo and Wedlin 2008; King 2009). In addition, international or supranational organisations, most notably perhaps the World Bank (El-Khawas and Shah 1998), the OECD (King 2009) and the EU (Corbett 2005; Erkkilä and Piironen 2014), are listing these topics at the top of their transnational policy agendas.

In higher education the appearance of soft rules has introduced new means to compare and to scrutinise organisational behaviour, and hence to govern the performance and quality of higher education institutions. Particularly salient is the increasing prominence of quality standards and accreditation as the dominant ways to ensure accountability (Schwarz and Westerheijden 2004; Stensaker and Harvey 2011). Rankings, particularly international rankings, are also important for spreading norms and values of what is expected in order to be categorised as a proper higher education organisation. With this development, governance efforts have shifted base from control-based to norm-based systems (Shore and Wright 2000; Czarniawska and Genell 2002), following the rise of what is often termed the 'audit society' (Power 1997).

Perhaps more salient in Europe than in the rest of the world, this development has led some to describe the development of an 'accountability market': a market where different systems and principles coexist and compete, and where actors and organisations involved in quality assurance and evaluation and the like also struggle for power, authority and voice

(Amaral and Rosa 2011; Sursock 2011). Because of their political character, systems for accountability and assessment have become important arenas for struggles over the conditions for, and quality of, higher education and research systems and procedures (Enders 2005).

This has led some to note the importance of accountability communities that evolve around these new governance mechanisms, which are 'composed of public and/or private organizations endowed with capacities to perform legislative, monitoring and compliance activities in specifically functionally-based regulatory regimes within – and beyond – national boundaries' (Jayasuriya 2010). Such communities are important for creating legitimacy for new, particularly transnational, regulatory regimes and for granting authority to new governance principles and fields.

Drawing on these findings we can argue that the growth of new governance mechanisms to evaluate higher education and research have become important for shaping what is considered good, appropriate and legitimate in these areas. The measurement and assessment systems being developed to define, promote and assess quality and excellence thus constitute a means of governing the field. In the following sections, we will investigate how these mechanisms – and the development of new measurement systems and practices – have been used in a European context, and by various actors, to argue for and shape a European governance field for higher education and research.

SHAPING THE NOTION OF QUALITY: A EUROPEAN DIMENSION OF QUALITY ASSURANCE IN HIGHER EDUCATION

In the 1980s and 1990s, when growing numbers of higher education systems across Europe were becoming deregulated, increasingly international and transformed into mass education systems, the topic of quality in higher education gained momentum (see for example, Kogan and Hanney 2000; Hedmo 2004). The expansion of student populations and institutions within and across systems raised concerns about trust and accountability. Consequently quality became a key issue on most policy agendas and raised public attention around the world.

The surge of interest in quality paved the way for a 'quality revolution' (Newton 2010), with a proliferation of new quality mechanisms, activities and agencies. The expansion was mainly located outside of state control, with the entrance of innovative and systematic external quality mechanisms resting on principles of voluntariness, independence and expertise. One such mechanism was professional accreditation, with roots in the

American context as the main quality model for accountability and/or quality improvement. One disciplinary area experiencing such a development in the European context was management education. In countries such as Spain, Italy and the UK, professional associations in the 1980s and 1990s introduced accreditation of master's degree programmes. Rather quickly, this quality model spilled over into the area of higher education more generally, and in Central and Eastern Europe, professional accreditation was adopted as a rational instrument in the transformation of higher education systems (Hedmo 2004). Despite severe criticism in academic circles, accreditation became a widely followed model in the spread of quality approaches in Europe, and especially beyond the national level.

European Developments

The expansion and variation of quality approaches across Europe were not solely responses to university reforms at the national level. Attempts to increase attention to quality and to stimulate an expansion of quality assurance approaches in Europe were also initiated by governmental and non-governmental actors operating at the transnational level, especially by EU authorities. The ideas and ideals of quality being issued by the EC were strongly interlinked with the belief in sharing and disseminating knowledge about EU members' higher education systems and constructing what was articulated as a 'European dimension' on the basis of shared values. By adding such a dimension to national higher education it could also be possible to reach the EU objectives of readability, comparability and compatibility of degrees (cf. Hedmo and Wedlin 2008).

In the early 1990s, specific projects and programmes were launched within the EU to encourage member states to cooperate and compare 'best practices' and to mutually recognise each other's quality approaches. In 1994–95 European pilot projects for evaluating quality in higher education were initiated by the European Council of Ministers, and in 1998 they issued a Recommendation (no 10212/98) on European cooperation in quality assurance in higher education. One outcome of these EU efforts was the establishment of the European Network for Quality Assurance (ENQA) in 1999. This membership organisation represented the interests of the increasing number of national quality assurance agencies operating in Europe, of ministries responsible for higher education in the EU and EFTA/EEA countries and of professional associations of higher education. The mission of the network was to promote the exchange of experiences and ideas in the field of external quality assurance in Europe. Rather soon ENQA also became a focal actor in another radical reform process taking place at the European level in the area of higher education, the Bologna Process (Hedmo 2012).

The Bologna Process was formally set in motion in 1999 following an intergovernmental agreement on constructing a comparable and transparent European Higher Education Area (EHEA) out of widely diverse national higher education systems by 2010. The process was largely triggered by the EU discourse and the EC policy agenda and the national governments' fear of losing their sovereignty to the supranational level. The belief in a European dimension in higher education was also central in the Bologna development, and a common approach to quality assurance was rapidly issued as a core means to achieve a more harmonised or unified European system (Hedmo and Wedlin 2008; Hedmo 2012).

The Bologna reform process nurtured the trend of assessment and quality evaluations in Europe. The intensity in quality activities was already increasing in the early 2000s as numerous seminars, conferences and specific projects were organised to exchange experiences, to compare quality assurance approaches and to spread ideas of best practices. As argued by ENQA:

> The process . . . is being more and more focused on quality assurance of higher education. Accordingly, serious interest for this issue is being demonstrated at more and more levels, many actors are positioning themselves for a place at the front of the debate, old themes are being redefined and new themes are being introduced. (ENQA Newsletter April 2002)

Different methodologies and procedures were compared and discussed during the Bologna events that took place between the ministerial meetings. A popular theme was accreditation, highlighted as the 'best practice' to achieve the goals of the Bologna Process (see for example, Lourtie 2001). The approach was strongly supported by some stakeholders, but also strongly resisted by others. Accreditation was referred to as covering a wide set of diverse concepts, procedures and missions. Most stakeholders preferred mutual recognition of national quality assurance procedures instead of a common European structure (Hedmo 2012).

Another recurrent theme was the European dimension, and how this unclear and abstract element could be appropriately concretised and understood. In line with the EU rhetoric it was expected that it should be based on a shared set of values and beliefs and that it should preserve and protect European diversity and consensus. The vagueness of the quality concept hence gave rise to debates about how to define quality at the European level, and it was clear that the concept needed further clarifications and agreements. In addition, it was argued that the formulation of a

European dimension presumed a multi-stakeholder approach, extending the participation of the Bologna signatory countries (Hedmo 2012).

A Multitude of Policy Actors

The quality agenda thus opened up for stakeholders operating beyond the scope of the nation states to mobilise and to take an active part in the process. For instance, in 2001 the European University Association (EUA) was created through a merger between the main university associations in Europe – the Association of European Universities (CRE) and the Confederation of European Union Rectors' Conferences – in order to give a strong and unitary voice to European universities in the process more generally. ENQA, representing the growing number of external quality assurance agencies across Europe, modified its membership criteria and activities. Also, new organisations such as the European Consortium for Accreditation (ECA) were set up in direct response to the Bologna Process. The ECA was created in 2003 to represent the interests of national accreditation agencies in the Bologna Process and to further the idea of accreditation.

In line with the ambitions, preferences and ideals of their members, these stakeholders drew up internal strategic plans for how to influence the notion of what constituted European-level quality. The EUA, for instance, protected and represented the core academic values of European universities in the process and argued that quality was a key responsibility of universities. The organisation supported the idea of mutual recognition of quality assurance at the European level, with accreditation being an option. ENQA, on the other hand, was sceptical about accreditation but supported the notion of external quality assurance in the form of transnational or pan-European evaluation criteria. The organisations also actively struggled to diffuse the idea of quality and to increase quality awareness in relation to the public at large and to their members in particular.

In parallel, they were involved in the quality activities going on within the EU. For instance, the EC launched a number of pilot schemes together with the EUA and ENQA in the early 2000s to stimulate external and transnational quality mechanisms in European higher education. For instance, the EU Socrates Programme supported the EUA's internal pilot project the 'Quality Culture Project' in 2002–06 and ENQA's pilot project the 'Transnational European Evaluation Project' (TEEP). Over time, the Bologna Process was increasingly intertwined with the EU Lisbon Agenda in 2000 and its supportive structure. It was considered an element of the EU policy agenda even though its scope transcended the borders of the EU. In line with the Bologna signatories and the policy-makers of the process, the EC promoted the spread of national quality assurance agencies across Europe. It also promoted the construction at the European level of agreed sets of standards, procedures and guidelines for external evaluations based on a European Qualification Framework in order to 'create a climate of trust based on transparency', also facilitating the recognition of diplomas and periods of study. By adding a 'trustworthy' European dimension of quality assurance to national systems, the expansion of mobility, employability, higher quality and increased attractiveness of European research and education would be realised (EC input to the Prague Report, 2001). The EU also demanded a development involving relevant stakeholders for achieving mutual trust and transparency across the continent (Hedmo 2012).

Designing the European Dimension

In 2003, it was declared that 'quality of higher education had proven to be at the heart of the setting up of the European Higher Education Area' (Berlin Communiqué 2003: 3). The role and meaning of European agencies in the process was strengthened and more formalised. At the Berlin meeting that year, the ministers of the Bologna Process adopted the ideals positioned by the EUA into the policy agenda and articulated that European universities should have the prime responsibility for quality assurance in higher education. At the same time, ENQA was asked to formally take command of the further development of the European dimension, meaning the construction of an agreed set of pan-European standards, guidelines and procedures on quality assurance (Berlin Communiqué 2003).

A precondition for this activity, however, was the use of a cooperative approach and the involvement of the main stakeholders in the process – in this case the EUA, the European Association of Institutions in Higher Education (EURASHE) and the European Student Information Bureau (ESIB[1]). Together with ENQA, these European associations formed the 'E4 group', being the founders of the European dimension of quality assurance. The Bologna management also recommended the inclusion of 'the expertise of other quality assurance associations and networks' (Berlin Communiqué 2003: 3) into this formative process, and consequently ENQA took the ideals of the EC, ECA and quality assurance networks operating in Central and Eastern Europe and Scandinavia into account.

This turn in the Bologna action lines harmonised with ENQA's vision, and also that of the EC, of being selected as the European platform for recognising higher education quality assurance agencies in Europe, spreading 'best practices' and advising national quality assurance agencies on appropriate procedures and initiating joint activities (ENQA 2003). ENQA had already started to initiate such activities with these organisations a few years before in order to consolidate their ideals into a common view on European quality assurance.

As an outcome, the European standards were shaped on the basis of the ideals and expertise of the E4 group and the 'outside' stakeholders. The European quality framework, formally adopted and implemented after the Bologna meeting in Bergen in 2005, was labelled the 'Standards and Guidelines for Quality Assurance in the European Higher Education Area (ESG)' and covered three separate parts: standards and guidelines for (1) internal and (2) external quality assurance, and standards and guidelines for (3) external quality assurance agencies. In order to be flexible and to preserve the diversity of the European higher education context and the national quality assurance agencies operating therein, the standards were formulated in an open and non-prescriptive manner. The European standards were also adopted as new membership criteria for ENQA.

At the London meeting in 2007, and partly as a response to input from ENQA, it was agreed that the E4 group should continue to develop and organise a European register covering those quality assurance agencies that were 'substantially' complying with the European-based standards (Secretarial Report – From Bergen to London 2007). It was important that such an operational model rest on a partnership approach in order to be trustworthy and legitimate. By developing such a register, the vision of a common EHEA could finally be realised. It was believed that EQAR could facilitate the mutual recognition of quality assurance agencies, promote student mobility, reduce the influence of 'accreditation mills' to gain credibility, and provide a basis for governments to authorise higher education institutions to choose any agency from the register (if compatible with national arrangements). In addition, the register could serve as an informative quality tool to enhance trust and transparency at the European level.

The setting-up phase of EQAR was funded by the EC. It was agreed, after some hesitant negotiations between the E4 members, that the register should rest on the principle of self-regulation and inclusiveness. The ENQA agency members, complying with the European standards, were automatically included on the list. It was also decided that the register should be organised as an independent, legal, international and non-profit organisation located in Brussels. Correspondingly, it was the first stakeholder-managed organisation, with non-governmental organisations playing a key role, to emerge directly from the Bologna Process. The register was designed as a web-based voluntary tool to be self-funded through fees from non-governmental and governmental members, applications, and the listed agencies.

In 2008, the leaders of the E4 group, the EC, and the Bologna Follow-Up Group (BFUG) formally launched the register at a ceremonial event in Brussels. During the first year, it received ten applications from invited quality agencies. Three of those agencies were recognised as complying with the quality standards for what was expected from a 'true' European agency. In 2015 the range of the list had increased to cover 36 agencies. The majority of the 'quality-stamped' and listed agencies were situated in the EU, and most of those (eight) were in Germany. The top decision-making body of the association is the General Assembly, consisting of various members being categorised into founding members, social partners and governmental members. Among other things, the Assembly approves the Register Committee managing the core objective of EQAR. The Committee members are viewed as independent experts in the area of quality assurance in higher education, and they evaluate and decide upon applications from national quality assurance agencies (EQAR 2015). As such, the EQAR does not simply operate as a novel mechanism for strengthening quality assurance in Europe, it also adds a second layer to quality assurance in two respects: first, by providing a European dimension based on a common set of shared pan-European standards for what constitutes higher education, and second, by adding a 'hierarchical level', opening up for an 'accreditation of accreditation agencies'.

CODIFYING NOTIONS OF EXCELLENCE: THE EUROPEAN RESEARCH COUNCIL

Around the turn of the millennium, and largely in parallel with the early phases of the Bologna Process, significant discussion and work to strengthen the European platform for research was started. Shaped largely by the agenda set in the discussions around the concept of a European Research Area (ERA, see Chapter 3) and the Lisbon Council declaration in 2000, these developments involved several initiatives to support the creation of a 'Europe of Knowledge' and a coherent space for research and researchers within Europe.

An important element in the work that took place within the frames of the EU is the development of a funding structure and mechanism to fund basic research at the European level, the ERC. The ERC was formally launched as part of the 7th Framework Programme (FP7) for research presented by the European Commission in 2005 (EC 2005). As one among several EU initiatives to increase policy and regulatory powers within the field of research, the ERC has become framed as one of the cornerstones for the creation of a European space for science and for the realisation of the ERA.

This was not, however, clear from the start, and for a long time the ERC was a contested and debated feature in the policy field, and well into the process the EC was not interested in being a candidate to host a pan-European funding initiative of the kind proposed by the ERC proponents (Nedeva 2013). However, as we move into the debates leading up to the creation of the ERC, we will see how the ERC became an important argument for the EC to increase its authority within the policy areas of research and science and a solution to some of the problems of the ERA. In particular we note two rhetorical elements of this work, centred on the notions of 'excellence' and 'competition', and how these became instrumental in moving this initiative forward.

Organised Efforts

Early initiatives and debates concerning the construction of something like an ERC originated in the scientific community. As significant criticism against the EC research funding programmes began to mount – particularly its focus on applied research, its bureaucratic structure and the politically laden 'distributional' approach to research funding – the idea of a pan-European funding mechanism to promote basic science started to grow. As ways to increase the funding base for basic science and to attempt to 'tap into' a larger share of the EU research money, members of the scientific community began to speak out for the idea of a European funding body, modelled largely on the national research councils common in many of the leading European countries as well as in the US (see for example, Abbott 1997; Pavitt 2000; Banda 2002). Presenting what he calls a 'radical proposal', Professor Pavitt, for instance, suggests that the EU should create a European agency for funding research at the transnational level that takes a new approach to research funding: independent from political intervention, run by the scientific community, and with a clear focus on high-quality original and basic research (Pavitt 2000).

Organised initiatives to move this idea forward came largely from the Scandinavian countries, in preparation for the Swedish and the Danish presidencies of the EU (in 2001 and 2002 respectively). A small group of representatives from research and funding organisations in these countries began to work to put this idea on the political agenda of the EU. Through workshops, meetings and conferences, this group managed to gather wide support among research funding organisations in some of the bigger member countries. For instance in France, the heads of the CNRS, the academy of the sciences and other science organisations, were publicly expressing their support for the idea (Gronbaek 2003: 396). Similarly in Germany, the heads of the Volkswagen Foundation, the Max Planck

Society and the DFG supported the initiative and helped to move it forward in their respective countries. This work also coincided with significant and ongoing reforms of systems of higher education and research within these countries (Banchoff 2002).

Other groups also formed to discuss options, present views, and push the idea of an ERC forward. Organisations such as Euroscience, Academia Europaea, ALLEA and others were all eager to pursue the idea and publicly speak out in favour of it (Gronbaek 2003). The European Union advisory board for research, EURAB, also spoke out in favour of it. Particularly visible and driving the debate within the scientific community was the life sciences community, with European organisations such as the European Life Sciences Forum (ELSF), the European Molecular Biology Organization (EMBO), the European Molecular Biology Laboratory (EMBL), and the Federation of European Biochemical Societies (FEBS) at the forefront. They organised conferences and events where the issue was debated (February and May 2003), which had a significant impact on the debate and the general awareness of the idea of an ERC. In a conference in October 2003, ELSF, together with Euroscience, organised a meeting aimed at including all areas of science and letting the 'scientific community speak with one voice' on the issue. For this community, the ERC idea thus provided an opportunity to ask for 'a much-needed tool for fostering curiosity-driven science', and a 'body that funds long-term research in all areas of human inquiry' (Connerade 2003: 4–7).

A Policy Discourse of Excellence and Competition

In the arguments presented to convince the political and the policy community that the idea of an ERC was appropriate, two concepts became central: excellence and competition. Beginning with the first, excellence, this became the main argument from the scientific community. The work of an 'expert group', convened by the Danish science minister to 'explore possible options' for the scope and purpose of an ERC, was particularly important in formulating this. They express the main mission of an ERC as follows: 'The mission of the European Research Council (ERC) is to promote excellence as a basis for social, cultural, and technological progress throughout Europe by funding world-class research' (ERCEG 2003: 15). Based on an analysis of the existing European research systems, the report outlines what is presented as 'shortcomings' of the existing system: a lack of a competitive 'quality setting' and funding scheme for research, a shortage of funding for basic and high-risk research, a shortage of high-quality researchers and a lack of career structures for scientists, and fragmentation in terms of organisation and funding of research. This was presented as a 'research gap' between Europe and other countries, most specifically the US: 'The European research is not strong enough: it does not match the research performance of the USA. Evidence suggests that a gap has emerged between Europe and the USA in performance of research' (ERCEG 2003: 21).

A report from another group, the High Level Working Group convened by the European Science Foundation, states similar arguments and presents their case for what they promote as a 'grand vision' for Europe. This report includes arguments for the ERC as the 'pan-European solution' to a number of problems related to European research, and it states that a fundamental requirement for this is that it be 'an institutional system which encourages and nurtures scientific excellence in Europe . . .' (ESF 2003: 6). Furthermore, it is stressed that '[a]n ERC must focus on excellence as the basis for its funding decisions' (ESF 2003: 8).

In this context, the notion of competition was introduced as the 'new' mechanism to promote and create excellence and to distribute funding on the European level. It was argued that by creating competition among researchers and research teams from different countries and regions, funding from a European source would create and foster excellence among European scientists and research communities. This would, it is argued, be the 'added value' of a European-level funding mechanism for science:

> So the European added value of the ERC is competition. We create European competition for the best brains to compete with each other, with the hope that excellence will be boosted from this competition. And the best one will become even better. So this is the whole idea behind it: boosting excellence through competition. (Interview, reported in Wedlin 2008)

The notion of 'added value' was an important recognition, and one that would become important in linking the ERC aims and missions to the political priorities of the EU. At the time, the understanding of 'added value' in the area was that anything that the EU does has to add value at the European level and contribute to networking and collaboration, or in other ways support the European integration project. This argument was often used by those opposed to the idea of an ERC: that any initiative in this area would have to contribute to the integration of research efforts or the coordination of national efforts. Since the EU, through the Treaty, was believed to have no formal authority to govern or fund basic science, this added-value argument was particularly salient in the EC's response to the initial idea of the ERC. Well into this process, the EC remained 'lukewarm' to the idea of an ERC, at least one that included the EC as the formal host (Wedlin 2008).

The work of the expert group and their attempt to reformulate the notion of added value was an important impetus to the change in the Commission's stance. Explicitly attempting to revise the understanding of the added-value argument, the group writes:

> It is now time to bring a new definition of added value, one that incorporates the principle of allowing a researcher in any European state to compete with all other researchers on the basis of excellence. Competition in order to achieve real excellence in research should become an essential part of a new, forward-looking definition of European added value. (ERCEG 2003: 9)

When the group delivered its final report to the Irish presidency in December 2003, the European Commission responded almost immediately with a formal communication entitled 'Europe and basic research' (EC 2004), fully endorsing the creation of a funding body for basic research. Building to a large extent on the recommendations and arguments of the expert group (also called the Mayor group), the communication argues that a funding mechanism for basic research, such as an ERC, would:

> ... make it possible to combat the effects produced by the compartmentalised nature of the national systems. By stimulating competition and encouraging innovation as well as experimentation in ideas and new approaches, including interdisciplinary ones, it would stimulate creativity, excellence and innovation by exploiting a form of European added value other than that produced by cooperation and networking: the added value which comes from competition at EU level ... converging on this point with the recommendations of the 'Mayor Group', the Commission plans to propose making the introduction of such a mechanism, as well as increased support for basic research, one of the main themes of the Union's future action in the field of research. (EC 2004: 13)

This rhetoric of competition and excellence, and its link to a revised formulation of the European added-value argument, were important in connecting the idea of the ERC to the overall political agenda of the EU and its member states. Here, the notion of the ERA and its links to the Lisbon Strategy goal to become the 'leading knowledge-based society' and to the Barcelona targets to increase public spending on research became important reference points for the debate on the ERC. The work of constructing the ERC opened a space both to argue for increased spending on research in general within the EU and to more clearly position science policy and basic issues of research funding and organising on the wider political agenda.

Revitalising the ERA Vision

On these grounds, the ERC debate, specifically its main features, became recognised as an important instrument to realise the vision of the ERA. With somewhat withering support for the ERA project during the early years of the new millennium (see EC 2002), the ERC was argued to be the mechanism that would see the vision of a coherent European research area finally come together (see for instance Gannon 2000; Banda 2002; Krull 2002; Smaglik 2003).

> In the long run, however, the ERA is likely to remain a bloodless vision unless there is an independent, flexible and self-administered pan-European funding body which – unlike the ponderous Framework – can react quickly to unexpected scientific developments. (*Nature* 2001: 871)

Seemingly seizing the opportunity to argue for an ERC within the framework of the ERA, both the ESF and EURAB (the European Research Advisory Board) argued forcefully for the creation of an ERC in this context:

> A strong recommendation is made for the creation of an ERC which should be regarded as being the cornerstone for the ERA and the key approach to developing a locus for basic research in Europe. (ESF 2003: 15)

> EURAB urges appropriate agencies and institutions within the EU, at both national and European level, to establish a European Research Council. This should be done after in depth debate (including with Europe's scientific research community) and careful planning, and as a significant new contribution to the development of ERA. (EURAB 2002: 3)

The arguments of European-wide competition and the need to increase European competitiveness by increasing spending on basic research seem to have caught the attention of the Commission, and with a formal communication in 2004 the idea of an ERC formally entered the EC and the political agenda of the EU.

TRANSNATIONAL EFFORTS TO CONSTRUCT EXCELLENCE AND QUALITY

In this chapter we suggest that transnational efforts – particularly the European ones we study – to establish pan-European quality assurance mechanisms and systems, and to define comparable criteria for quality and excellence, have been important in defining and legitimising an expanding

European governance field for higher education and research. The policy work to set jointly agreed upon standards and principles for quality and excellence, and the rhetoric guiding these dialogues, has involved a large set of transnational actors being organised in networks of constellations, working both in relation to but also in parallel with the EU. Their efforts have had a triple role: constructing and positioning themselves and their actions as governance mechanisms for the field; supporting and legitimising an expanding European governance field for higher education and research; and strengthening (although this was not necessarily the intention) the power and centrality of the EU as a governance actor within the field.

In our analysis, we have drawn attention to the influential role played by interest groups, networks and partial organisations, as they take the lead in forming criteria and principles for what constitutes quality and excellence in academic systems and, hence, norms and standards for what represent appropriate behaviour for higher education institutions. While national initiatives and systems for quality assurance and excellence are still believed to formally shape fundamental principles that guide claims for legitimacy for higher education institutions and the allocation of resources, these are increasingly coordinated and intertwined with initiatives being taken by a constellation of actors operating beyond the national level (cf. Grande and Peschke 1999).

In addition, the two empirical initiatives analysed in this chapter are largely shaped outside of, but not independently of, formal political systems. The shaping of European dimensions of quality and excellence being essential for a European governance field demands expertise and the bringing and maintaining of legitimacy, attention and knowledge by non-governmental actors. On the other hand, these processes are highly intertwined with the shaping of political institutional frameworks at the EU and international levels and below, and hence politicians and public agencies are also operating on these levels. Analysing these initiatives and the construction of quality and excellence in these complex organisational constellations helps us to better understand the dynamics and reciprocity characterising the transnational landscape of research and science activities and its multilevel and multi-actor organising. In these complex settings, accountability communities being developed around measurement systems and practices become influential actors in both formal and informal policy processes. These communities seem to play a double role: to legitimate the development of a transnational governance field on the basis of common European policy frameworks, and to legitimate actors, ideals and mechanisms operating within that field.

The findings also highlight the dynamics of legitimacy and prestige in the academic field, and the complexity in and importance of transnational governance mechanisms and principles in shaping such efforts. The work of non-governmental organisations such as accreditation agencies, ranking organisations, funding organisations and others may in this context ultimately have an influence on the creation and relationships of authority and power (Whitley et al. 2010) and the creation or reproduction of scientific elites within the academic system (Gläser 2007). Consequently, these organisations take the role as legitimating agencies (Durand and McGuire 2005), constructing, validating or supporting claims of legitimacy among actors in the academic field.

ACKNOWLEDGEMENT

This research was carried out with financial support for both authors from RJ (P2005-1189:1).

NOTE

1. Since 2007 renamed and reformed into the European Students' Union, ESU.

REFERENCES

Abbott, A. (1997), "New DFG head vows to back Germany's young scientists – and genetics research", *Nature*, 388, (7 August): 507.
Ahrne, G. and Brunsson, N. (2010), "Organization outside organizations: The significance of partial organization", *Organization* 18(1): 83–104.
Amaral, A. and Rosa, M.J. (2011), "Transnational accountability initiatives: The case of the EUA audits", in Stensaker, B. and Harvey, L. (eds) *Accountability in higher education: Global perspectives on trust and power*, New York and Abingdon UK: Routledge, pp. 203–20.
Banchoff, T. (2002), "Institutions, inertia and European Union research policy", *Journal of Common Market Studies* 40(1): 1–21.
Banda, E. (2002), "Implementing the European Research Area", *Science* 295: 443.
Bleiklie, I. (2011), "Excellence, quality and the diversity of higher education systems", in Rostan, M. and Vaira, M. (eds) *Questioning excellence in higher education: Policies, experiences and challenges in national and comparative perspectives*, Rotterdam: Sense Publishers, pp. 22–35.
Boli, J. and Thomas, G.M. (eds) (1999), *Constructing world culture: International nongovernmental organizations since 1875*, Stanford: Stanford University Press.
Brunsson, N. and Jacobsson, B. (eds) (2000), *A world of standards*, Oxford: Oxford University Press.

Connerade, J.P. (2003), "Will Europe have its research area?", *Euroscience News* 22(Winter 2003) 1: 4–7.

Corbett, A. (2005), *Universities and the Europe of knowledge: Ideas, institutions and policy entrepreneurship in European Community higher education policy 1955–2005*, Basingstoke: Palgrave MacMillan.

Czarniawska, B. and Genell, K. (2002), "Gone shopping? Universities on their way to the market", *Scandinavian Journal of Management* 18(4): 455–74.

Djelic, M.L. and Sahlin-Andersson, K. (eds) (2006), *Transnational governance: Institutional dynamics of regulation*, Cambridge: Cambridge University Press.

Durand, R. and McGuire, J. (2005), "Legitimating agencies in the face of selection: The case of AACSB", *Organization Studies* 26(2): 165–96.

EC, European Commission, (2002), COM 2002/0565 Final, "The European Research Area: Providing new momentum", http://eur-lex.europa.eu/legal-content/EN/TXT/PDF/?uri=CELEX:52002DC0565&from=EN [Accessed on 2015-06-08].

EC, European Commission, (2004), COM 2004/9 Final, "Europe and basic research", http://ec.europa.eu/transparency/regdoc/rep/1/2004/EN/1-2004-9-EN-F1-1.Pdf [Accessed on 2015-03-10].

EC, European Commission, (2005), "European Commission develops its plans for future research programme", IP/05/1171,http://europa.eu/rapid/press-release_IP-05-1171_en.htm.

El-Khawas, E. and Shah, T. (1998), "International review to assure quality. Comparative perspective on evolving practice", *Tertiary Education Management* 4(2): 95–101.

Enders, J. (2005), "Border crossings: Research training, knowledge dissemination and the transformation of academic work", *Higher Education* 49(1–2): 119–33.

ENQA (2002), Newsletter No 7, April.

ENQA (2003), "Statement of the European Network of Quality Assurance in higher education (ENQA) to the conference of European ministers of education in Berlin 18–19 September 2003", http://www.enqa.eu/wp-content/uploads/2013/06/030918-19STATEMENT_ENQA.pdf [Accessed on 2015-05-03].

ENQA (2014), "The concept of excellence in higher education", *Occasional papers 20*, http://www.enqa.eu/indirme/ENQA+Excellence+WG+Report_The+Concept+of+Excellence+in+Higher+Education.pdf.

EQAR (2015), "EQAR structure", http://www.eqar.eu/about/eqar-structure.html [Accessed on 2015-04-03].

ERCEG (2003), "The European Research Council. A cornerstone in the European Research Area", Report from the ERC Expert Group, also called the "Mayor group", Published by Ministry of Science, Technology and Innovation, Denmark.

Erkkilä, T. and Piironen, O. (2014), "Shifting fundamentals of European higher education governance: Competition, ranking, autonomy and accountability", *Comparative Education* 50(2): 177–91.

ESF (2003), "New structures for the support of high-quality research in Europe", ESF position paper.

EURAB (2002), "European Research Council", EURAB input 02.055, p. 3, http://ec.europa.eu/research/eurab/pdf/recommendations3.pdf [Accessed at 2015-03-10].

Finnemore, M. (1993), "International organizations as teachers of norms: The

United Nations Educational, Scientific, and Cultural Organization and science policy", *International Organization* 47(4): 565–97.

Gannon, F. (2000), "Does Europe exist?", *EMBO reports*, September 15, 1(3): 197. Available DOI: 10.1093/embo-reports/kvd056 [Accessed on 2015-03-10].

Gläser, J. (2007), "The social order of research evaluation systems", in Whitley, R., and Gläser, J. (eds) *The changing governance of the sciences*, Dordrecht: Springer, pp. 245–66.

Grande, F. and Peschke, A. (1999), "Transnational cooperation and policy networks in European science policy-making", *Research Policy* 28(1): 43–61.

Gronbaek, D. (2003), "A European Research Council: An idea whose time has come?", *Science and Public Policy* 30 (6): 391–404.

Hedmo, T. (2004), *Rule-making in the transnational space. The development of European accreditation of management education*, Doctoral Thesis no 109, Uppsala University, Department of Business Studies.

Hedmo, T. (2012), "Towards a European quality assurance system", in Vukosovic, M., Maassen, P., Nerland, M., Pinheiro, R., Stensaker, B. and Vabø, A. (eds) *Effects of higher education reforms: Change dynamics*, Rotterdam: Sense Publishers, pp. 185–201.

Hedmo, T. and Wedlin, L. (2008), "New modes of governance: The re-regulation of European higher education and research", in Mazza, C., Quattrone, P. and Riccaboni, A. (eds) *European universities in transition: Issues, models and cases*, Cheltenham, UK and Northampton, MA, USA: Edward Elgar, pp. 113–32.

Jayasuriya, K. (2010), "Learning by the market: Regulatory regionalism, Bologna and accountability communities", *Globalisation, Societies and Education* 8(1): 7–22.

King, R. (2009), *Governing universities globally: Organizations, regulation and rankings*, Cheltenham, UK and Northampton, MA, USA: Edward Elgar.

Knill, C. and Lehmkuhl, D. (2002), "Private actors and the state: Internationalization and changing patterns of governance", *Governance* 5(1): 41–64.

Kogan, M. and Hanney, S. (2000), "Reforming higher education", *Higher Education Policy Series 50*.

Kohler-Koch, B. and Eising, R. (eds) (1999), *The transformation of governance in the European Union*, London: Routledge.

Krull, W. (2002), "A fresh start for European science", *Nature* 419 (19 September): 249–50.

Lourtie, P. (2001), "Furthering the Bologna Process", *General report commissioned by the Follow-Up Group of the Bologna Process*.

Meyer, J.W. (1994), "Rationalized environments", in Scott, W.R. and Meyer, J.W., and associates (eds) *Institutional environments and organizations, structural complexity and organizations*, Thousand Oaks, CA: Sage, pp. 28–54.

Mörth, U. (2004), *Soft law in governance and regulation: An interdisciplinary analysis*, Cheltenham, UK and Northampton, MA, USA: Edward Elgar.

Nature (2001), "Storm clouds over Brussels", 411 (21 June): 871, http://www.nature.com.ezproxy.its.uu.se/nature/journal/v411/n6840/pdf/411871a0.pdf [Accessed on 2015-03-10].

Nedeva, M. (2013), "Between the global and the national: Organising European science", *Research Policy* 42(1): 220–30.

Newton, J. (2010), "A tale of two 'qualitys': Reflections on the quality revolution in higher education", *Quality in Higher Education* 16(1): 51–3.

Nicolaidis, K. and Egan, M. (2001), "Transnational market governance and regional policy externality: Why recognize foreign standards?", *Journal of European Public Policy* 8(3): 454–73.

Pavitt, K. (2000), "Why European Union funding of academic research should be increased: A radical proposal", *Science and Public Policy* 27(6): 455–60.

Power, P. (1997), *The audit society: Rituals of verification*, Oxford: Oxford University Press.

Risse, T. (2007), "Transnational actors and world politics", in Zimmerli, W.Ch., Richter, K. and Holzinger, M. (eds) *Corporate ethics and corporate governance*, Berlin: Spring Verlag, pp. 251–86.

Rostan, M. and Vaira, M. (eds) (2011), *Questioning excellence in higher education: Policies, experiences and challenges in national and comparative perspectives*, Rotterdam: Sense Publishers.

Schwarz, S. and Westerheijden, D. (eds) (2004), *Accreditation and evaluation in the European higher education area*, Dordrecht: Kluwer.

Shore, C. and Wright, S. (2000), "Coercive accountability: The rise of audit culture in higher education", in M. Strathern (ed.) *Audit cultures: Anthropological studies in accountability, ethics and the academy*, London: Routledge, pp. 57–89.

Smaglik, P. (2003), "Europe goes back to basics", *Nature*, 426 (20 November): 365.

Stensaker, B. and Harvey, L. (2011), *Accountability in higher education: Global perspectives on trust and power*, New York and Abingdon, UK: Routledge.

Sursock, A. (2011), "Accountability in Western Europe: Shifting quality assurance paradigms", in Stensaker, B. and Harvey, L. (eds) *Accountability in higher education: Global perspectives on trust and power*, New York and Abingdon, UK: Routledge, pp. 111–32.

Tamm-Hallström, K. (2004), *Organizing international standardization: ISO and the IASC in quest of authority*, Cheltenham, UK and Northampton, MA, USA: Edward Elgar.

Wedlin, L. (2006), *Ranking business schools*, Cheltenham, UK and Northampton, MA, USA: Edward Elgar.

Wedlin, L. (2008), "Creating a European space for science: The development of the European Research Council", paper presented at the 24th EGOS Colloquium in Amsterdam, July 2008.

Whitley, R., Gläser, J. and Engwall, L. (eds) (2010), *Reconfiguring knowledge production: Changing authority relationships in the sciences and their consequences for intellectual innovation*, Oxford: Oxford University Press.

Reports

Aarhus Declaration (2012), http://www.excellence2012.dk/fileadmin/www.excellence2012.dk/pdf/exc_declaration_FINAL_screen.pdf.

Berlin Communiqué (2003), http://www.ehea.info/Uploads/about/Berlin_Communique1.pdf.

Prague Report (2001), http://www.ehea.info/Uploads/Declarations/PRAGUE_COMMUNIQUE.pdf.

The Secretarial Report – From Bergen to London (2007), http://www.ehea.info/Uploads/Related%20EU%20activities/Report-from-BergentoLondon-May-2007.pdf.

7. Organising knowledge institutions – standardising diversity

Ivar Bleiklie, Gigliola Mathisen Nyhagen, Jürgen Enders and Benedetto Lepori

INTRODUCTION

The point of departure of this chapter is the statement by the editors of this volume on a previous occasion that universities are increasingly expected to play a crucial, multifaceted role in the development of modern society. The aim is to analyse the relationship between changing conceptions of knowledge, higher education reform policies and changing university organisation in Europe.[1] We question two common assumptions about the implications of this development: a) that the growing size and importance of higher education promote one specific rather than a wider diversity of knowledge ideals; and b) that universities are becoming more closely steered and tightly managed hierarchical organisations. We argue further that because governments tend to pursue the twin goals of efficiency and academic quality they tend to promote different mechanisms of governance depending on which goal is emphasised in specific contexts. Conceptually and empirically, we draw on organisation theory and comparative research on higher education reforms and their impact on academic systems and institutions in the last decades, comprising data from eight European countries. The chapter is divided into two main sections. In the first part the idea of a changing concept of knowledge is put into a political and social context of rapid growth of higher education and the way in which it relates to major developments in society at large. The second and last part analyses the organisational implications for modern university institutions.

HIGHER EDUCATION EXPANSION – TOWARDS A COMMON KNOWLEDGE IDEAL?

In the mid-1990s Gibbons et al. (1994) gave one of the most sweeping and widely known statements about the widening concept of knowledge and its implications in their book *The New Production of Knowledge*. Here they argue that a new form of knowledge production, "*. . . a distinct set of cognitive and social practices is beginning to emerge*" (Gibbons et al. 1994: 3). They call this set of cognitive practices 'Mode 2' knowledge production. Compared to Mode 1, the traditional mode of scientific knowledge production, Mode 2 is "*. . . more socially accountable and reflexive. It includes a wider, more temporary and heterogeneous set of practitioners, collaborating on a problem defined in specific and localised context*" (Gibbons et al. 1994: 3).

The argument has been criticised for being too simplistic, as it did not specify the content of the concept of knowledge, and overstated both the novelty and the universality of the movement from Mode 1 to Mode 2 (Bleiklie and Byrkjeflot 2002). However, in a follow-up to *The New Production of Knowledge*, members of the same author team published *Re-Thinking Science* (Nowotny et al. 2001), a book that gives a more contextual and 'thick' description of the topic and nuanced, less normatively biased analyses. Their analyses bring forth the complexity of the issue of knowledge and changes in knowledge production. The authors seek to demonstrate that although they hold on to their notion of an emerging Mode 2 knowledge production, the process is neither deterministic nor uniform, and its implications vary across academic fields and social settings. One of their major claims is that 'science' or 'research' is becoming more 'contextualised': Whereas science traditionally has been regarded as an inner-directed, intellectually self-propelled enterprise that has 'spoken' to society, it now increasingly finds itself integrated in society, embedded in a context that increasingly 'speaks back' to science. The process whereby this happens is extremely complex, as are its implications.

The expansion of higher education from elite to mass phenomenon makes it very easy and straightforward to understand why this integration happens and why its implications must necessarily be complex. This transition of higher education in North America, Europe and elsewhere meant that a system that for centuries catered to a very small fraction of the population, the educated elites of the learned professions and top civil servants, in the matter of four decades grew from serving a few per cent to encompassing about one half of each new generation. Research has experienced a similar growth, which means that employers – private companies, organisations and public enterprises – increasingly need research in order to do their job properly. They express this need in various ways. Partly they start to buy or produce their own research. Partly they need research-trained employees in order to apply research-based products. But as higher education institutions become more influential because research and scientific values become more widespread in society, they also become exposed to a stronger and more diverse influence from their surroundings – a steadily more informed and better educated public. Thus there is a two-way development of steadily stronger inter-relationships and mutual influences. This development also affects our notions about what research and academic activity is about. Although it may expose universities to a pressure to becoming more 'useful', this utilitarian pressure is not uniform because the needs of those who express them are more varied than ever.

Among a number of factors that add to this development is the inclusion of a wide array of previously distinct vocational schools into the higher education system. This brings in new constituencies with their often idiosyncratic ideas about knowledge that contribute to the dilution of traditional scientific conceptions. Put differently: as society becomes more 'knowledgeable', higher education has come under pressure to expand the kinds and types of knowledge it provides and to diversify the criteria by which it is judged. Traditional ideals about what counts as knowledge thus tend to be diluted. To put it shortly: as society becomes more 'knowledgeable', knowledge becomes more 'social' (Nowotny et al. 2001).

We have argued until now that the developments behind the widening and more utilitarian concept of knowledge that is emerging are a complex mix of diversifying and unifying trends. As the level of education increases in a society, employers increasingly hire people with higher education degrees and research training, while research-based products make up an increasing share of the economic output, and scientific knowledge production caters to the needs of an increasingly wide array of stakeholders. The implication is that as scientific knowledge gains influence in society, traditional research ideals are gaining influence in the definition of knowledge. Stakeholders will by the same token increasingly have research training, but because thcy also represent a wider variety of expectations based on an increasing diversity of needs and interests, universities will also be faced with a wider diversity of knowledge traditions and demands. These latter trends are likely to increase the diversity of ideas about what useful knowledge means (Bleiklie 2005; 2007). These arguments point to the following conclusion. The degree of standardisation and diversity of knowledge ideals in modern higher education systems are shaped by the tension between and relative strength of a scientific knowledge ideal and the way in which it interacts with the practices and ideals of a growing array of disciplinary and professional communities within higher education institutions.

The way in which the tension between these ideals plays out is likely to have organisational implications, because they are associated with power structures within academic institutions and higher education systems. From this point of departure we shall make two somewhat simplistic assumptions. In distinguishing between processes that generate diversity and those that push for standardisation, the former is likely to depend on the degree of decentralisation of power and influence, based on the autonomy of higher education institutions, disciplines and professional groups to shape the higher education system from 'below'. The push for standardisation is on the other hand more likely to depend on the capacity of governments to implement such policies in a top–down process regardless of the preferences of actors further down in the system. This leads us to the next point in our analysis.

MORE TIGHTLY MANAGED UNIVERSITIES?

In the 1960s and 1970s organisation theorists made universities sites of important academic studies that produced path-breaking contributions to organisation theory by developing concepts such as 'resource dependency', 'organised anarchies', 'loosely coupled organisations', and 'garbage can decision-making' (Cohen et al. 1972; Meyer and Rowan 1977; Pfeffer and Salancik 1974; Weick 1976). Universities were portrayed as a specific kind of organisation, loosely coupled and fragmented with decentralised structures, with weak leadership capacities to govern decision-making processes from the top. The picture depicted by organisation theorists is clearly of a specific organisational type characterised by bottom–up decision-making. However, since then, university reformers in most Western countries have implemented measures designed to remove these characteristics that were considered peculiar to universities. In their place the goal was to provide universities with stronger leadership capabilities and capacity for stronger top–down management. These processes of organisational change, which in some countries started as early as the 1980s, have accelerated in the last decade. They are characterised by parallel developments of rationalisation, promoted by the introduction of New Public Management rationales and steering instruments, and of intra-organisational processes of hierachisation of organisational structures (de Boer et al. 2007; Ferlie et al. 2008; Paradeise et al. 2009). While much of the recent debate has been inspired by these notions, some scholars have pointed to the pervasive and growing external penetration of universities through horizontal relationships linking organisational and individual actors with external constituencies often (but not always) dominated by academics (Theisens and Enders 2007; Whitley 2008; Bleiklie et al. 2015).

The claim that academics, as a consequence of recent reforms, have lost power (Bleiklie and Kogan 2007; Paradeise et al. 2009) therefore is an answer to a question that is framed in a particular and we believe too narrow way. Traditionally the focus has been on the extent to which academics gain or lose formal decision-making power within individual academic institutions. We claim that this perspective misses a wide range of decisions made by bodies that are heavily influenced by horizontal relationships among academics in areas such as research funding, evaluation, quality control, and promotion that have a real impact on the institutions and their members. These decision-making activities often limit the ability of institutional leaders to control their organisations and are at the same time part and parcel of the quality measures promoted by national governments alongside efficiency-oriented measures aiming at transforming universities into powerfully led strategic actors.

Therefore we argue that a study of organisational change in universities cannot be reduced to the question of the distribution of decision-making power among academics, administrators and other actors within individual institutions (Brunsson and Sahlin-Andersson 2000). The reason is that internal processes are inextricably linked to horizontal relationships and networks into which individual universities are integrated at several levels, from institutional leaders, via leaders of faculties and basic units to individual academics.

When we formulate assumptions about the relationship between knowledge ideals and organisational forms we should take these observations into consideration. Whereas we may assume that a process of stronger hierarchies and standardisation promotes convergence towards a common ideal and give less room for diversity, the influence of horizontal relationships and the increased diversity of academic subjects included in modern higher education institutions may, but will not necessarily, increase diversity. We shall return to this after a closer look at the organisational implications of these processes.

Although studies of the internal development of stronger managerial structures may strengthen the argument that universities have become more tightly managed and increased the influence of managers at the expense of academics (Paradeise et al. 2009; Bleiklie et al. 2015), the argument may hold less well against evidence that includes the horizontal cross-institutional national and international relationships into which universities are integrated. Consequently we argue that different coordinating principles coexist in today's universities. Furthermore, the interaction between organisational hierarchies and external relationships generates new sources of loose coupling, and the penetration of institutional hierarchies by inter-organisational networks entails new forms of interdependencies between environment and organisational processes. Before we return to the question of the relationship between changing knowledge ideals and organisational change, we will briefly develop the idea of more complex processes of organisational change a bit further. In addition to the already mentioned processes of strengthened organisational hierarchies and strengthened horizontal relationships among organisations, we also add the process of rationalisation.

Intra-organisational Hierarchisation

Organisational hierarchies may be defined as a mode of coordination of activities within formal organisations where positions are arranged vertically, where leaders use command and control to steer activities within their organisations, and managers handle the command and control line on behalf of the leadership. Since the early 1980s and what Keller (1983) called the managerial revolution in higher education, intra-organisational hierarchisation has also occupied a central position on public university reform agendas (Bleiklie and Kogan 2007). Universities have, partly at the initiative of ministries, partly at their own initiative, started to formulate goals, develop strategies and strengthen leadership, administrative structures and top–down steering of internal decision processes while reducing rank and file academic influence. Historically, attempts by reformers at securing better managerial control over internal decision-making in universities are nothing new, and the power balance has varied over time and across countries (Paradeise et al. 2009). Two issues are easily identified. One issue turns on representation on decision-making bodies. The other turns on the authority of elected bodies, at departmental, faculty and institutional levels. They came traditionally under many different names, such as board, council or collegium, but as a rule the system of elected bodies with decision-making authority was built up in such a way that higher-level bodies consisted of representatives from units at the level below. Whereas a department board was typically made up of representatives of some or all different employee groups, a faculty board was made up of representatives from the departments, and the university board of representatives from the faculties. In the last 30 years, the tendency is twofold. First, during the 1970s we saw an extension of the privileges of representation from full professors to all members of the university community (Clark 1987). Second, since the 1980s there has been a tendency in some countries (Netherlands, Norway and the United Kingdom for instance) to reduce the size of elected bodies and more recently to turn these bodies, except institutional boards, into advisory rather than decision-making bodies (Bleiklie et al. 2015; Paradeise et al. 2009). Institutional boards have by the same token changed character from being internally recruited representative bodies, usually dominated by academics, to being more influenced by external (stakeholder) representatives, making them more similar to corporate boards of business enterprises (Kretek et al. 2013). The process of hierarchisation is furthermore represented by the abolition of shared leadership structures, replacing elected academic leaders (rectors, deans and department chairs) by appointed ones equipped with stronger managerial capacities and decision-making powers (Bleiklie et al. 2015). Hierarchisation turned internal decision processes upside down from a system that was designed to representing the aggregate preferences of organisation members in a bottom–up process to a system designed to impose preferences of and decisions made by organisational leaders on organisation members at subordinate levels in a top–down process.

Emerging Inter-organisational Horizontal Relationships

Important relationships between universities and external actors are no novelty in the academic world. The increasing importance of inter-organisational networks can be seen in the context of the increasingly distributed organisation of higher education systems as well as a broader tendency to establish semiautonomous agencies, including agencies dedicated to funding, evaluation and quality assurance. Several studies have emphasised the importance of external linkages of university faculty for university life, for example, through direct connections to political power (Musselin 1999; Kogan et al. 2006), acquisition of external funding (Pfeffer and Salancik 1974) and quality assurance (Henkel 1991; Stensaker and Frølich 2012). In some countries, like France (Musselin 1999) and Italy (Reale and Poti 2009), the strong co-management and intertwined relationships between the ministry and the academic profession weakened the capacity for internal governance of universities. Here we argue that the influence of *inter-organisational relationships* has increased and is often formalised in the shape of various boards and panels closely connected to academic and/or stakeholder networks that often play a crucial role in the selection of their members. Thus power is being spread beyond the borders of individual organisations, residing in relations, both formal and informal, across organisations. The strengthened role of networks in public administration literature is associated with the development of new forms of governance since the 1980s, conceptualised as an alternative to traditional bureaucratic top–down steering (Addicott et al. 2006; Paradeise et al. 2009; Rodríguez et al. 2007; Rhodes and Marsh 1992). There are ample reasons to consider decision-making power based on horizontal networks as an alternative form and a possible challenge to top–down bureaucratic power. Nevertheless, network influence may emerge from needs that are felt and expressed by traditional hierarchic power holders as well (Kogan et al. 2006).

The promotion and maintenance of quality is such a need that is catered to by collegial bodies recruited from academic networks. Thus while governments seek to make universities more efficient by strengthening hierarchical university structures, quality tends to be promoted through processes that strengthen horizontal relationships at different levels of the organisation. Decisions on research funding, evaluation, quality assurance and staff recruitment are typically based on recommendations resting on quality considerations from academic review panels. Although academic power has been weakened within individual universities, it is making itself increasingly felt through decisions made by international (and national) peer review mechanisms related to research funding, evaluation and publication (Bleiklie et al. 2011; 2015). Another manifestation of stronger network influence is increasing stakeholder involvement through external representation on the boards of university institutions (Paradeise et al. 2009). Finally, during the last decades we have witnessed a tremendous growth, differentiation and formal integration of higher education systems, and with it a differentiation of government bodies involved in higher education governance (Bleiklie 2007; Guri-Rosenblit et al. 2007).

Horizontal power relations are thus promoted by several developments: growth and differentiation of the higher education system itself; differentiation of public bodies involved in higher education governance; increasing stakeholder involvement in higher education and increasing number of bodies related to evaluation, funding and publishing; and growing importance of the supranational level, for example, with the emergence of funding and evaluation mechanisms at the European level. Decisions concerning control over major resources, such as funding, organisational strategies and human resources, are therefore heavily affected by horizontal relationships.

One example of how horizontal relationships interfere with the hierarchical line of authority may be the way in which acquisition of increasingly important external funds affect the budget control of top leaders. Parallel to the strengthening of hierarchical authority in European universities, they have become increasingly dependent on external third party funding, mostly from funders like national and European research funding organisations. In countries like the Netherlands, Norway and Switzerland, between one fifth and one third of university budgets now come from third party funding (Bleiklie et al. 2015). This weakens, formally at least, the control of top leaders over the economy of their institution. The acquisition of such funds depends rather on researchers who are able to write successful research proposals and on members of funding panels (academics and sometimes other stakeholders) who make decisions on the allocation of funds. Furthermore, some large allocations like EU Framework Programme grants or National Centre of Excellence grants often come with a demand for matching funds that require the receiving institution to allocate funds to match the external funding. Recruitment of individual researchers to funding panels is often based on reputation and academic standing in the research community. Thus, the more successful the institution in the competition for external funding, the less formal control institutional leaders have over their budgets.

Other important academic bodies where academic judgement plays an important role and that may have an impact on and affect internal hierarchical structures are evaluation panels that may pass judgement and recommend measures that are necessary to improve the academic quality of individual institutions that their institutional leaders hardly can ignore. This may imply, for instance, recommendations to institutions or disciplines on strategically important issues like the profile of their teaching programmes or research portfolios (Stensaker and Frølich 2012). A third example is the practice of using academic hiring committees the recommendations of which may determine the hiring practices of the institutions.

Rationalisation

Rationalisation – in the Weberian sense of an increasing formalisation and standardisation of social relations and procedures (Weber 1978) – forms an essential element in organisational change affecting the contemporary university. Historically rationalisation can be seen as an on-going process, a long-term movement from the typical orientation of traditional groups towards a modern orientation that has been in the making since the sixteenth century. In the field of national and institutional university policy, this movement implied the slow replacement of decision ideals based on local, intramural, familial, personal and short-range considerations with decision ideals based on cosmopolitan, extramural, occupational, impersonal and long-range considerations (Clark 2006: 294f). Currently it is represented by such phenomena as the introduction and proliferation of quality assurance, evaluation, accountability procedures and incentive systems in which scientific quality is increasingly expressed in terms of standardised and quantifiable criteria. The bodies involved in these activities increasingly base their decisions on formal criteria and the collection of standardised data in order to measure and visualise the performance of academics and academic institutions. The various systems of formula funding of public universities that have been introduced in European countries usually encompass rules defining standardised criteria that determine the size of such components as the basic grant and compensation based on output measures such as number of new candidates and number of scientific publications (Kogan et al. 2006; Lepori et al. 2013; Paradeise et al. 2009). Accreditation and quality standards are increasingly administered by national bodies that oversee a standardised set of criteria and procedures for ascertaining quality and applying sanctions in order to achieve the standards they seek to achieve (Stensaker and Frølich 2012). Rationalisation in this sense is often justified in the name of improved democratic control and increased transparency that are supposed to make more efficient use of (public) funds. Public sector movements, such as New Public Management and the ensuing transformation of the discourse on public sector reform in general and higher education governance in particular, represent this trend (Bleiklie et al. 2011).

Interaction between the Three Processes

Taking rationalisation into account adds a new dimension to our understanding of processes of organisational change in academic institutions.

Standardised social orders negotiated at the policy level tend to replace local social orders related to different academic communities and expand into realms traditionally subject to control by academics, such as the evaluation of the quality of research activities. Accordingly, rationalisation entails a potential for external control of organisational processes, while it makes decoupling as a strategy to shield technical operations of universities from external control more difficult (Kogan et al. 2006). Evaluation and quality standards offer a telling illustration. Traditionally quality evaluation turned on assessment of the content of individual pieces of academic work, be it student papers and exams, or the scientific publications of applicants for tenured positions. Only academics in the relevant scientific fields were deemed competent to question the decisions made by academic evaluators. Standardised systems of evaluation and quality assurance, however, have two fundamental implications: First, quality assessments are not just made at the individual level, but also at the organisational level in terms of combined standardised performance measures that are assumed to express the capacity of the organisation to produce output at a given quality, such as number of candidates produced at bachelor, master's and PhD level, number of scientific peer-reviewed publications in recognised journals, amount of external funding acquired from research funders and so on. The second implication is that academic performance measured in this way is accessible to scrutiny by actors outside the academic community, to administrators, politicians and the public at large. No specific academic qualifications are required in order to compare and pass legitimate judgement on the performance of individual academics as well as of university organisations when expressed by easily accessible quantitative measures.

Thus formal rules and procedures embody and consolidate interests and power relationships and define the role of individual actors in decision-making processes. Accordingly, rationalisation creates new instruments for social control also inside universities themselves, because it renders decision premises accessible to managers and stakeholders that previously could only be assessed by academic professional judgement. The new instruments can, in turn, be used strategically by academic leaders to exercise power (for example, through incentive systems) in more indirect ways than direct command.

Rationalisation makes it easier to understand how hierarchies and horizontal relationships interact and how government policies aim at strengthening both.

Firstly, government policies have aimed at improving the efficiency of individual institutions and their academic quality. Whilst the former goal is pursued by stronger leadership and management structures, the latter is pursued by the use of academic peer-review mechanisms. However, efficiency and quality are both increasingly pursued by using formalised tools in order to establish goals and measure performance. Multiple goals and the coexistence of different coordinating principles are characteristics that universities share both with public sector agencies (Christensen and Lægreid 2011; Hood et al. 2004; Verhoest et al. 2010) and complex organisations in general. The study of organisational change in universities has been deeply concerned with this kind of tension between coordinating principles (Clark 1983; Neave 1998). Despite this wide recognition, the interaction of intra- and inter-organisational relationships in organisational processes has been offered surprisingly little attention.

Secondly, there are a number of reasons to assume that the discussed processes of rationalisation and hierarchisation entail a profound change in the structure and functions of horizontal relationships, which are pointed out by Bleiklie et al. (2015). Traditional conceptions of relevant networks associated with universities were mostly concerned with networks of academics, divided along the borders between epistemic communities whilst cutting across organisational as well as national borders. Rationalisation has created and strengthened new social orders that cross epistemic borders and generate a potential for new types of networks.

They do so *inter alia* by creating languages that allow communication across epistemic boundaries, for example standard ways of measuring and communicating academic performance, like we have seen in connection with the European Bologna process (Corbett 2005), and international ranking exercises (Paradeise and Thoenig 2013; Wedlin 2006). Another and more telling example is the European Framework Programmes for research funding that also contributed to opening new spaces, connecting social groups, like academics, policymakers and bureaucrats, in new ways. Growing national arenas for funding of research and innovation partnerships between universities and industry is another potential type of site for network formation and strengthened horizontal bonds among representatives of academia, industry and bureaucracy (Brown 2011).

Furthermore, the emergence of universities as strategic actors – a movement often strongly promoted by governments – generates an interest in networks and strategic alliances between universities as well as between universities and other actors such as members of evaluation bodies and funding agencies. Expected improvements of strategic positioning and organisational performance as well as improvements in overall system governance motivate the call for inter-organisational networking (Bleiklie 2007). Hence, with the emergence of organisational hierarchies, the impact of external university linkages will (also) be mediated by the structural position of the persons involved in the internal hierarchy, while external networks and social relationships at the same time will influence internal careers and nominations to positions like those of rectors or deans. This kind of interaction between internal hierarchies and external relationships may be illustrated by the implications of the emergence of new centres of power around centres of excellence and large externally funded projects.[2]

Dimensions of Networks

The concept of 'network' in social science analysis has many uses, and many attempts have been made at distinguishing between different types of networks and developing schemes for classification of networks (e.g. Rhodes and Marsh 1992; Van Waarden 1992). In order to specify better how external relationships and associated actor networks interact with decision-making in universities, we distinguish between three dimensions along which external relationships and network characteristics may vary: level, function, and membership.

The first dimension refers to the *level* at which decisions are made. If we think of public universities as parts of the structure of democratic representative systems, the institutional design implies a vertical line of authority, from the electorate, via elected assemblies and central government ministries to the different branches and national government agencies, and further down to individual institutions such as universities and colleges (Koppenjan et al. 2009). Thus we are dealing with a hierarchical chain of decisions that goes beyond single universities, but is relevant to better understand how individual university organisations operate. As for our argument about penetrated hierarchies it is important to point out the different access points at which decisions made by external bodies may enter and interfere with the vertical chain of decisions: from policy-making via policy implementation to institutional and intra-institutional levels. Taken together these network-based collegial decision arenas penetrate and limit the power of university leaders in many different ways.

From what is said above it is already clear that decisions made by external bodies differ not just in terms of the level, but also in terms of the *functions* that are served by the decision-making activity. Such functions may range from the formulation of supranational and national higher education and research policies, allocation of research funds, judgements made in evaluation reports on the quality of academic institutions, disciplinary fields, single university departments or research centres and decisions made by hiring committees or referees on publication in scientific journals. In all these contexts, academic influence is based on specialised knowledge and the privileged access granted to persons deemed to be particularly knowledgeable and influential in order to assure that decisions made in these areas promote legitimacy as well as quality. As already pointed out, one of the reasons why networks have gained importance in new and more formal ways in recent decades is political priorities that have emerged regarding the importance of promoting academic quality in order to promote competitive knowledge economies in Europe (Gornitzka 2009). The main organisational mechanisms by which these quality concerns are accommodated are two: strong academic representation on decision-making bodies or by the use of advice from academic peer review panels. This brings us to the last dimension.

The kind of networked bodies we are dealing with in the context of universities brings together actors from different organisations either ad hoc (for example, review panels, white paper commissions and evaluation panels) or based on temporary *membership* (funding agency and programme boards, institutional boards). They recruit members from different organisations, but whilst bodies with managerial and strategic functions (for example, institutional boards) tend to have a stakeholder character, bodies whose main function is to sustain or improve academic quality tend to recruit senior academic members.

In sum, the tightening of hierarchical control over decisions made within individual institutions as well as within the entire chain of authority envisaged by theories of representative democracy has been paralleled by dependence upon and penetration by decisions made by outside actors. Horizontal external relationships interfering with vertical authority chains are nothing new, but the current relationships are more strongly embedded in government policies in a more formalised way than previously. While external bodies and networks may affect internal decision processes on different levels of authority, and have different functions and membership, they are increasingly given formalised roles in order to promote specific public policies aiming at improving the accountability and quality of academic institutions.

UNIVERSITIES AS PENETRATED HIERARCHIES AND KNOWLEDGE IDEALS

Academic institutions across Europe are changing. The dominant account of change holds that universities are in the process of becoming more tightly coupled and less anarchic; more centralised, autonomous, strategic actors; hierarchically integrated and tightly managed where the position of academics is closer to that of any employee group in a business enterprise (Bleiklie and Kogan 2007; Paradeise et al. 2009).

The concept of *penetrated hierarchies* coined by Bleiklie et al. (2015) indicates that organisations with formal hierarchical structures with which leaders control key organisational processes like strategy, budgeting, internal career, at the same time are characterised by the presence of horizontal connections. Those connections run between actors who occupy specific positions in the organisational hierarchy and actors located at the policy and agency levels, which control relevant parts of the institutional and resource environment of the organisation itself.

We argue that the penetration of universities by external relationships is likely to strengthen old and to generate new sources of anarchy and loose couplings. If university governance arrangements traditionally have been perceived as some sort of compromise between academic collegial power and administrative power internally and institutional autonomy and government steering externally, the emerging relationships have complicated the picture in two ways: universities are integrated in horizontal as well as hierarchical governance patterns, and the division between academic collegial jurisdictions and those of administrators and outside actors are becoming blurred (Bleiklie 2007).

Redesigning Academic Hierarchy and Emerging New Sources of Power

One of the consequences (as well as causes) of this development of universities as 'penetrated hierarchies' is the reconfiguration of the academic profession (Musselin 2011). According to Bourdieu (1988) the academic field in which the profession operates is structured by two sets of antagonistic forces. The first set puts the inherited, economic and political capital (mainly present in law and medicine) against the scientific and intellectual capital (characteristic for the sciences and the humanities). The second set puts the academic capital (control over the academic profession) against the intellectual and scientific prestige rewarded outside universities themselves. Bourdieu thus stressed how antagonistic forces across the academic field organise the academic profession into different categories: from the scholar driven by scientific prestige (and in some cases looking for recognition from society at large) to the academic leader-manager sitting in all kinds of bodies regulating access and trajectories within the profession.

Recent developments experienced by universities run together with the internal ordering of the academic profession (Musselin 2004). Some categories of academics become more numerous, are recognised as filling more important roles and constitute emerging new groups of academic gatekeepers regulating individual access to funding, prestige and positions, and affecting organisational priorities and strategies. A first category consists of the wide range of reviewers sitting on the numerous scientific committees of research councils and/or on editorial boards of major journals and/ or on assessing teams of evaluation agencies. These partly overlapping groups play an increasing role in the regulation of the academic profession by setting the norms to be applied, by rewarding 'the best' but also by publicising the results and by classifying the activities of their colleagues.

Another category consists of co-opted elites (Kogan et al. 2006), i.e. academics involved in the design of higher education and research policies pushing their own views and conceptions. They might be influential individuals acting as institutional entrepreneurs or associations, groups and bodies taking on this role. Let us think for instance of the increasing influence of the conference of university rectors (presidents/vice chancellors). One example is their crucial influence during the preparation of the 2007 act that reformed the internal governance of French universities.

A further development is linked to the emergence of a specific group of academics at the frontier between academia and management. The traditional 'primus inter pares' who occupied deanships, rectorates (presidencies/vice chancellorships) or other forms of academic leadership positions, increasingly become full-time managers who still invoke their membership in the academic profession, but hardly any engagement in academic activities such as research and teaching. The sphere of activity of this specific group also expanded. Evaluation agencies, research councils or support functions are led by individuals of this group that mix academic and management capacities to structure and define the activities of these bodies, to fix the rules and work with bureaucrats to design the 'right' procedures. One example of the normative and organising power of this group may be illustrated by policies designed to enhance quality through various initiatives promoting excellence by offering highly competitive funding initiatives at the European level (ERC) or nationally (like the German *Exzellenzinitiative* where the main operators of the peer review process are the German research council (*Deutsche Forschungsgemeinschaft*) and the German scientific council (the *Wissenschaftsrat*) (Bleiklie and Lange 2010).

The emergence, evolution and strengthening of these sub-groups within the academic profession redistribute the power balance among academics in two ways. First, it confirms that scientific prestige is only one among several ways to get recognition and make a career: Different paths relying on different types of expert knowledge and power can be observed. Second, the reconfiguration of the academic profession goes along with the development of the intra-organisational hierarchisation of universities. As shown by Musselin (2011), university managers need the legitimacy and decisions of the new academic power-holders to exercise their authority within their institutions. By doing so, they become dependent on two categories of faculty members. The first is constituted by those who participate in external decision-making bodies and can influence decisions within and outside their university. The second are made up by those who are being rewarded by such bodies, and the more they are rewarded in terms of funding and/or prestige the more negotiating power they get vis-à-vis their university.

CONCLUSION

The development of knowledge ideals and organisational forms in the academic world is complex. We started from the rather simplistic premise that diversity of knowledge ideals is likely to be promoted by decentralised organisational structures that permit bottom–up processes based in an increasing number of academic subjects, disciplines and basic units, sometimes in close collaboration with strong and active stakeholders (for example, professional associations, employers and influential customers), to create political upward push and create sufficiently strong pressure to allow a diversity of knowledge ideals to flourish. Conversely, convergence and standardisation of knowledge ideals is likely to occur in higher education systems dominated by traditional scientific ideals in terms of which all academic subjects and fields are evaluated and structured. We conclude that we have observed forces pushing in both directions. The influence conveyed by more powerful leaders and stronger managerial structures are to some extent countered by the influence of external penetration by external decision-making bodies often dominated by groups of influential academics. However, we also pointed out the role of rationalisation which affects both the two former processes, not so much in terms of the knowledge ideals that are ostensibly promoted, but rather in terms of the way in which academic performance including research and teaching is measured and evaluated. These procedures for measuring and evaluating performance often entail specific prescriptions for what kind of research funders prefer (international and cross-disciplinary, problem-oriented research), for how new knowledge is presented (article rather than monograph format) and communicated (through peer-reviewed journals rather than reports or books) and for what kind of achievements are considered worthy of merit (research rather than teaching). This process of rationalisation is powerful in the sense that it creates spaces for communication of knowledge, evaluation of new knowledge and academic performance that can include a wider set of actors than previously. This may promote more openness and more democratic scrutiny of the activity of universities as crucial institutions in modern knowledge economies. They may also promote administrative structures in which considerable time and resources are spent on developing ways of communication and evaluation of academic performance that promote conformity by supporting fulfilment of formal standards rather than development of new ideas and critical knowledge. The changing organisation of academic institutions also has implications for the academic profession. Although rank and file academics may have less influence within their own universities than previously, new groups of more powerful academics are emerging. Their power is based on positions in external bodies that make decisions affecting universities in important ways. This renders the questions of whether the academic profession is losing or gaining power less interesting than the questions of the changing ways in which academic power is exercised and the ways in which it affects the management of national and supra-national systems of funding and evaluation, of communication of research and of hiring of personnel in individual universities.

NOTES

1. Although we draw on an increasing body of literature on changes in higher education in European higher education, three research projects in which the authors have participated are particularly important, a comparative research project on higher education reforms in England, Norway and Sweden during the 1980s and 1990s (Kogan et al. 2006), a comparative study of university governance in England, France, Germany, Italy, the Netherlands, Norway and Switzerland (Paradeise et al. 2009), and a comparative study of organisational change in universities and higher education policies in England, France, Germany, Italy, the Netherlands, Norway, Portugal and Switzerland (Bleiklie et al. 2011; 2013).
2. Bleiklie, I., N. Frølich, K.L. Hope, S. Michelsen and G. Mathisen Nyhagen (2013), TRUE Case Study Monograph: Developing a university strategy – a Norwegian case, p. 26.

REFERENCES

Addicott, Rachael, Gerry McGivern and Ewan Ferlie (2006), 'Networks, Organisational Learning and Knowledge Management: NHS Cancer Networks', *Public Money & Management*, 26:2, 87–94.

Bleiklie, Ivar (2005), 'Organizing Higher Education in Knowledge Society', in I. Bleiklie and W.W. Powell (eds), 'Universities and the Production of Knowledge', Special issue *Higher Education*, 49(1–2): 31–59.

Bleiklie, Ivar (2007), 'Systemic Integration and Macro Steering', *Higher Education Policy*, 20: 391–412.

Bleiklie, Ivar and Haldor Byrkjeflot (2002), 'Changing Knowledge Regimes – Universities in a New Research Environment', *Higher Education*, 44(2–3): 519–32.

Bleiklie, Ivar and Maurice Kogan (2007), 'Organisation and Governance of Universities', *Higher Education Policy*, 20: 477–93.

Bleiklie, Ivar and Stefan Lange (2010), 'Competition and Leadership as Drivers in German and Norwegian University Reforms', *Higher Education Policy*, 23(2): 173–93.

Bleiklie, Ivar, Jürgen Enders, Benedetto Lepori and Christine Musselin (2011), 'New Public Management, Network Governance and the University as a Changing Professional Organization', in Tom Christensen and Per Lægreid (eds), *Ashgate Research Companion to New Public Management*, Aldershot: Ashgate, pp. 161–76.

Bleiklie, Ivar, Jürgen Enders and Benedetto Lepori (2015), 'Organizations as Penetrated Hierarchies. Institutional Pressures and Variations in Patterns of Control in European Universities', *Organization Studies*, 36(7): 873–896. DOI: 10.1177/0170840615571960.

de Boer, Harry, Jürgen Enders and Uwe Schimank (2007), 'On the Way towards New Public Management? The Governance of University Systems in England, the Netherlands, Austria and Germany', in Dorothea Jansen (ed.), *New Forms of Governance in Research Organisations – Disciplinary Approaches, Interfaces and Integration*, Dordrecht: Springer.

Bourdieu, Pierre (1988), *Homo Academicus*, Cambridge: Polity Press.

Brown, Roger (ed.) (2011), *Higher Education and the Market*, New York and Milton Park: Routledge.

Brunsson, Nils and Kerstin Sahlin-Andersson (2000), 'Constructing Organizations: The Example of the Public Sector Reform', *Organisation Studies*, pp. 721–46.

Christensen, Tom and Lægreid, Per (eds) (2011), *Ashgate Research Companion to New Public Management*, Aldershot: Ashgate.

Clark, Burton R. (1983), *The Higher Education System: Academic Organisation in Cross-National Perspective*, Berkeley and Los Angeles: University of California Press.

Clark, Burton R. (ed.) (1987), *The Academic Profession*, Berkley, Los Angeles, London: University of California Press.

Clark, William (2006), *Academic Charisma and the Origins of the Research University*, Chicago and London: The University of Chicago Press.

Cohen, Michael D., James G. March and Johan P. Olsen (1972), 'A Garbage Can Model of Organizational Choice', *Administrative Science Quarterly*, 17(1): 1–25.

Corbett, Anne (2005), *Universities and the Europe of Knowledge*, Houndmills, Basingstoke: Palgrave Macmillan.

Ferlie, Ewan, Christine Musselin and Gianluca Andresani (2008), 'The Steering of Higher Education Systems: A Public Management Perspective', *Higher Education*, 56(3): 325–48.

Gibbons, Michael, Camille Limoges, Helga Nowotny, Simon Schwartzman, Peter Scott and Martin Trow (1994), *The New Production of Knowledge. The Dynamics of Science and Research in Contemporary Society*, London, Thousand Oaks, New Dehli: Sage.

Gornitzka, Åse (2009), 'Networking Administration in Areas of National Sensitivity: The Commission and European Higher Education', in Alberto Amaral, Guy Neave, Christine Musselin and Peter Maassen (eds), *European Integration and Governance of Higher Education and Research*, Dordrecht: Springer, pp. 109–32.

Guri-Rosenblit, Sarah, Helena S. Sebkova, and Ulrich Teichler (2007), 'Massification and Diversity of Higher Education Systems: Interplay of Complex Dimensions', *Higher Education Policy*, 20: 373–89.

Henkel, Mary (1991), *Government, Evaluation and Change*, London and Philadelphia: Jessica Kingsley Publishers.

Hood, Christopher, Oliver James, B. Guy Peters and Colin Scott (eds) (2004), *Controlling Modern Government*, Cheltenham, UK and Northampton, MA, USA: Edward Elgar.

Keller, George (1983), *Academic Strategy. The Management Revolution in American Higher Education*, Baltimore and London: The Johns Hopkins University Press.

Kogan, Maurice, Marianne Bauer, Ivar Bleiklie and Mary Henkel (eds) (2006), *Transforming Higher Education. A Comparative Study* (2nd edition), Dordrecht: Springer.

Koppenjan, Joop, Mirjam Kars and Haiko van der Voort (2009), 'Vertical Politics and Horizontal Policy Networks: Framework Setting as Coupling Arrangement', *The Policy Studies Journal*, 37(4): 769–92.

Kretek, Peter M., Zarco Dragsic and Barbara M. Kehm (2013), 'Transformation of University Governance: On the Role of University Board Members', *Higher Education*, 65(1): 39–58.

Lepori, Benedetto, John Usher and Marina Montauti (2013), 'Budgetary Allocation and Organisational Characteristics of Higher Education Institutions:

A Review of Existing Studies and a Framework for Future Research', *Higher Education*, 65(1): 59–78.

Meyer, John W. and Brian Rowan (1977), 'Institutionalized Organizations: Formal Structure as Myth and Ceremony', *The American Journal of Sociology*, 83(2): 340–63.

Musselin, Christine (1999), 'State/University Relations and How to Change Them: The Case of France and Germany', in Mary Henkel and Brenda Little (eds), *Changing Relationships Between Higher Education and the State*, London and Philadelphia: Jessica Kingsley.

Musselin, Christine (2004), *The Long March of French Universities*, London and New York: RoutledgeFalmer.

Musselin, Christine (2011), 'European Universities' Evolving Relationships: The State, the Universities, the Professoriate', Contribution for the 24th CHER Conference, University of Reykjavik, 23–25 June.

Neave, Guy (1998), 'The Evaluative State Reconsidered', *European Journal of Education*, 33(3): 265–84.

Nowotny, Helga, Peter Scott and Michael Gibbons (2001), *Re-Thinking Science. Knowledge and the Public in an Age of Uncertainty*, Cambridge: Polity.

Paradeise, Catherine and J.C. Thoenig (2013), 'Academic Institutions in Search of Quality: Local Orders and Global Standards', *Organization Studies*, 34(2): 189–218.

Paradeise, Catherine, Emanuela Reale, Ivar Bleiklie and Ewan Ferlie (eds) (2009), *University Governance: Western European Comparative Perspectives*, Dordrecht: Springer.

Pfeffer, Jeffrey and Gerald R. Salancik (1974), 'Organizational Decision Making as a Political Process: The Case of a University Budget', *Administrative Science Quarterly*, 19(4): 135–51.

Reale, Emanuela and Bianca Poti (2009), 'Italy Local Policy Legacy and Moving to an "In Between" Configuration', in Catherine Paradeise, Emanuela Reale, Ivar Bleiklie and Ewan Ferlie (eds), *University Governance: Western European Comparative Perspectives*, Dordrecht: Springer.

Rhodes, R.A.W. and David Marsh (1992), 'New Directions in the Study of Policy Networks', *European Journal of Political Research*, 21: 181–205.

Rodríguez, Charo, Ann Langley, Francois Béland and Jean-Louis Denis (2007), 'Governance, Power, and Mandated Collaboration in an Interorganisational Network', *Administration and Society*, 39: 150.

Stensaker, Bjørn and Nicoline Frølich (2012), 'University Strategizing: The Role of Evaluation as a Sensemaking Tool', in Stensaker, Bjørn, Jussi Välimaa and Cláudia Sarrico (eds), *Managing Reform in Universities. The Dynamics of Culture, Identity and Organisational Change*, Basingstoke: Palgrave Macmillan.

Theisens, Hans and Jürgen Enders (2007), 'State Models, Policy Networks and Higher Education Policy', in Georg Krücken, Anna Kosmützky and Marc Torka (eds), *Towards a Multiversity? Universities between Global Trends and National Traditions*, Bielefeld: Transcript Verlag, pp. 87–107.

Verhoest, Koen, Paul G. Roness, Bram Verschuere, Kristin Rubcksen and Muiris MacCarthaigh (2010), *Autonomy and Control of State Agencies. Comparing State Agencies*, Houndmills, Basingstoke: Palgrave Macmillan.

Van Waarden, Frans (1992), 'Dimensions and Types of Policy Networks', *European Journal of Political Research*, 21: 29–52.

Weber, Max (1978), *Economy and Society. An Outline of Interpretive Sociology*, Berkeley, Los Angeles, London: University of California Press.

Wedlin, Linda, (2006), *Ranking Business Schools. Forming Fields, Identities and Boundaries in International Management Education*, Cheltenham, UK and Northampton, MA, USA: Edward Elgar.

Weick, Karl (1976), 'Educational Organizations as Loosely Coupled Systems', *Administrative Science Quarterly*, 21(1): 1–19.

Whitley, Richard (2008), 'Constructing Universities as Strategic Actors: Limitations and Variations', in Lars Engwall and Denis Weaire (eds), *The University in the Market*, Colchester: Portland Press Limited, pp. 23–37.

8. Academies and their roles in policy decisions

Lars Engwall

INTRODUCTION[1]

Standing on the shoulders of Plato and his school in Academia outside Athens, modern academies emerged from Renaissance Italy in the fifteenth century and onwards, and can today be found all over the world. Although not always very visible, they play an important role in policy decisions. They do so in two respects: policy for science and science for policy (Engelbrecht and Mann 2011: 19), that is, providing input for decisions (1) on the allocation of resources, academic governance and other conditions for research, and (2) on other significant political issues.[2] In the first case it is a question of to what extent and how tax-payers' money should be allocated to higher education and research, while the second type of input implies the offering of expertise to politicians regarding issues such as energy, the environment, and health.

Of these two tasks the former, science policy, can be regarded as promoting the latter: i.e. the more attention society pays to research and higher education, the more opportunities to provide input for other strategic decisions. It can even be argued that science policy to a certain extent, particularly before Putin came to power, has taken over the role of defence policy during the past few decades (Engwall 2005): military expenses have been on the decline in many countries, while spending on research and higher education has gone in the other direction. In other words, economic power in relation to other countries (Porter 1990) has become more in focus than the military power. Competitiveness based on knowledge supremacy is the gospel. As stated by the 1965 Nobel Laureate in Medicine and Physiology, François Jacob:[3]

> The power of a nation was long measured by that of her army. Today, it is rather evaluated by her scientific potential. (my translation)

Like defence policy, science policy is facing increasing challenges (Lane et al. 2011). In this struggle, all voices are not listened to with equal effectiveness. Therefore reputation is an important feature of the system. And, this reputation is built on the gradual admission into successively more prestigious scientific elites. In this process, universities through their career systems are crucial, but so are academies. Although many of them were once founded as a complement to, or in competition with, universities, today they constitute important devices for the selection of scientific elites. In this way these organisations have also acquired a signficant impact on policy decisions. The reason is that academies are supposed to host the outstanding members of scientific disciplines.

Against the above backdrop, *the present chapter aims at demonstrating the role of academies in policy decisions.* For this purpose the following section will briefly summarise the development of academies over time. This exposition will be followed by an analysis of the characteristics of academies. It will point to the two important roles expressed in mission statements of academies: (1) international collaboration and (2) interaction with society. These roles are played both by individual members and the national academies themselves. However, like many other organisational fields, that of academies has seen the emergence of organisations that gather individual organisations into meta-organisations (Ahrne and Brunsson 2008). The development of these international organisations will be summarised in a subsequent section, followed by one dealing with the relationship between European academies and society. A final section will present conclusions.

The Emergence of a Population of Academies

As pointed out by way of introduction, academies constitute a successful organisational form diffusing from Renaissance Italy to other European countries and the rest of the world (Figure 8.1 and Table 8.1). Academies were thus founded in Italy as early as the fifteenth century, although many of them disappeared. The oldest still existing academy is therefore Accademia dela Crusca, which was founded in 1583. Oriented towards languages, it published a first cdition of an Italian dictionary in 1612, and became the role model for many other academies, among them the French l'Académie française from 1635. Later in the seventeenth century this academy was followed by two others in France, both founded by Jean-Baptiste Colbert: l'Académie des inscriptions et belles-lettres in 1663 and l'Académie des sciences in 1666.[4]

Parallel developments occurred in Germany and the United Kingdom. In 1652 the oldest continuously existing academy of sciences – as of 2007 Deutsche Akademie der Wissenschaften Leopoldina – was founded as

Sources: http://www.accademiadellacrusca.it, http://www.institut-de-france.fr/fr/une-institution/son-histoire. Hahn (1971), Leopoldina (2010), Bryson and Turney (2010), http://www.bbaw.de, Engwall (2012), http://www.rae.es, Hildebrand (1939, p. 45), http://www.royalacademy.dk, http://www.amphilsoc.org/, http://www.ngzh.ch/, http://www.khmw.nl, http://www.dknvs.no, http://www.academieroyale.be, http://www.acad-ciencias.pt, http://www.royalsoced.org.uk, http://www.cas.cz/o_avcr/historie/, http://www.ria.ie and Grau (1988).

Figure 8.1   Geographical distribution of the early academy foundations

Table 8.1　Academy pioneers in different countries

Year	Name	Country	Location
1583	Accademia dela Crusca	Italy	Florence
1635	l'Académie française	France	Paris
1652	Academia Naturae Curiosorum	Present Germany	Schweinfurt
1660	Royal Society	United Kingdom	London
1700	Preußische Akademie der Wissenschaften	Prussia	Berlin
1710	Royal Society of Sciences at Uppsala	Sweden	Uppsala
1713	Madrid Real academia española	Spain	Madrid
1724	Rossi'iskaya akade'miya nau'k	Russia	St. Petersburg
1742	Det Kongelige Danske Videnskabernes Selskab	Denmark	Copenhagen
1743	American Philosophical Society	USA	Philadelphia
1746	Naturforschende Gesellschaft	Switzerland	Bern
1752	De Hollandsche maatschappij der wetenschappen	The Netherlands	Haarlem
1760	Det Kongelige Norske Videnskabers Selskab	Norway	Trondheim
1779	Academia das Ciências de Lisboa	Portugal	Lisbon
1783	Royal Society of Edinburgh	Scotland	Edinburgh
1784	Die Böhmische Gesellschaft der Wissenschaften	Bohemia	Prague
1785	Royal Irish Society	Ireland	Dublin

Sources:　See Figure 8.1.

Academia Naturae Curiosorum.[5] As an academy of sciences, it was followed by the Royal Society in Britain in 1660 and the above-mentioned l'Académie des sciences in France in 1666.

In the eighteenth century, as also shown in Figure 8.1 and Table 8.1, the academy as an organisational form spread all over Europe from Trondheim in the north (1760) to Lisbon in the south (1779). It started out with Preußische Akademie der Wissenschaften founded in Berlin by Gottfried Wilhelm von Leibniz in 1700. And, an early follower with direct inspiration from the Berlin academy was the Swedish Royal Society of Sciences from 1710.[6] Academy foundations in most European countries thus followed. The academy form also spread to the United States in 1743 through the American Philosophical Society in Philadelphia.[7]

Further development in the nineteenth century included the diffusion of academies to Eastern Europe: Budapest (1825), Zagreb (1861),

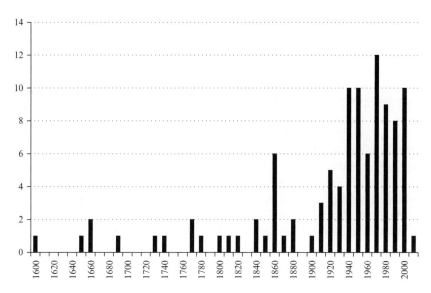

Source: Adaptation of data provided on http://www.interacademies.net. Foundation years for a few members are missing, but that will not influence the general picture.

Figure 8.2 Decades of establishment for InterAcademy Panel Members

Warszaw (1872), and Belgrad (1886).[8] In addition, the academy form spread outside Europe within the British Empire (New Zealand, 1867; South Africa, 1877; and Canada, 1882) and to South America (Argentina, 1869; Brazil, 1916; Colombia, 1933).[9] However, as can be seen in Figure 8.2, which provides further data for most national members of the InterAcademy Panel (see further below), relatively few of the members were founded before the twentieth century. Only one-fourth were thus created before 1900, and they were predominantly European (80 per cent). Then, there were establishments in the Americas and Asia, and in the 1950s and onwards also in Africa.

Although Figure 8.2 can be considered to provide a general picture of developments, it is just a part of the world academy population, since it is limited to InterAcademy Panel members. This is important to note, as there is a much larger number of other academies worldwide, some with other orientations and others constituting competing or supplementary national academies.[10] An example of a new orientation is the Royal Swedish Academy of Engineering Sciences, which was the first of its kind at its foundation in 1919. Eventually there were successors, first in the Nordic countries, later on in the rest of the world, counting nowadays more than twenty sister academies.[11]

The existence of competing and supplementary academies can be illustrated by developments in Sweden. As can be seen in Table 8.2 the number of Swedish academies with Royal charters is presently 18 with different orientation and recruitment: six have broad orientation, six are oriented towards the humanities, four gather professional groups and two are artistic. Eleven have a national recruitment, while seven basically recruit members from four university communities. Even if not all countries have the Swedish broad spectrum of academies, this is a further demonstration of the successful diffusion of the academy as an organisational form.

It is also appropriate to mention that academy foundations in the twentieth century crossed national borders. A relatively new entrant to the population of academies is thus Academia Europaea, which is a transnational academy with members mostly from European countries but also from some non-European ones. It was founded in 1988 at a meeting of the European Ministers of Science in 1985, at the initiative of a number of departing members of the Board of the European Science Foundation. Twenty-five years later it had more than 2,000 members from a very wide range of disciplines and is managed from an office in London.[12] As is often the case, other initiatives appeared at the same time. In 1990 thus a group of Austrians founded the European Academy of Sciences and Arts, located in Salzburg, also transnational and interdisciplinary in character. And, in the first years of the present century another European academy was created: the Belgium-based European Academy of Sciences.[13]

This tendency to create transnational academies is not unique to Europe. For the developing countries a project of this kind was thus launched in 1983 through the foundation of the Academy of Sciences for the Developing World (TWAS). Thirty years later it has 588 members from 76 countries and a secretariat in Trieste, Italy.[14] Likewise the Islamic World Academy of Sciences (IAS) was founded in 1987; today it has about 100 fellows representing 35 nationalities.[15] As a matter of fact, as early as in 1960 the World Academy of Art and Science (WAAS) was created "for distinguished scientists and scholars to discuss the vital problems of mankind, independent of political boundaries or limits – whether spiritual or physical; a forum where these problems will be discussed objectively, scientifically, globally and free from vested interested or regional attachments". Presently it has 650 individual members "from diverse cultures, nationalities, and intellectual disciplines".[16]

This brief summary not only demonstrates a diffusion of the academy as an organisational form, it also points to the fact that it includes different types. Some, like Leibniz's academy Preußische Akademie der Wissenschaften, are broad, comprising both the natural sciences and the

Table 8.2   Orientation and recruitment of Swedish academies with royal charters

Recruitment Orientation	National (11)	Local (7)
Natural sciences, medicine, humanities and social sciences (6)	The Royal Academy of Sciences (1739)	The Royal Society of Science at Uppsala (1710), the Royal Physiographical Society at Lund (1772), the Royal Society of Arts and Sciences in Gothenburg (1778), the Royal Society of Arts and Sciences of Uppsala (1954), the Royal Skytteanian Society at Umeå (1956)
Humanities (6)	The Royal Swedish Academy of Letters, History and Antiquities (1753), the Swedish Academy (1786), the Royal Society for the Publication of Manuscripts concerning Scandinavian History (1815), the Royal Gustav Adolf Academy (1932)	The Royal Society of the Humanities at Uppsala (1889), the Royal Society of the Humanities at Lund (1918)
Professional groups (4)	The Royal Society of Naval Sciences (1771), the Royal Swedish Academy of War Sciences (1796), The Royal Swedish Academy of Agriculture and Forestry (1811), the Royal Swedish Academy of Engineering Sciences (1919)	
Artistic (2)	The Royal Swedish Academy of Fine Arts (1735), the Royal Swedish Academy of Music (1771)	

Sources: http://www.kva.se; http://www.vetenskapssocietetenuppsala.se; http://www.fysiografen.se; http://www.kvvs.se; http://www.kvsu.se; http://www.skytteanskasamfundet.se; http://www.vitterhetsakad.se; http://www.svenskaakademien.se; http://www.kungligasamfundet.se; http://www.kgaa.nu; http://www.khvsu.se; http://www.lu.se/lucat/group/017080600; http://www.koms.se; http://www.kkrva.se; http://www.ksla.se; http://www.iva.se; http://www.konstakademien.se; and http://www.musakad.se.

humanities. Others concentrate on either the natural sciences (like the Royal Society) or on the humanities, especially languages (like l'Académie française). There are also a number of academies oriented towards the arts (like l'Académie des beaux-arts). This diversity makes it appropriate to look more closely at the common characteristics of academies.

CHARACTERISTICS OF ACADEMIES

Governance

A basic question in relation to all types of organisations concerns the rules for their creation. For academies we may note that, in contrast to banking, where a charter is required to start a bank, there are in principle no formal barriers to entry. However, as is evident from the above, most of the old academies received official support from the monarch, manifested in the prefix "Royal". Some of them, like the Swedish Academy founded in 1786, were even founded on the initiative of the sovereign. Needless to say, the support from the head of state has been crucial for the trust in these institutions. And this trust and a related reputation are key variables for academies, as they are closed to an extent that is not found elsewhere. First, in comparison to corporations, they differ by not having any owners to which they are responsible. Second, in comparison to most associations they differ by having restricted membership. Of these two characteristics, the latter is particularly important for the building of reputation. New members are selected through cooptation by those who are already members. As a result academies and their members live in symbiosis: members gain in reputation by being elected into the academy, while academies gain in reputation by electing distinguished members of the academic community. And the latter is particularly important for their role in giving policy advice in general and the selection of experts for policy decisions in particular, a topic to which we will return below.

Traditionally, academies have in their statutes a specified number of members without consideration of age. As a result renewal can only occur at the decease of a member. However, in order to avoid petrification in modern times, many academies have chosen to adopt new members as old members pass retirement age. Although this has the disadvantage of diluting the exclusivity of membership, it has the advantage of the academies gaining in reputation by adding well-reputed active academic scholars. Some academies, like the Royal Society, solve the renewal problem by adding a specified number of new members every year.[17]

In order to enhance their reputation, academies also need to reflect the development of the wider scientific community. It is therefore important to guarantee that members from different disciplines are represented. In many academies this is achieved by a structure with different classes or divisions. Obviously, for old academies such structures have undergone considerable change over time.[18]

The fact that academies base their reputation on their members may also entail a problem when an elected member is suspected of misconduct in one way or another. A basic question is then whether a member can be excluded. The argument against this is obviously the risk that rules of exclusion may be used by those in power to expel their enemies and that it would be in conflict with the freedom of speech. Such rules do exist, however. For instance, Deutsche Akademie der Wissenschaften Leopoldina and the Royal Society have the following statement in their statutes, respectively:[19]

> In the event of gross misconduct that is damaging to the Academy's reputation, a member can be expelled from the Academy.
>
> If, in the opinion of Council, the conduct of any Fellow, Foreign Member or Honorary Fellow is injurious to the character or interests of the Society, Council, after due consideration and after giving the Fellow, Foreign Member or Honorary Fellow an opportunity to state his or her case in person, in writing or by representation, may require him or her to resign.

Since academies and their members live in symbiosis, the opposite of exclusion may also arise, that is, that an academy member does not like the activities or points of view of her or his academy. The most practical way for the individual to deal with this is of course to abstain from taking part in the activities of the academy, as academies, unlike organisations like Rotary, do not have rules of minimum participation. However, sometimes members like to distance themselves officially from the organisation. Again, Deutsche Akademie der Wissenschaften Leopoldina has a rule in its statutes addressing this:[20]

> A member may apply to retire from his or her duties for a limited or unlimited period. The Presidium decides on the acceptance of the application. All rights to vote and all duties then expire.

A counter example is the Swedish Academy, well known through its role as the institution that awards the Nobel Prize for Literature. In the wake of a conflict regarding the lack of support for the author Salman Rushdie after he received the Islamic fatwa, three of the 18 members declared that they wished to leave the Academy. As this was not granted, they choose to abstain from taking part in the meetings.[21]

The above implies that academies can be expected to have considerable intellectual capital through the reputation of their members. However, in many cases their financial capital is not equally impressive. Membership fees are not very common. Donations occur but are often directed towards awards and other specific projects rather than the general financing of the organisation. Corporate sponsoring as well as government support both create problems of credibility, since it may hamper the independence of the academy. At the very least, such economic support may lead to the suspicion that critical views may be suppressed or that the views expressed are related to economic transactions.[22] However, academies may also have trouble activating their intellectual capital, since, as already mentioned, in most cases there are few obligations associated with academy membership. This is particularly important to note in relation to policy activities of academies, for which it is crucial to mobilise the star academicians.

Missions

A reading of mission statements of academies reveals in principle three basic tasks: (1) to promote science in various ways (among them to publish research results and to distribute prizes), (2) to provide expertise and advice, and (3) to foster international cooperation.[23] For instance, Deutsche Akademie der Wissenschaften Leopoldina declares that:[24]

> Its mission is that of promoting science in national and international co-operation, traditionally "for the benefit of humankind and nature".
> For this purpose, it runs academic events, appoints commissions, and publishes the results obtained. It awards honours and prizes and promotes junior scientists.
> With its appointment as National Academy of Sciences, the Leopoldina officially assumes the representation of German scientists in the international committees in which other Academies of Sciences are represented, and it contributes to the science-based consulting of the public and politics. This does not affect the missions or activities of the German Research Foundation, the Max Planck Society or the other members of the alliance.

And similar statements can be found for other academies such as the Royal Society and l'Académie des sciences.[25]

In terms of the first task (to promote science in various ways), academies have over time been active to varying degrees with their own research institutes. This has particularly been the case in Central and Eastern Europe, but also to some extent in countries like Austria, the Netherlands and Sweden.[26] However, this task has also to a large extent entailed the strengthening of the influence of the sciences in society, that is, to be active regarding policy for science and science for policy. In both cases, however, academies may find it difficult to provide clear-cut opinions, as, like all academic institutions, academies host members with many different views. Therefore, when it comes to the second task (to provide expertise and advice) it is often individual members who act rather than the organisation. However, in so doing, their relationship to prestigious academies is an asset that means that they are listened to. Academies have in this way been instrumental in the identification of scientific elites. This has increasingly been the case in quality assessments.

The third task (to foster international cooperation) has obviously become more important in modern society with its increasing international links between individuals as well as organisations. An important feature in this context is meta-organisations (Ahrne and Brunsson 2008), that is, organisations whose members are organisations rather than individuals. Since such organisations have become increasingly important for the interaction between academies and society, in the next section we will look more closely at their development, before we turn to the policy activites of European academies.

ACADEMIES IN INTERNATIONAL COOPERATION

International cooperation has traditionally been an important task for academies, particularly as manifested through the exchange of publications and scientific results. However, with the growth of the number of academies an increasing formalisation of international cooperation has taken place through the foundation of meta-organisations. A few of them were created in the twentieth century (Table 8.3), while a large number emerged in the present century (Table 8.4).

Among the meta-organisations of academies, the first appears to have been the International Association of Academies (IAA), founded in 1899 and dissolved after the First World War in 1919.[27] In its place two other organisations were created: Union Académique Internationale (UAI) for the humanities and the International Research Council (IRC) for the sciences (Campbell 1920). In 1931 the latter was turned into the still existing International Council for Science (ICSU), which presently has a membership of 120 national scientific bodies of 140 nationalities and 31 International Scientific Unions.[28]

The second half of the twentieth century saw the creation of three meta-organisations of academies (see again Table 8.3): International Foundation for Science (IFS) in 1972, InterAcademy Panel on International Issues

Table 8.3   Early meta-organisations of academies

Year	Name	Mission	Members
1899–1919	International Association of Academies (IAA)	To link various academies around the world	Specific membership not available
1919	Union Académique Internationale (UAI)	To promote the advancement of knowledge, development of scientific exchanges and initiatives of its academies	About 100 academies of 60 nationalities in the humanities and the social sciences
1919–1931	International Research Council (IRC)	(a) To coordinate international efforts in the different branches of science and its applications, (b) to initiate the formation of international associations or unions, (c) to direct international scientific activity in subjects [outside] existing international associations, (d) to enter through the proper channels into relation with the governments	Specific membership not available
1931	International Council for Science (ICSU)	To strengthen international science for the benefit of society	120 national scientific bodies of 140 nationalities and 31 International Scientific Unions
1972	International Foundation for Science (IFS)	To contribute towards strengthening the capacity of developing countries to conduct relevant and high-quality research on the sustainable management of biological and water resources	IFS has 135 affiliated organisations in 86 countries, mainly in the developing world
1993	InterAcademy Panel on International Issues (IAP)	IAP is a global network of the world's science academies [with the] goal to help member academies work together to advise citizens and public officials on the scientific aspects of critical global issues	105 academies

Table 8.3   (continued)

Year	Name	Mission	Members
1993	Federation of European Academies of Medicine (FEAM)	To promote cooperation between the national Academies of Medicine; and to extend to the political and administrative authorities of the EU the advisory role on matters concerning medicine and public health	13 academies in EU member states
1994	All European Academies (ALLEA)	(1) To promote cooperation between member academies through exchange of information and experience, and (2) to collaborate in giving advice on policy issues to particular audiences	52 academies in more than 40 countries from the Council of Europe region

Sources: *Science* (1904), Alter (1980), http://www.uai-iua.org; http://www.icsu.org; http://www.ifs.se; http://www.interacademies.net; http://www.feam.eu.com; http://www.allea.org.

(IAP) in 1993 and All European Academies (ALLEA) in 1994. Of these IFS is oriented towards the developing world, IAP with its 100 members aims at giving advice "on the scientific aspects of global issues", while ALLEA brings together some 50 European academies (see further below).

While the twentieth century brought about the foundation of a number of organisations with academies as members, the first decade of the twenty-first century signified an even larger expansion of such organisations (cf. Table 8.4). Many of the new meta-organisations, like the European ALLEA, have involved the gathering of academies of a particular region for cooperation: Association of Academies of Sciences in Asia (AASA; 2000), the Caribbean Scientific Union (CCC; 2000), Network of African Science Academies (NASAC; 2001), InterAmerican Network of Academies of Sciences (IANAS; 2004), Network of Academies of Science in the Islamic Countries (NASIC; 2004) and Euro-Mediterranean Academic Network (EMAN; 2010). Another phenomenon is the bringing together of specialised academies: Federation of European Academies of Medicine (FEAM; 1993), InterAcademy Medical Panel (IAMP; 2000) and International Council of Academies of Engineering and Technological Sciences (CAETS; 2000). Finally, two of the twenty-first century organisations were particularly oriented toward policy-making: InterAcademy Council (IAC; 2000) and European Academies Science Advisory Council

Table 8.4   Meta-organisations of academies founded in the twenty-first century

Year	Name	Mission	Members
2000	InterAcademy Council (IAC)	To provide advice on the scientific, technological and health aspects of issues of global, regional or national importance to intergovernmental organisations, to other international bodies and institutions, to national governments and to other decision-makers	About 20 academies with global representation
2000	InterAcademy Medical Panel (IAMP)	To strengthen the role of all academies to alleviate the health burdens of the world's poorest people; build scientific capacity for health; and provide independent scientific	A network of the world's academies of medicine, science, engineering and others having medical members
2000	International Council of Academies of Engineering and Technological Sciences (CAETS)	To promote engineering sciences and provide expertise in international cooperation	21 engineering academies world-wide
2000	Association of Academies of Sciences in Asia (AASA)	To establish an international interdisciplinary network for scientific and technological cooperation, and to play a pivotal role in promoting cooperation for the development of science and technology in the region	27 academies with science and technology interests
2000	The Caribbean Scientific Union (CCC)	To integrate, consolidate and promote the academies of the wider Caribbean region and their impact on the strengthening of scientific communities there, and to increase their impact on local communities	Academies in the Caribbean region

Table 8.4   (continued)

Year	Name	Mission	Members
2001	European Academies Science Advisory Council (EASAC)	To provide authoritative reports and assessments on scientific topics relevant to European policy needs	26 national science academies of every EU Member State, Academia Europaea and ALLEA
2001	Network of African Science Academies (NASAC)	To act as an independent African forum that brings together the nine merit-based academies of science in the continent	Nine African academies
2004	InterAmerican Network of Academies of Sciences (IANAS)	To support cooperation towards the strengthening of science and technology as a tool for advancing research and development, prosperity and equity in the Americas	A regional network of Academies of Sciences
2004	Network of Academies of Science in the Islamic Countries (NASIC)	To catalyse the development of collaborative programmes among OIC member countries	17 academies in Islamic countries
2010	Euro-Mediterranean Academic Network (EMAN)	To promote the growth and coordination of a Mediterranean science area	Academies of science of the Mediterranean countries

Sources: http://www.interacademycouncil.net; http://www.iamp-online.org; http://www.caets.org; http://www.aasa-net.org; http://www.interacademies.net; http://www.easac.eu; http://www.nasaconline.org; http://www.interacademies.net.

(EASAC; 2001). Their policy orientation is evident from their mission statements:[29]

> The IAC shall provide advice on the scientific, technological and health aspects of issues of global, regional or national importance to intergovernmental organizations, to other international bodies and institutions, to national governments and to other decision-makers.

> The main business of the Council shall be to provide authoritative reports and assessments on scientific topics relevant to European policy needs.

Interest in taking part in policy-making appears to be shared to varying degrees by the other meta-organisations mentioned above. This in turn seems to represent a change in the role of these organisations. While at the beginning of the twentieth century they were basically oriented towards research projects, policy-making has become increasingly important for them. This in turn can be explained by the increasing role of research in modern societies and the development of various types of lobbying and communication efforts.[30]

ACADEMIES IN EUROPEAN POLICY-MAKING

Global Transnational Organisations

It should be evident from the previous section that there are a multitude of global organisations that bring academies together for cooperation. They are all very important for the relationship between scientific communities and society. Many European academies belong to several of these. However, although the most general of them (ICSU and IAP) have their offices in Europe (Paris and Trieste, respectively), the formal European influence is limited. Only about one third of the ICSU Excutive Board and about one fifth of the IAP Exective Committee are Europeans, which is not remarkable since the two organisations are global in orientation.[31] Needless to say these two organisations may nevertheless have an impact on European policy decisions through projects and initiatives on global issues such as climate change, ecosystems, biodiversity, and so on. ICSU thus declares that it is particularly promoting closer relationships between its historically strong members in North America and Europe, on the one hand, and less developed countries, on the other.[32] IAP also has clear European connections by having among its partners two organisations that appear particularly important for the development of European policy-making, that is, ALLEA and EASAC.[33]

European Transnational Organisations

Discussions regarding the formation of an organisation for European academies started in the early 1990s after the fall of the Berlin Wall in 1989. On the initiative of l'Académie française, the Royal Society, the Royal Swedish Academy of Sciences and the Royal Netherlands Academy of Arts and Sciences, ALLEA was officially launched in 1994.[34] The idea was to raise the mission of the national academies to the European level. It started out as a clearinghouse for member academies at the Royal

Society. It got a permanent office at the Dutch Academy in 2000 through support from the Dutch government and the Royal Netherlands Academy of Arts and Sciences (KNAW), and moved in 2012 to Berlin and the Berlin-Brandenburg Academy of Sciences and Humanities (the academy founded by Leibniz). Throughout its existence ALLEA has focused on what Engelbrecht and Mann (2011: 19) label policy for science rather than science for policy, that is, on conditions for European research.[35] This has been manifested through standing committees on "Science and Ethics" and "Intellectual Property Rights" as well as working groups on "Research Cooperation", "Science and the Media", "Privacy in the Information Society", "Evaluation for Science", and "Science Education". ALLEA has also been an active proponent of the European Research Council as well as a partner in dialogues with the European Commission regarding the Framework Programmes and related matters. ALLEA differs from most other of the transnational meta-organisations of academies by having academies with different orientations as its members.[36]

While ALLEA has been oriented towards policy for science, EASAC, the European Academies Science Advisory Council, is providing science input to policy. Founded in 2001 by national science academies of the EU Member States and Academia Europaea, it is also a more narrow organisation in terms of discipline representation. Thus while the board of ALLEA is constituted by a fairly balanced distribution of members from the natural sciences and medicine, on the one hand, and the humanities and social sciences on the other (55 per cent vs. 45 per cent), the Council of EASAC is dominated by the former disciplines (93 per cent vs. 7 per cent). EASAC conducts programmes in three fields: energy, biosciences and environment, each with a steering panel and a secretary. As of 2010 the Secretariat is located at Deutsche Akademie der Wissenschaften Leopoldina. In order to facilitate interaction with EU politicians, which is crucial for its activities, EASAC has set up an office in Brussels sponsored by the Belgian academy the Royal Academies for Science and the Arts.[37]

In addition to ALLEA and EASAC, it is appropriate to mention two other organisations on the European scene: the European Science Foundation (ESF) and Academia Europaea. The first of these was founded in 1974 with a mixed membership of European academies and research councils. As the research councils had the financial resources, they became more dominant in the ESF than the academies, and therefore in 2008 a joint ALLEA-ESF workshop was organised to strengthen the role of the academies. However, developments have gone in another direction. As a consequence, several European academies left the ESF, and the activities of the ESF have gradually been transferred to the new organisation Science Europe, "an association of European Research Funding

Organisations (RFO) and Research Performing Organisations (RPO), based in Brussels".[38]

While the organisations discussed so far are meta-organisations of academies, Academia Europaea, mentioned above, is based on individual membership. However, it nevertheless has ambitions to play a role in policy-making. In its mission statement it thus declares that:[39]

> [It will make] recommendations to national governments and international agencies concerning matters affecting science, scholarship and academic life in Europe [and that it will endeavour to promote] a better understanding among the public at large of the benefits of knowledge and learning, and of scientific and scholarly issues which affect society, its quality of life and its standards of living.

Academia Europaea, like ALLEA, has in comparison to EASAC a stronger representation for the humanities and the social sciences in its board: 41 per cent.[40] At the same time it can be noted that Academia Europaea was a founding member of EASAC.[41]

All in all, it is very easy to agree with the statement by Staffan Helmfrid at the ALLEA meeting in Stockholm 1992: "There is certainly no lack of organizations for scientific cooperation and exchange in Europe."[42]

National Academies

European academies have thus been able to influence policy decisions through ALLEA and EASAC, and earlier to some extent through the ESF. However, the European academies have also played a policy role through their own activities. This can be demonstrated by the three oldest European academies of science, that is, Deutsche Akademie der Wissenschaften Leopoldina, the Royal Society, and l'Académie des sciences. Far from being ivory towers, they have long interacted with society at large through publications and other expressions of views.

The policy advice of Deutsche Akademie der Wissenschaften Leopoldina is mainly directed towards issues such as "climate change, energy supply, disease control and health, demographic change, global economic systems, conflict research and the use of natural resources". And, there are reasons to believe that the advice of the academy is listened to. According to its web-page:[43]

> Leopoldina's voice is respected. For example, its statement on the energy and research policy implications of the nuclear disaster in the Japanese prefecture of Fukushima in spring 2011 impacted on the work and the recommendations of Chancellor Angela Merkel's Ethics Commission on a Safe Energy Supply. Another statement published in 2011 focusing on preimplantation genetic

diagnosis (PGD) met with great interest among the members of the German Bundestag and was widely discussed in the media and in the society.

Due to the significance of the German economy and its central geographical position within the European Union, we can also expect that the views of the academy also have an impact outside Germany. National and international trust based on the reputation of the academy probably contributes to this, but they would seem to be more specifically based on the four specific guidelines for the policy advice of the academy:[44]

- Transparent working methods that are documented in a reproducible way.
- Open and unbiased design of advisory process through inclusion of different disciplines.
- Statements that are developed independently of any economic and political interests giving recommendations on how to approach specific problems facing society.
- Clear presentation and broad dissemination of recommendations in order to encourage public debate.

The policy work is undertaken in working groups and standing committees. In addition, international cooperation constitutes a significant part of the policy work of the German academy. Deutsche Akademie der Wissenschaften Leopoldina thus has links to six of the organisations listed in Tables 8.3 and 8.4: ALLEA, EASAC, FEAM, IAC, IAP and IAMP.[45] In addition to hosting the EASAC Head Office, as mentioned above, the links to EASAC are also manifested by representation by Leopoldina members on EASAC steering panels and working groups as well as a great number of meetings at the academy.[46]

The Royal Society, for its part, can claim that its first scientific advice to policy-makers (on the state of Britain's forests) appeared as early as 1664.[47] And, some 350 years later these activities go on in various forms, among which the Science Policy Centre, founded in 2010, constitutes a basic platform. It deals with four flagship themes: sustainability, diplomacy, innovation and governance.[48] Again we can see the ambitions to strengthen the position of science in society by giving advice regarding urgent problems and by providing a better understanding for the role of science. It is particularly worth noting that there are few geographic limitations in the programme. Most problems are global, and in addition we can note that the Royal Society expresses a particular interest in alliances of academies, Islamic world science and innovation as well as capacity-building in Africa. As a result, the Royal Society can claim that their "spheres of influence include decision makers in Westminster and Whitehall; business leaders; research funders and bodies such as the European Commission, OECD, World Bank and UN agencies".[49]

As far as the French l'Académie des sciences is concerned, one of its five missions is to ensure "a dual role of expertise and advice". This is accomplished through:[50]

> Arbitrating among possible scientific and technological options [. . .] within the remit of elected politicians, but they must be enabled to do so, on sound, reasoned bases. The Academy is called upon by public authorities to intervene as an expert, advisory body; it can likewise self-commission studies on similar questions, as it sees fit. Its conclusions are duly published: in reports, in advice notes and recommendations; in the form of expertise.

In 2010–11 these efforts resulted in 14 reports on topics like the Fukishima accident, education, vaccination, climate change, and space research.[51] Like its British sister academy, the French one is trying to stimulate a dialogue between researchers and politicians. This is accomplished through the programme "Pairing between Members of the French Parliament, Members of the Académie des sciences and young scientists".[52] Also, like the Royal Society, l'Académie des sciences aims at fostering international collaboration. Means for this are constituted by membership or participation in international organisations, bilateral or multilateral cooperation and partnerships with developing countries. In terms of the international organisations l'Académie des sciences particularly points to the International Council for Science (ICSU), the InterAcademy Panel on International Issues (IAP), the European Academies Science Advisory Council (EASAC) and the All European Academies (ALLEA).[53]

In addition to the involvement of the national academies in policy-making, we should also note the role of individual academy members from the different nations. This can be demonstrated by an analysis of the links between European academies and the 22 members of the governing body of the European Research Council (ERC) in 2013. Among them two-thirds (15) are elected members of Academia Europaea, and together they have 40 elections to other academies, among them the Royal Society and the National Academy of Sciences.[54] So even if academies are not directly represented in the ERC, they have close links through their members. It could also be argued that through their selection processes the academies have been helpful by signalling excellence among their academic compatriots to ERC recruiters.

Concluding Remarks

The above implies that we have been able to identify considerable activities from European academies in policy-making. This is accomplished both through meta-organisations, like ALLEA and EASAC, and directly through initiatives of national academies. In addition, individual academy members tend to be elected to hold significant posts on the basis of the reputation gained from academy membership. All this may indicate that the influence of academies has increased and will increase over time. However, it is important also to point out that the environment of the academies has changed with the passage of time. The field of higher education and research has undergone strong growth in most countries, and many actors are trying to make their voice heard. In addition, there are indications that academic excellence is not always appreciated in the selection of academic leaders (Engwall 2014a). At the same time it appears important to keep in mind that selectivity, which is a key feature of academy membership, may be even more important for individuals in a world crowded with scientists.

CONCLUSIONS

Our analysis of the role of academies in policy-making has provided a number of conclusions:

1. The academy as an organisational form, emerging from Renaissance Italy, has been successfully adopted all over the globe, before the twentieth century particularly in European countries, later spreading to Asia and the Americas, and since the 1950s also to Africa.
2. Academies have special opportunities to take part in policy-making, as they are closed organisations to which members are elected on the basis of their scholarly reputation. In this way academies and their members live in symbiosis: members acquire reputation through membership and academies gain in reputation from their members.
3. Our analysis of mission statements has demonstrated that academies basically focus on three tasks: (1) to promote science in various ways, (2) to provide expertise and advice, and (3) to foster international cooperation.
4. In terms of the involvement of academies in policy-making, it is important to make a distinction between (1) policy for science and (2) science for policy. In the former case academies are involved in discussions regarding the conditions for scientific work, and in the latter case they offer input from their expertise for other significant political decisions.

5. The past hundred years have entailed not only the foundation of a considerable number of academies, but also the creation of a large number of meta-organisations of academies, that is, organisations for transnational cooperation between various national academies.
6. In policy-making we have been able to identify efforts both through the transnational organisations and also through national academies, particularly those based in the major European countries. We have also noted that academies have indirect influence through their members, who are recruited to important positions with policy implications.
7. Finally, it is appears fair to conclude that the world of academies is characterised by competition. This has been evident in the development of the academies themselves with many different intitiatives over time. This appears to be equally true, or perhaps even more so, regarding the meta-organisations of academies, for which there are a number of competing alternatives. Sometimes, as in the case of ALLEA and EASAC, this has led to a division of labour.

After these conclusions it may be appropriate to speculate somewhat on the future role of academies in policy-making. It is obvious that they are highly likely to continue to express their views on the policy for science, since the strengthening of the influence of science in society is a basic concern for all academies. To what extent they will be listened to on this matter is another question. Even if, as mentioned by way of introduction, science policy has tended to become the modern defence policy, excessively high expectations on deliveries that do not materialise may constitute a risk that politicians will become less sensitive to the arguments of academies.

Then, in terms of science for policy, there are also reasons to believe that academies will continue to be active. It is a question of communicating research results to decision-makers and contributing to a better world. However, as already indicated above, academies are not monoliths and, due to the uncertainty associated with research, are not always characterised by consensus. This may be difficult to understand for outsiders, who therefore may prefer to talk to commercial consultants rather than academies. It is important that academies be aware of this competition.

For both types of advisory roles we may expect academies to increase their communication efforts by adding new staff for that purpose. Such a development is in line with a general trend in society entailing that communication activities – in the form of persuasion, promotion and protection – have become increasingly common (Engwall 2014b). This has been observed for corporations but also for other institutions such as universities (Engwall 2008). And, academies cannot be expected to be an exception to this general trend. The followers of Plato are therefore likely to express their views on policy issues increasingly through various channels.

NOTES

1. I am grateful for valueable comments on an earlier draft from Pieter Drenth, Jüri Engelbrecht, Jürgen Mittelstrass, Helga Nowotny, Stig Strömholm and Sten Widmalm.
2. See also Drenth (2006, pp. 183–95).
3. "Longtemps, la puissance d'une nation s'est mesurée à celle de son armée. Aujourd'hui, elle s'évalue plutôt à son potentiel scientifique." (Le Monde, 2003, April 8, p. 1).
4. Since 1832 they are part of l'Institut de France, which also includes two other French academies created in 1795: l'Académie des beaux-arts and l'Académie des sciences morales et politiques.
5. In terms of age, it is true that the Italian Accademia dei Lincei was founded as early as 1603. However, it was closed down in 1651 and re-established in 1875. (http://www.lincei.it/modules.php?name=Content&pa=showpage&pid=21).
6. On the early period of this academy, see further Engwall (2012). The internationally better-known Royal Swedish Academy of Sciences was founded in 1739.
7. http://www.amphilsoc.org/. For further information on the development of the academies in the eighteenth century, see McClellan (1985).
8. http://mta.hu, http://www.hazu.hr, http://pau.krakow.pl and http://www.sanu.ac.rs. As was pointed out to me by Helga Nowotny, under Communism in Eastern Europe the Academy Presidents became politically very important, since the academies were the only institutions for research. See also Proukakis and Katsaros (1997).
9. http://www.royalsociety.org.nz/organisation/; http://www.royalsocietysa.org.za; http://rsc-src.ca; http://www.anc-argentina.org.ar; http://www.abc.org.br; and http://www.accefyn.org.co/sp/history.htm.
10. Among more recent supplementary academies it is particularly worth mentioning the founding of young academies in Austria, Germany, the Netherlands, Poland and Sweden (Engelbrecht and Mann 2011, p. 32). Since December 2012 the Young Academy of Europe organises the ERC starting grant holders (http://yacadeuro.org/about-yae.htm).
11. DeGeer (1978, pp. 117–19) and http://www.caets.org.
12. http://www.ae-info.org/. See also Burgen (2009) and *European Review* (2011).
13. Its statutes were approved by the Belgian King in 2003 (http://www.eurasc.org/aboutus/statutes.asp). Before that the whole organisation was seriously questioned in an article in *Nature* (Adam, 2002).
14. http://www.interacademies.net/About/Committees/15444/TWAS.aspx.
15. http://www.interacademies.net/Academies/11798/11025/IAS.aspx.
16. http://www.worldacademy.org.
17. The Royal Society thus every year invites members to propose new members by 30 September. Candidates are then reviewed through a sophisticated screening procedure including reference letters from members of the Royal Society and other academies. And, at the end of the process 44 fellows, eight foreign members and one honorary fellow are elected (http://royalsociety.org/uploadedFiles/Royal_Society_Content/about-us/fellowship/130810_ElectionProcess.pdf).
18. Cf. e.g. Frängsmyr (1989) for the development of the class structure within the Royal Swedish Academy of Sciences.
19. http://www.leopoldina.org/en/about-us/presidium-boards/statutes/, third paragraph and http://royalsociety.org/uploadedFiles/Royal_Society_Content/about-us/governance/Statutes.pdf, Chapter IV.
20. http://www.leopoldina.org/en/about-us/presidium-boards/statutes/, third paragraph.

21. Two of them boycotted the Academy completely, while the third one had some limited contacts with the Academy.

22. As was pointed out to me by Pieter D.J. Drenth, academy members in many Eastern European academies receive a yearly salary (often on top of their professorial salary). Needless to say, this creates additional problems, with respect to the budget as well as the selection of new members.

23. For discussions of these missions, see Drenth (2006, pp. 183–251).

24. http://www.leopoldina.org/en/about-us/presidium-boards/statutes. For a discussion of the role of academies, see the speech at Deutsche Akademie der Wissenschaften Leopoldina by Jürgen Mittelstrass (2010).

25. See http://royalsociety.org/about-us and http:/www.academie-sciences.fr/en/mission. htm. On the role of the French academy of sciences, see Grunberg-Manago (1997).

26. In terms of Sweden, the Royal Swedish Academy of Sciences has during the last decade transferred a considerable part of their research facilities to universities.

27. *Science* (1904) and Alter (1980).

28. http://www.icsu.org/about-icsu/about-us.

29. http://www.interacademycouncil.net/23450/24788/24801.aspx and http://www.easac.eu/about-easac/easac-statutes.html, respectively.

30. Some, like Quére (2010), also argue that it is a responsibility of academies to engage with society.

31. Calculations based on the information provided at http.//www.icsu.org and http://www.interacademies.net.

32. ICSU (2011, pp. 36–7).

33. http://www.interacademies.net/About/18456.aspx.

34. On the contributions of ALLEA, see Drenth (2006, pp. 231–8).

35. Cf. e.g. All-European-Academy Meeting (1993).

36. Engelbrecht and Mann (2011, pp. 18–20) and http://www.allea.org/Pages/ALL/4/982. bGFuZz1FTkc.html.

37. http://www.easac.eu/home.html and http://www.leopoldina.org/en/international-issues/ihttp://www.ae-info.org/nternational-academy-associations/easac/.

38. http://www.esf.org, Engelbrecht and Mann (2011, pp. 31–2), Clery (2011), ESF (2009), http://www.esf.org/esf-today/recent-developments.html and http://www.scienceeurope. org/.

39. http://www.ae-info.org/ae/Acad_Main/About_us/Mission_Statement.

40. The corresponding figure for IAP Executive Committee is 0 per cent, for the ICSU Executive Board 22 per cent and for ERC Scientific Council 23 per cent.

41. http://www.acadeuro.org

42. All-European-Academy Meeting (1993, p. 8).

43. http://www.leopoldina.org/en/policy-advice/science-for-politics-and-society/. Note that it was not until 2007 that the Leopoldina academy became the German national academy of sciences.

44. http://www.leopoldina.org/en/policy-advice/science-for-politics-and-society/.

45. http://www.leopoldina.org/en/international-issues/international-academy-associations/.

46. http://www.leopoldina.org/en/international-issues/international-academy-associations/ easac/.

47. http://royalsociety.org/policy/.

48. http://royalsociety.org/uploadedFiles/Royal_Society_Content/policy/Science-Policy-Cen tre-Prospectus.pdf.

49. http://royalsociety.org/uploadedFiles/Royal_Society_Content/policy/Science-Policy-Cen tre-Prospectus.pdf.

50. http://www.academie-sciences.fr/en/mission.htm.

51. Un an avec l'Academie des sciences *2010–2011*, p. 37.

52. Floc'h (2009) and Un an avec l'Academie des sciences 2010–2011, p. 22.

53. Un an avec l'Academie des sciences 2010–2011, pp. 25–6.

54. Calculations based on the information on http://erc.europa.eu/about-erc/organisation.

REFERENCES

Adam. D. (2002), 'Suspicions Intensify over Elusive European Academy of Sciences', *Nature*, **419**, (31 October 2002), 865.

Ahrne, Göran and Nils Brunsson (2008), *Meta-organizations*, Cheltenham, UK and Northampton, MA, USA: Edward Elgar.

All-European-Academy Meeting (1993), *The Role of Academies as Learned Societies in the New Europe, 17–18 March 1992: the All-European-Academy Meeting in Stockholm at the Royal Swedish Academy of Sciences: Summaries and Statements*, Stockholm: Kungl. Vetenskapsakademien.

Alter, P. (1980), 'The Royal Society and the International Association of Academies 1897–1919', *Notes and Records of the Royal Society*, **34** (2), 241–64.

Bryson, Bill and Jon Turney (eds) (2010), *Seeing Further. The Story of Science & the Royal Society*, London: Harper Press.

Burgen, Arnold (2009), 'Academia Europaea: Origin and Early Days', *European Review*, **17** (3–4), 469–75.

Campbell, W.W. (1920), 'Report of the Meetings of the International Research Council and the Affiliated Unions Held at Brussels, July 18–28, 1919', *Proceedings of the National Academy of Sciences of the United States of America*, **6** (6), 340–8.

Clery, D. (2011), 'ESF Moves Towards Rebirth, but Change Worries Some', *Science*, **331** (7 January), 16.

De Geer, Hans (1978), *Rationaliseringsrörelsen i Sverige: effektivitetsidéer och socialt ansvar under mellankrigstiden* (The rationalization movement in Sweden: Efficiency programs and social responsibility in the interwar years), Stockholm: SNS (diss.).

Drenth, Pieter J.D. (2006), *Walks in the Garden of Science: Selected Papers and Lectures*, Amsterdam: ALLEA.

Engelbrecht, Jüri and Nicholas Mann (2011), *The Sum of the Parts: ALLEA and Academies*, Amsterdam: ALLEA.

Engwall, Lars (2005), 'Hur har vi det med beredskapen idag? Utbildning och forskning som modern försvarspolitik' (What's the Preparedness Today? Higher Education and Research as Modern Defence Policy), in Anders Björnsson, Martin Kylhammar and Åsa Linderborg (eds), *Ord i rättan tid* (Words at the Right Time), Stockholm: Atlantis, 281–300.

Engwall, Lars (2008), 'Minerva and the Media. Universities Protecting and Promoting Themselves', in Carmelo Mazza, Paolo Quattrone and Angelo Riccaboni (eds), *European Universities in Transition: Issues, Models, and Cases*, Cheltenham, UK and Northampton, MA, USA: Edward Elgar, 31–48.

Engwall, Lars (2012), 'From Collegium Curiosorum to Royal Society', in Lars Engwall (ed.), *Scholars in Action: Past-Present-Future*, Acta Universitatis Upsaliensis. Nova Acta Regiæ Societatis Scientiarum Upsaliensis, Ser. V, Uppsala: Uppsala University, 17–27.

Engwall, Lars (2014a), 'The Recruitment of University Leaders: Politics, Communities and Markets in Interaction', *Scandinavian Journal of Management*, **30** (3), 332–43.

Engwall, Lars (2014b), 'Corporate Governance and Communication', in Josef Pallas, Lars Strannegård and Stefan Jonsson (eds), *Organizations and the Media*, London: Routledge, 220–33.

ESF (2009), 'Strengthening the Role of Academies in ESF. An ESF–ALLEA High Level Workshop on ESF and the Academies, Brussels, 7 March 2008', Strasbourg: ESF.

European Review (2011), 'Focus: Academia Europaea: Founders and Founding Visions', *European Review*, **19** (2), 153–253.

Floc'h, Benoit (2009), 'Science+politique=intérêt général', *Le Monde*, 28 October, 3.

Frängsmyr, Tore (1989), 'Gubben som gräver – Vetenskapsakademien 250 år' (The Digging Man – the Royal Swedish Academy of Sciences 250 Years), in Tore Frängsmyr, *Gubben som gräver: Människor och miljöer i vetenskapens värld* (The Digging Man: Persons and Settings in the World of Science), Stockholm: Författarförlaget Fischer & Rye.

Grau, Conrad (1988), *Berühmte Wissenschaftsakademien: von ihrem Entstehen und ihrem weltweitem Erfolg*, Leipzig: Edition Leipzig.

Grunberg-Manago, Marianne (1997), 'The Role of the French Academy of Sciences', in Charalambos Proukakis and Nikos Katsaros (eds), *The New Role of the Academies of Sciences in the Balkan Countries*, Dordrecht: Kluwer Academic Publishers, pp. 7–13.

Hahn, Roger (1971), *The Anatomy of a Scientific Institution. The Paris Academy of Sciences, 1666–1803*, Berkeley, Los Angeles, London: University of California Press.

Hildebrand, Bengt (1939), *Kungl. Svenska Vetenskapsakademien: förhistoria, grundläggning och första organisation* (The Royal Swedish Academy of Sciences: Prehistory, Foundation and the Early Organization), Stockholm: Kungl. Vetenskapsakademien.

ICSU (2011), *ICSU Strategic Plan II, 2012–2017*, Paris: International Council for Science.

Jacob, François (2003), 'Recherche: jusqu'où ira le déclin?', *Le Monde*, April 8, 2003, p. 1.

Lane, Julia, Kaye Fealing, John Marburger III, and Stephanie Shipp (eds) (2011), *The Science of Science Policy: A Handbook*, Palo Alto, CA: Stanford University Press.

Leopoldina (2010), *A Tour of the German National Academy of Sciences Leopoldina*, Halle: Leopoldina Nationale Akademie der Wissenschaften.

McClellan, James E. III (1985), *Science Reorganized: Scientific Societies in the Eighteenth Century*, New York: Columbia University Press.

Mittelstrass, J. (2010), 'The Culture of Science: On Reason in Scientific Institutions', *Nova Acta Leopoldina*, NF, **113** (385), 65–77.

Porter, Michael E. (1990), *The Competitive Advantage of Nations*, New York: Free Press.

Proukakis, Charalambos and Nikos Katsaros (eds) (1997), *The New Role of the Academies of Sciences in the Balkan Countries*, Dordrecht: Kluwer Academic Publishers.

Quéré, Y. (2010), 'Academies Must Engage with Society', *Nature*, **465** (24 June), 1009.

Science, 17 June 1904, **19** (494), 930–1.

Un an avec l'Academie des sciences 2010–2011, Paris: Institut de France (Available at http://www.academie-sciences.fr/RA_sources/index-35.html).

Websites accessed in March 2013 and revisited in February 2014:
http://erc.europa.eu/about-erc/organisation.
http://mta.hu.
http://pau.krakow.pl.
http://royalsociety.org/about-us.
http://royalsociety.org/policy/.
http://royalsociety.org/uploadedFiles/Royal_Society_Content/about-us/governance/
    Statutes.pdf.
http://royalsociety.org/uploadedFiles/Royal_Society_Content/about-us/fellowship/
    130810_ElectionProcess.pdf.
http://royalsociety.org/uploadedFiles/Royal_Society_Content/policy/Science-Policy-
    Centre-Prospectus.pdf.
http://rsc-src.ca.
http://www.aasa-net.org.
http://www.abc.org.br.
http://www.acad-ciencias.pt.
http://www.academieroyale.be.
http://www.academie-sciences.fr/en/mission.htm.
http://www.accademiadellacrusca.it.
http://www.accefyn.org.co/sp/history.htm.
http://www.ae-info.org/.
http://www.ae-info.org/ae/Acad_Main/About_us/Mission_Statement.
http://www.allea.org.
http://www.allea.org/Pages/ALL/4/982.bGFuZz1FTkc.html.
http://www.amphilsoc.org/.
http://www.anc-argentina.org.ar.
http://www.bbaw.de.
http://www.caets.org.
http://www.cas.cz/o_avcr/historie/.
http://www.dknvs.no.
http://www.easac.eu.
http://www.easac.eu/about-easac/easac-statutes.html.
http://www.easac.eu/home.html.
http://www.eurasc.org/aboutus/statutes.asp.
http://www.feam.eu.com.
http://www.fysiografen.se.
http://www.hazu.hr.
http://www.iamp-online.org.
http://www.icsu.org.
http://www.icsu.org/about-icsu/about-us.
http://www.ifs.se.
http://www.institut-de-france.fr/fr/une-institution/son-histoire.
http://www.interacademies.net.
http://www.interacademies.net/About/18456.aspx.
http://www.interacademies.net/Academies/11798/11025/IAS.aspx.
http://www.interacademycouncil.net.
http://www.interacademycouncil.net/23450/24788/24801.aspx.
http://www.iva.se.
http://www.kgaa.nu.
http://www.khmw.nl.

http://www.khvsu.se.
http://www.kkrva.se.
http://www.koms.se.
http://www.konstakademien.se.
http://www.ksla.se.
http://www.kungligasamfundet.se.
http://www.kva.se.
http://www.kvsu.se.
http://www.kvvs.se.
http://www.leopoldina.org/en/about-us/presidium-boards/statutes/.
http://www.leopoldina.org/en/international-issues/
     international-academy-associations/easac/.
http://www.leopoldina.org/en/international-issues/
     international-academy-associations/.
http://www.leopoldina.org/en/policy-advice/science-for-politics-and-society/.
http://www.lincei.it/modules.php?name=Content&pa=showpage&pid=21.
http://www.lu.se/lucat/group/017080600.
http://www.musakad.se.
http://www.nasaconline.org.
http://www.ngzh.ch/.
http://www.rae.es.
http://www.ria.ie.
http://www.royalacademy.dk.
http://www.royalsoced.org.uk.
http://www.royalsociety.org.nz/organisation
http://www.royalsocietysa.org.za.
http://www.sanu.ac.rs.
http://www.skytteanskasamfundet.se.
http://www.svenskaakademien.se.
http://www.uai-iua.org.
http://www.vetenskapssocietetenuppsala.se.
http://www.vitterhetsakad.se.
http://yacadeuro.org/about-yae.htm.

9. The internationalisation of research institutes

Laura Cruz-Castro,[1] Koen Jonkers[2] and Luis Sanz-Menéndez

INTRODUCTION

Governments continue to be key players in research, despite the significance of private investments. Governments' direct funding, regulations and incentives are essential factors and mechanisms in steering and funding research (OECD 2012a). However, countries differ in the basic features and the institutional arrangements of their public sector research (PSR) (Senker 2000; Whitley 2003) and in the extent to which universities and non-university research organisations are key research performing actors in PSR.

While in the US, and some other countries, research universities have become the central institution in PSR, in many continental European countries, in addition to the traditional government laboratories, a different type of "non-university" public research organisation (PRO) is also a central actor of the PSR. In countries like Germany, France, Spain, Italy, Poland, Slovak Republic, Hungary, Romania and others, a specific type of institution, public research centres, have complemented, and historically at some time replaced, the research functions of the universities.

In recent years in all European countries, PSR has been undergoing important changes. The first one is that universities have gradually become the major research performing actor in almost all European public research (Paradeise et al. 2009; Nedeva 2013), with increasing competition and environmental pressures for the PRO. Secondly, PSR has experienced a changing balance between block and project funding (Lepori et al. 2007; OECD 2011b), the increased use of performance-based funding mechanisms (OECD 2010; Hicks 2012; Whitley 2008) and, in Europe, the growing role of EU funding. Finally, the PRO has been subject to significant reforms and transformations, including deregulation and transfer of ownership from governments to other actors (Boden et al. 2006). PROs are estimated to be spending over 40 per cent of the total public research funds allocated by governments to research in the EU.[3]

While the transformations of universities have attracted a lot of attention, the focus on the change in PROs has been more limited (Cox et al. 2001). Besides the concerns about the effects of privatisation and new public management (Boden et al. 2004) or the adaptation responses to changes in funding (Sanz-Menendez and Cruz-Castro 2003), most of the contributions have addressed a specific type of PRO (for example, mission oriented research, the national laboratories (Crow and Bozeman 1998) or the research technology organisations (RTOs) (Sharif and Baark 2011)), while the issue of the role of European research policy in changes has been mostly overlooked. In fact, while PROs have traditionally been considered as very responsive to national governments' demands, despite their relevance in terms of public expenditure, no significant efforts have been made to better understand the impact of the European research policy and the emergence of a new space for research on the functioning, structures and strategies of PROs. In this chapter we are interested in how public research organisations address internationalisation pressures and Europeanisation dynamics.

Whereas internationalisation of research (with a focus on individual research collaboration and, more recently, on researcher mobility) has been widely analysed, we do not know that much about internationalisation processes and strategies at the organisational level of research institutes. The conditions under which organisational actors engage and invest resources in international activities are understudied. The structure of the PSR (Senker 2000) and the organisational features of PROs (Whitley 2008) are intervening variables that condition the internationalisation process; here we will try to build an analytical framework to provide a better understanding of the role of key organisational attributes of PROs in the internationalisation process.

Firms have attracted most of the attention in the scholarly analysis of strategic organisational behaviour related to internationalisation and globalisation of R&D activities (Gassmann and von Zedtwitz 1999; von Zedtwitz and Gassmann 2002); additionally, the literature on research collaboration presents evidence on the exponential growth of international co-authorship as an indicator of this trend (Katz and Martin 1997). Literature on higher education institutions also provides us evidence about the increasing role of international competition for talent, students and academics, and the attempts to develop an overseas presence by more and more universities (Bartell 2003; Stromquist 2007).

Despite the existence of some literature analysing the PRO, very few authors have specifically addressed the internationalisation process, its features and consequences for different types of research institutes (Ebersberger and Edler 2009; Jonkers and Cruz-Castro 2011; Van den Besselaar et al. 2012). Even in the very few analyses of a mostly descriptive nature (Berger and Hofer 2011; Edler et al. 2012) there is some evidence of an increase in non-nationally based operations of PROs growing in parallel with the internationalisation or globalisation of their "national systems".

The aim of this chapter is to understand how different types of research institutes (PROs) engage in processes of internationalisation, paying attention to the interplay between EU research policy and research organisations. The chapter is organised as follows. In the next section we review the drivers of internationalisation and build up the analytical framework on the role of some key features of PROs in the internationalisation process. After that, we revise the emergence and changes of the EU research policy as part of the changing environment of PROs and describe some Europeanisation developments. We then apply our classificatory framework to analyse the internationalisation capabilities of four types of PRO that differ in specific organisational characteristics which have direct implications for the ways in which the PROs internationalise. The chapter ends with some concluding remarks.

CONCEPTS, DRIVERS AND ANALYTICAL FRAMEWORK

This chapter is based on the premise that organisational differences generate variations in internationalisation processes, and that those very features will also influence the ways in which the process of internationalisation emerges and evolves. To analyse these processes we propose a framework for understanding the internationalisation processes of PROs based on organisational and institutional theory; this approach provides us with theoretical grounds for addressing the key issue of the relationship between the organisation and its environment(s) and how organisations internationalise in two distinct ways: responsive vs. strategic. In this section we set up the framework for the analysis; we begin with some definitions, followed by the identification of the main drivers of internationalisation, and finally we present our typology of PROs according to some key organisational attributes.

By internationalisation we understand a process of increasing involvement in international (non-nationally based) operations and actions by the PRO, its sub-units or its employees and an increasing openness of the PRO to 'non-national' influences, with the effect of transforming the attributes of the organisation and of modifying its resource dependence features (for example, funding composition). It may also be understood as different forms of commitment with regards to resources to be invested or acquired from abroad outside the traditional national markets or sources of resources. In the literature on Europeanisation, the concept has been mainly used in analyses of changes in national policy-making in response to the emergence of a European level of policy-making (Olsen 2002). Here we understand Europeanisation as consisting of processes of growth in the interaction of PROs with research performing actors in other EU Member States and EU level actors (policy-makers, funding agencies and political actors) through various forms of collaboration, competition, adaptation and influence.

The means through which the PRO can exert its potentiality for internationalisation are a) material: through decisions on the internal distribution of its resources, b) institutional: through political influence and negotiation and c) discursive: through mission statements and discussion of goals/aims/ambitions it can attempt to interactively engage in setting an agenda for future action. In doing so, the PRO can, on the one hand, contribute to the socialisation of its researchers and stimulate them to engage in particular forms of behaviour, such as collaboration and competition for resources at the European level. On the other hand, it can engage in setting an external discourse that may have some influence on decisions at the national and European level.

Most of the evidence about the internationalisation of scientific research often considered it to have been driven primarily through individual-level self-organised networks of scientists. This, however, is not the only aspect of the internationalisation/Europeanisation process. Organisational-level strategies can also play a role. Here, strategic internationalisation understood as the commitment of resources at the organisational level is different from encouraging or rewarding individual 'spontaneous' international collaborations.

The process of PRO internationalisation can be understood as an adaptation to technological, economic, political and cultural change (Slipersaeter and Aksnes 2012). Much of the empirical analysis and theory development regarding internationalisation has referred to firms and their R&D functioning. Dominant views in business and management studies have adopted a theoretical approach that emphasises responses to reduce uncertainty in a changing environment, with a focus on rational calculations of the benefits and costs of the process; very few studies have made the attempt of developing organisational models for understanding internationalisation processes (e.g. Malhotra and Hinings 2010). In organisational theory, a stream of literature (Drori et al. 2003) has addressed the processes of globalisation and internationalisation from the perspective of diffusion dynamics and adoption of new normative models. From this view, PROs, like firms, may engage in learning/imitation to implement the structures and strategies developed by their domestic and foreign counterparts to engage in internationalisation. However, it is our contention that management and economic approaches do not fully capture the variety of strategic drivers of public and semi-public research organisations to engage in internationalisation.

We consider that the main driving goal of organisational behaviour is preservation/maintenance and potential expansion. This motivation is strongly tied up with access to resources. Both firms and PROs internationalise as a way of accessing markets, clients and resources. PROs develop internationalisation mainly as a way to reduce resource dependency, to increase the diversification of their resources or expand their resource base. PROs may also have other objectives, including their organisational/ political missions, societal impact and reputation, visibility or search for excellence. Their need for material resources refers mainly to funding but also to the maintenance and expansion of their scientific and technological human capital (Bozeman et al. 2001). Although accessing markets may be a driver for PROs too, it is important to acknowledge that PROs operate in different types of spaces. Firstly, the research space/research system in which they get their public and private funding, and secondly, the research field in which they (also) disseminate and valorise their products and through which they access other resources: new knowledge, feedback and so on (Nedeva 2013). Like individual researchers, PROs are at the interface of the two domains. The PRO's need for resources is not restricted to the material (funding) but also includes cognitive and institutional resources.

For PROs the goal of internationalisation/Europeanisation has traditionally been linked to the search for new funding sources (diversification and reducing the dependence of traditional sources), though increasing their international reputation which can be tied to the accumulation of cognitive, institutional and symbolic resources also plays an important role. International funding has been mostly competitive (especially at the EU level) although there are instances of international block grant funding, for example in the cases of international cooperative research facilities. However, apart from funding and the increasing costs of research, the drivers for internationalisation of PROs have multiplied over the last decade (see also Boekholdt et al. 2009). Related to the increasing costs of (large-scale) research comes the need of most PROs to engage in the sharing of costs and risks. Internationalisation can also provide PROs with access to non-financial resources including infrastructure, human resources recruitment, data and partners with complementary capabilities and resources.

Additional to expanding and accessing resources, a second driver for internationalisation is related to the changing dynamics of research, the changing demands made by the principals of PROs (for example, to enhance their contribution to innovation activities) and the environmental changes in the research space of PROs, such as the emergence of research funding agencies and the growing role of research universities in many countries. The compounded effect of these dynamics have stimulated and enabled PROs to increase their links with other actors in their national innovation systems. PROs may also find these other actors outside their national research space. Related to this, a third driver, namely the increasing commercialisation of research outputs in global markets, is also relevant.

Several additional drivers can be identified. The globalisation of scientific fields and the associated motivation to increase the visibility and impact of their research, combined with the increasing role of transnational research funding as well as the emergence of new actors at the European level and the policies made at this level. National policies and institutional changes can also provide important motivations for expanding their activities to the European level. Interacting with PROs in other countries can be a source of institutional learning and can lead to the formation of alliances that can increase the PROs' potential to influence the development of their national and European research space too. Finally, related to policies and institutional dynamics but also tied to technological developments, are the increasing opportunities for mobility and long-distance communication that can enable PROs and their researchers to engage in long-distance collaboration, competition and international recruitment.

All PROs have been exposed to these environmental dynamics and yet we see diversity in the ways and extent to which they are internationalising. While recent studies on internationalisation have drawn the attention to various factors that are likely to cause variations in the process, we need to understand more systematically why such variations occur. A missing element in current research on internationalisation/Europeanisation of PROs is an understanding of how the organisational characteristics of a PRO may influence its internationalisation process.

It has become traditional to identify three types of PRO: government laboratories, academic, and research and technology organisations (Arnold et al. 2010; OECD 2011b). Based on their diverse nature, here we distinguish four organisation (ideal) types of PRO: the public research centre (PRC) (academic or basic research), the mission-oriented research centre (MOC) (applied and use-oriented), the research technology organisation (RTO) (commercially oriented) and the independent research institute (IRI) (Pasteur quadrant type of research (Stokes 1997)) (OECD 2011c).

Table 9.1   *Classification of (ideal types) PRO according to attributes a (external autonomy) and b (internal authority)*

PRO management		Internal authority	
		+	−
External autonomy	+	*RTO*	*IRI*
	−	*MOC*	*PRC*

In order to address the questions of what would be the expected responses of PROs to the pressures for internationalisation, we advance an analytical framework to interpret organisational variation. Based on diverse contributions from the organisational, institutional and sociology of science literature (March 1994; Whitley 2003) we have identified a few attributes of the different types of organisations that are likely to condition the forms and dynamics of the internationalisation process: a) the degree of external autonomy and resource dependence of the organisation – in terms of funding, human resources, access to external knowledge, for instance – and the associated degree of autonomy and discretion over resources; b) the type of internal authority structure that characterises the functioning of the organisation; and c) the nature of the knowledge production, dissemination and use processes. The forms adopted (modes of operation of internationalisation that can be more or less strategic) will also be influenced by these three basic organisational attributes; consequently we expect to observe different levels of attention and resource commitment for internationalisation by the different PROs over time.

Building on these attributes, we developed a table (Table 9.1) that classifies the different ideal types of PRO according to (a) their external autonomy and (b) their internal authority, the two attributes that shape the opportunities of PRO management to develop strategic internationalisation.

Additionally, the type of knowledge produced by RTOs and MOCs tends to be applied in nature and to either be commercialised or offered to other stakeholders/principals/clients (including governmental actors). In the case of PRCs the main knowledge products tend to be fundamental in nature and be published in academic journals, although they may also engage in applied research, consultancy work, patenting and so on. IRIs aim to produce knowledge products in Pasteur's quadrant (scientific excellence and potential for application). They will mainly publish in academic journals as well, but potentially produce relatively more of the other types of knowledge products (mainly patents) than PRCs (Martinez et al. 2013).

There are limits for strategic action that the PRO has to engage in an interactive way (through adaptation and interaction) with its changing environment. Here we build on the notion of organisational actorhood (Krücken and Meier 2006; Whitley 2008). The concept of strategic action emphasises external autonomy and internal integration. For research institutes to develop internationalisation as an independent organisational goal they need to have some autonomy with respect to the state, but also with respect to the scientific elites. Whether and how managers/directors can use authority and incentives to coordinate and direct initiatives towards internationalisation, not necessarily in a hierarchical way, also influence their capacity to engage strategically with this process.

It is thus important to note that we are dealing with two levels (or units of analysis) that we could identify with internationalisation: the individuals/sub-units and the organisation as a whole. From the literature on research collaboration we find that the levels of internationalisation of different sub-units in organisations are very diverse and probably conditioned by the disciplines or research areas (Nedeva 2013). Also related to the attributes identified above, internationalisation processes thus depend on field dynamics that occur at the sub-unit level.

Later in this chapter we apply this framework to analyse the internationalisation processes of four types of PRO that differ in specific organisational characteristics that have direct implications for the ways in which the PROs internationalise. More specifically, we should be able to generate plausible predictions about the ways in which research institutes allocate their own resources (investments, researchers and other staff, opening up of facilities, and so on) to improve their production and expand their activities (in some cases following clients) or search for international resources (such as clients, funding, and incoming researchers) to continue their internal production.

EUROPEANISATION OF THE PRO EXTERNAL ENVIRONMENT: THE ROLE OF THE EU RESEARCH POLICY

In the last 30 to 50 years research policy[4] developed at the European level has modified the environment of all research actors in Europe, including PROs. As in the case of universities, PRO interactions with European research policy develop at two levels: on the one hand, at the level of teams and researchers (sub-units within the organisations) who interact directly, in the context of research funding, with the policy instruments and, on the other hand, with the strategies that PRO managers develop either to take advantage of, or to shape, European research policy. However, we should not take for granted that policy interventions at the European level produce organisational effects, because the primary environment of most research organisations continues to be national or local.

The aim is to highlight that, in the context of a policy historically shaped by direct implementation and distributive functions, recently complemented by regulatory and coordination activities (Banchoff 2002), the main research policy instruments have been focused on researchers and teams, more than on research institutions. European research policies have traditionally been built on the principle of improving conditions for research, with a strong emphasis on collaboration and networking (Guzzetti 1995). The traditional research and innovation support activities of the EU have had a focus on joint research collaboration and improving European competitiveness through financing mainly transnational research collaboration and mobility of researchers (Sanz-Menéndez and Borrás 2001); in this context the Europeanisation of research organisations has been an indirect effect of increasing links and networks. We believe that European research policy has, in general terms, been ill-equipped to produce strong structural effects at the level of the research organisations, which have continued mainly to respond to national pressures; in this context most of the impact on organisations has been through indirect effects.

When building expectations about the influence of the European policies in the Europeanisation of PROs, it is important to take into account the way research organisations are funded and their internal authority structures. Despite their steady growth, the EC contribution to the overall European budget on R&D is about 16 per cent while national sources account for 84 per cent of public civil research and development (R&D) budget in the European Union (EC 2011: 79). However, the EU's share of competitively allocated project funding is considerably higher and those additional resources have attracted the interest of researchers and research organisations. Nonetheless, the main policy environment of PROs across Europe continues to be the national one and nationally based funding remains by far the most important source of resources for them.

Together with large multilateral research facilities in particular fields, like the CERN or the EMBL, the Framework Programmes (FP) institutionalised European research policy from the 1980s onwards, through funding research collaboration in specific fields (see Chapter 2 of this volume). The FPs developed with the rationale of fostering collaboration among member countries in particular programmatic areas, and with an emphasis on cross-national networks. The main actors were the researchers and teams and not the organisations. As a funding source highly dependent and contingent on micro dynamics, this type of instrument could hardly become a strong driver of organisational change.[5]

Likewise, although very competitive, mobility programmes such as Marie Curie actions were targeted at individuals as well, with marginal institutional control on the inflows, and, especially, outflows. In this context, PROs have been highly dependent on the researchers' international networks and their interest and decisions to apply to funding calls. Thus the capacity of those instruments to generate structural and strategic effects at the level of the organisation is limited, except in the case of institutions that effectively value international mobility and grant-raising capacities in their evaluation, recruitment and promotion systems.

Some argue that in the 1990s the policy networks of research organisations, researchers and administrators which had formed around and relied on the existing FP instruments resisted change that could have led to further European integration (Banchoff 2002: 3). The launching of the Lisbon Strategy and the European Research Area (ERA) initiative represented an attempt to redefine the objectives and targets of EU research policy (see Chapter 3 of this volume). The development of the idea of the ERA was structured around three main objectives: to increase integration, to reduce fragmentation and to create a strong European science base. One of the basic ideas of the ERA was the creation of an internal market for research within which knowledge would circulate freely and some efforts have been made during the last decade to remove barriers against researcher mobility: in 2005 the Council adopted the scientific visa package.[6] In 2005 the Commission recommended the European Charter for Researchers and the Code of Conduct for their recruitment.[7] On a voluntary basis, by 2008 more than 150 institutions had signed their interest in implementing the principles of the Code of Conduct. Meanwhile the EC has also attempted to redirect funding to promote further integration: Networks of Excellence and Integrative Projects were two new instruments of the 6th Framework Programme. As regards the actor level, Edler (2003: 118) argued in 2003 that only if European research organisations and other national actors believed in the added value of long-term European large-scale, largely self-organised projects, would the ERA materialise beyond the logic of extra money. Overall, Chou (2012) argues, the evolution of the EU research policy has mainly been characterised by gradual institutional change through "layering" rather than through "displacement", in the sense that new rules have been progressively adopted in co-existence with the old ones.

The set-up of the European Research Council (ERC) in 2007 signalled a new, complementary, approach based on scientist-driven research, frontier knowledge and excellence, rather than on the traditional mission-oriented competitiveness (see Chapters 2 and 4 of this volume). One of the explicit objectives of the ERC as regards research organisations was to *develop their research strategies and priorities to become global players in research*. Recent empirical evidence suggests that ERC grants strengthen the position of excellent researchers within their organisations by binding the granted funds to the specific activities proposed by the principal investigators. Research groups are built around lines of research that may or may not be part of the strategic planning of the management of the organisation (Edler et al. 2012: 39). There thus appears to be an internal contradiction between the normative pressures on the organisations to provide the conditions to attract and retain grantees (autonomy and support) and the binding of resources and development of autonomous trajectories that this implies. The limited actorhood of some major kinds of PRO[8] helps to explain why in some cases additional European money does not add to organisational authority over resources. Despite this tension research institutions may use the ERC as a motivation and justification for making internal reforms. Edler et al.'s study thus suggests that the emergence of this new funding mechanism on the European landscape can have a positive effect on the internationalisation/Europeanisation of this type of PRO (Edler et al. 2012; Edler et al. 2014; see also Nedeva et al. 2012: 7).

Current European-level science policy still combines cooperation and competition, scientific excellence and political goals (Nedeva and Stampfer 2012). In theory, increasing competition should provide a push towards internationalisation. PROs, universities and researchers are supposed to compete for researchers, students and research funds. International collaboration is seen as a means to stay at the frontier of knowledge-creation and gain reputation, which is a self-reinforcing process. And often, internationalisation is perceived as a quality indicator per se.

The empirical descriptive study of Europeanisation has traditionally been based on input and output indicators (e.g. Van den Besselaar et al. 2012), reflecting activities that can develop as the result of either bottom–up activities of individual researchers or research units, or as the result of top–down policies.

While reflecting Europeanisation, however, these indicators do not necessarily reflect the type of organisational change that is of interest in this chapter. For example, a large share of European funding in a PRO's budget can in some cases be the product of the sum of multiple initiatives by individual researchers, the result of the strategic actions of the PRO management, or of the effect of the actions and demands of policy-makers which fund, steer and exploit the abilities of the PRO. A small share of European funding in a PRO's budget may be a reflection of a lack of incentives for individual researchers to compete/collaborate internationally, of a lack of competitiveness/abilities/means of individual researchers or the organisation as a whole, of a continued reliance on national sources in the absence of the previous three strategies, and/or of the limited freedom given to the PRO leadership by its principal to engage with actors outside the national system. While an increase in the budget share indicates some Europeanisation/internationalisation, it does not necessarily imply strategic Europeanisation/internationalisation at the organisational level.

A second group of developments can be associated more clearly with a process of organisational change related to Europeanisation/internationalisation of the PRO as it refers to changes in organisational structures and strategies; these are, among others, access to resources or sharing (joint infrastructures), and the set-up of facilities abroad.

Other organisational changes, including changes in structures governing the recruitment, evaluation and promotion of researchers and the allocation of human and capital resources more generally, reflect the strategic aim to engage in internationalisation/Europeanisation, when they are aimed, for example, at attracting European funding or excellence strategies. This can also include the use of foreign experts in the evaluation of personnel and organisations.

PROs may establish representations at international organisations (including the European institutions), engage in international or Europe-wide networks to influence European policies/strategies that affect them (for example, EARTO, ALLEA, ESF, EUROHORCS), or engage in ad hoc joint initiatives aimed at the EU policy level.

In order to study organisational change and strategic internationalisation one would need to develop indicators capable of capturing processes. For example: open recruitment practices, or the existence of organisational structures for the support of Europeanisation, the presence of Europeanisation objectives in strategic plans or internationalisation criteria in evaluation procedures, or the existence of incentives for the researchers or managers to internationalise.

A question remains about the right policies and instruments to promote the transformation of local actors into European and global ones, not necessarily through setting up facilities abroad but through servicing globally. The EMBL and the European University Institute are examples of European funded research organisations playing globally and operating under rules, which make them distinctive in comparison to most European universities and PROs. But there are also instances of nationally funded organisations that have been able to evolve into this type of global actor and change some of their functioning rules (for example, the German Max Planck Society (MPG) or the French National Center for Scientific Research (CNRS)). Since national funding is likely to remain the principal funding source of existing PROs, the interplay between national funding and the change of organisational objectives and internal management towards internationalisation is of greatest importance. This does not imply that there is no room for European-level policies to impact on this process. On the contrary, as we will conclude later, the combination of legislative and non-legislative measures might trigger the commitment to Europeanisation goals at the national level, even for organisations that will continue to be primarily funded by national sources.

INTERNATIONALISATION OF RESEARCH INSTITUTES AS STRATEGIC ADAPTATION

In this section we apply the framework developed above (variations in external autonomy and internal authority) to characterise the internationalisation of the different types of PRO identified (PRC, MOC, RTO and IRI) and make some plausible predictions based on their strategic capacities and constraints.

Regarding external autonomy, a first relevant condition for strategic action at the PRO level is related to the amount of resources that organisations are entitled to manage in a discretionary way. If they lack such a control and in the absence of slack resources they can devote to particular goals, it is very difficult for the PRO to even think about internationalisation as a real strategic option beyond "rhetorical discourses" and implementation designs based on delegation to researchers (Edler et al. 2011); in general, poor research organisations are unlikely to internationalise and PROs under financial strain are likely to reduce their internationalisation activities. A case study of the internationalisation of a North American university highlighted the potential conflict between organisational goals or objectives regarding internationalisation and the practices and behaviour of the faculty, when the organisation lacks discretionary resources to devote to these aims (Dewey and Duff 2009). Similar dynamics are likely to occur in PROs. When considering the typology shown in Table 9.1, it is important to realise that between the organisations that fall under the different ideal types there are considerable differences in both the relative size of their research budget and the amount of autonomy they have in deciding how to use it.

A second condition related to the external autonomy refers to the "clients" or "users" of their research activities. If the clients are firms that contribute with significant resources to the functioning of the research institute, and moreover there is an internal hierarchical managerial direction, it is very likely that the institute will "follow" the firms on which it depends, also if it implies internationalising. The notion of "clients" is, however, rather alien in the knowledge production of many PROs. Moreover, many of them (particularly MOCs and PRCs) still receive a large share of their funding through block grants earmarked for the maintenance of infrastructure and the payment of the salaries of their permanent researchers, who have civil servant status. In this context, capacities for strategic actorhood at the organisational level are likely to be very limited, if not marginal. As a general rule, those PROs that are fundamentally financed through project-based funding and have a small proportion of their funding portfolio coming directly from the state, face greater incentives to internationalise (fundraising or fund applications). Overall, it seems that access to additional discretionary resources and access to users and clients are catalysts of strategic internationalisation. RTOs seem to combine both.

A third condition affecting external autonomy refers to the funding regime predominant in the system. About 85 per cent of public research investment still goes only to national endeavours[9] and the research space in which PROs operate thus maintains a strong national dimension, especially as regards block funding. However, over the past decades European funding sources have become increasingly important: and the share of transnational public R&D programmes in the total competitively allocated public project funding is significant. PROs receive a considerable share of these resources. For example, in an interim evaluation of the Framework Programme, it was shown that the CNRS, the Fraunhofer Gesellschaft, the CEA[10] and the MPG were the largest recipients of FP7 funding (Annerberg et al. 2010). Changes in the funding regimes and the emergence of European-level funding sources are likely to have affected the various types of PRO in different ways. Depending on their specific sector or field, but also the level of control they have over their own budgets and their size, some types of PROs are better equipped to compete, collaborate and contract with other (including foreign) actors and engage in strategic interaction with national and European policy-makers to negotiate and influence the outcomes of this process of Europeanisation.

Many PRCs (mostly academic research institutes and science academies) have internationalised as a way to access resources (funding and human capital) rather than as a way to access markets or clients. These PRCs were searching for research complementarities (and capacities they lacked) through specific collaborations and strategic alliances – *to increase their ability to acquire resources from domestic and international sources.* For example, the Spanish CSIC, the French CNRS and German MPG (all basic academic science-oriented centres) are increasingly open to "inward internationalisation" focused on recruitment and co-authorship, and outward internationalisation focused on getting funding from abroad and getting access to foreign physical and human capital to search for complementarities. Most of the initiatives have been developed from below.

However, if organisations grow in a rich environment (in terms of funding) they may also make decisions to develop strategic alliances and even to establish joint research facilities or funding their own networks in third countries. Examples include the joint units established by the German MPG and the French CNRS in both European and third countries (for example, China, India, and Argentina) (Jonkers and Cruz-Castro 2010). In these types of PROs, organisational slack (either related to funding or staff) will create more propensities for internationalisation; budgetary reductions on the other hand will change the priorities: for example, in the context of the financial crisis, the Spanish CSIC will mainly focus on actions involving a low level of consumption of local resources, such as opening up the recruitment or searching for funding.

In general, PRO internationalisation strategies are likely to be stronger if there is some organisational slack coupled with the potential for discretionary allocation of resources.

Most of the internationalisation activities in PROs have a limited link with entry in "foreign markets" (or direct investments, allocation of owned resources in classical terms of foreign direct investments). For a PRO to access markets beyond the national environment means basically to recruit, to sell knowledge and services, and to be funded internationally, as well as to associate with foreign partners. However, there is a type of PRO (the RTO) in which we do find that sometimes access to foreign markets and following customers may be a relevant driver for internationalisation, for example the case of the Fraunhofer Gesellschaft in various Asian and American countries (supported by the German Government) or Tecnalia in Scotland (following Iberdrola).

Apart from the establishment of alliances and other organisational-level collaborations, there are even examples of the set-up of foreign subsidiaries, cross-border mergers or investments to obtain stakes in foreign RTOs. An example of the latter is the acquisition by the Netherlands Organisation for Applied Scientific Research (TNO) of 10 per cent of an Austrian RTO, the Joanneum Research. The motivation for this action was that the greater autonomy over resources from non-national actors gave TNO a greater potentiality to further engage strategically in a process of internationalisation. It aimed to increase its market links and facilitate cooperation in different Member States (EC 2007).[11] Furthermore, four RTOs – the TNO, the Technical Research Centre of Finland (VTT), the Joanneum Research and Tecnalia – also established a Joint Institute for Innovation Policy (JIIP), presumably to become a more attractive partner for international clients.

In some countries, MOCs have become RTOs as a result of the evolution and reforms implemented by governments granting them more autonomy and independence; for example, TNO used to be a traditional mission-oriented research organisation but configured as an umbrella organisation; in other countries the RTOs have evolved from independent private entities or associations into RTOs.

The mission-oriented centres (MOCs), such as the Spanish National Institute for Agronomic Research (INIA), the French National Institute for Agricultural Research (INRA), and the Netherlands Organization for Agricultural Research (DLO), are by definition neither multi-sectorial nor multi-technological. They develop applied research linked to users or sectors, meaning that they have strong links with local sectors and they tend to function as local knowledge providers. However, some of them may also be quite active internationally. INRA, for example, is an active player at the European level and engages in organisational-level collaboration with partners in other European countries. It has, for example, two joint laboratories in China and a permanent representative office together with the French CIRAD (Agricultural Research for Development). Wageningen UR was formed out of a merger of a research university and a former MOC (DLO) and is international in its orientation at the organisational and sub-unit level. Rothamsted Research, an agricultural experimental station and research centre in the UK, is also international in nature and, for example, established a joint laboratory in China.

The group of IRIs (basic knowledge with links with users; Pasteur quadrant model), such as the Spanish CNIO (Spanish National Cancer Research Centre), the Dutch NKI (Netherlands Cancer Institute) or the French Institute Pasteur, has high levels of external autonomy in comparison with PRCs and MOCs; by design, they show high levels of internationalisation in terms of recruitment, funding and international collaboration. As a result of the openness emerging from frontier science, the IRIs will increase their active involvement in international activities to increase their funding and in that way reduce their dependence on local sources.

In sum, autonomy-related conditions to engage strategically with their environments with respect to the process of Europeanisation/internationalisation include, among others, funding structures, rules regarding employment and high degrees of management autonomy that prevent locking in institutes at the national level. Conversely, a strong dependence on the state and little discretionary authority over resources limit the capability of PROs to establish new internationalisation goals, unless the state directly allocates new resources (Whitley 2010). There are considerable variations between the levels of external autonomy across European PROs even for those that are classified under the same 'ideal type'. As shown in Table 9.1, in MOCs this level of external autonomy is expected to be low. However, it is not high in the case of some PRCs either, because governments tend to keep a considerable degree of control over employment and funding. When considering block funding it is important to realise that PRO leadership tends to have limited discretionary authority over it, since most of these resources are earmarked for salary and infrastructure costs. IRIs and RTOs usually have more flexibility to determine employment conditions, resource allocation and organisational structures. This greater autonomy gives these types of PRO, which often operate as non-profit foundations, more room for strategic manoeuvre. The emergence of new patrons in the form of European-level research funders can provide all PROs opportunities to lessen their dependency on the national/regional states – provided they have the political/organisational autonomy to do so.

Turning to the dimension of internal authority, PRCs share with universities some strong barriers to developing competences on internationalisation on the basis of their (limited) authoritative internal coordination capacities and control of the research activities within their organisation (Whitley 2010). In research organisations where the distribution of authority is decentralised and researchers are very autonomous, PROs may find it harder to develop strategic approaches towards internationalisation. As a result, the Europeanisation of this type of PRO will tend to be the aggregate of the individual preferences and orientations of its researchers. Additionally, in these organisations we can expect Europeanisation to be driven to a large extent by external factors, including changing scientific dynamics, the availability of European funding sources, greater mobility and communication possibilities. The PRO can provide stimulation to its researchers to engage in these activities through material, institutional and discursive actions.

The capacity of many PRCs to direct research activities to international arenas is limited by their need to rely on collective judgement to evaluate possible options. This echoes the analysis of Van der Meulen (2002), who argues that the Europeanisation of universities mainly takes place at the level of organisational sub-units. Similar arguments can be found in the analysis of Edler et al. (2012) and Whitley (in Edler et al. 2012); in PROs in which scientific logics and scientific dynamics are particularly important (PRCs and IRIs), strategic decisions with respect to internationalisation tend to be made or at least shaped at lower levels of research organisations (schools, departments, units or even individual researchers). At this level the interaction between the scientific field and the research space (Nedeva 2013) is more pronounced than at higher levels because of the differences in the dynamics between different scientific fields.

PROs that have a greater degree of internal centralisation in the form of managerial leadership (for example, many RTOs and MOCs) may be able to engage more strategically with their changing external environment by making decisions that are binding upon their staff members and commit resources to internationalisation objectives. Combining the two attributes, we could argue that PROs that are characterised by a lack of both external autonomy and internal authority are heavily dependent on their tutelary public authorities. This was traditionally the case for many MOCs, though over time this dependency has been decreasing for some organisations. Even in the instance of a reduction in the availability of public funding, such organisations are less likely to supplement their finances by competing for European/international funding. Over the years, however, many PROs have sought or have been forced to accept an increase in autonomy from their ministries. Some preliminary evidence was found that MOCs that do have a higher degree of autonomy do engage in strategic internationalisation activities at the organisational level (Arnold et al. 2010). Additionally, some policy-led developments, as in the case of metrology under article 185 of the Treaty on the Functioning of the European Union (ex article 169 of the Treaty establishing the European Community) which enables the EU to participate in research programmes undertaken jointly by Member States, can also promote European integration (Barker et al. 2012).

PROs with a combination of limited autonomy and low levels of internal authority have difficulties engaging strategically with their changing environment through internationalisation. As a consequence, while they may profess internationalisation as a strategic goal at the discursive level, this is not always translated in structural changes within the organisation. One may wonder whether internationalisation processes are sustainable without an organisational strategy or whether this type of organisation will continue to adapt mainly passively, through bottom-up processes – processes which are likely to occur to a more limited extent than in organisations in which real changes in both strategies and structures with regard to internationalisation are made. PROs with higher levels of organisational autonomy (and resources), possibly in combination with higher levels of internal authority, have a higher potential for strategic internationalisation and are therefore expected to have changed their respective strategies and structures and to be more successful in directing or facilitating their researchers to engage with their changing environment.

CONCLUDING REMARKS

Organisational differences regarding external autonomy and internal authority generate variations in the capabilities of PROs to internationalise in a more adaptive or strategic way. From what came out of our analysis there are some initiatives, linked to European research policies that could shape and help increase the level of Europeanisation (internationalisation) of PROs at the organisational level. Considering that we are dealing with structural attributes of national institutions, organisational change can only occur either as an effect of incentives or from the application of rules; the history of European research policy has shown that funding incentives are a necessary but not sufficient condition to trigger institutional transformation.

The integration of the distributive stream of EU research policy with a regulatory stream seems necessary for advancing towards a European science space, mainly with the rationale of reducing the barriers for developing international strategies and structures at the PRO level.

We have identified that the level of resources, its sources and destination, as well as its control and management, are determinants of the opportunities for promoting strategic Europeanisation. Therefore, more European resources and "tuned instruments" could help the PRO (and other actors) to become more engaged in the European arena (versus the local ones).

We have also argued that the limited organisational autonomy and managerial discretion of most PROs are (especially in the context of limited resources) major constraints for PROs to become seriously engaged in strategic Europeanisation. Thus, effective changes promoted at national level to enhance organisational autonomy and managerial discretion (in the context of fair assessment of accomplishments related to their missions and responsibilities) of the PRO would be needed to advance strategic Europeanisation.

In the current context, also in line with the approach of EU policy associated with the ERA and the open method of coordination (see also Chapter 5 of this volume) and implementation measures in research policy (Kaiser and Prange-Gstoehl 2010), it would be sound to attempt to reduce national regulations inhibiting Europeanisation as a strategic organisational development, or replace them with rules, perhaps voluntarily agreed as a code of good practices, set up at European level. This would entail changing some employment, promotion, and evaluation systems linked to national models of civil service which structurally inhibit strategic Europeanisation and actors playing in the global arena.

We cannot conclude our final remarks without setting some note of caution on the possible outcomes of the strategic Europeanisation process. The PSR in Europe will become more stratified, with more actors playing in the international/European arena of research even if they still remain mainly funded by national sources. At the same time, some PROs are likely to remain national or local players only.

Additionally, it could also be the case that a process of internal differentiation occurs at PRO level, especially if the capabilities of managers and their discretion over the use of resources remain limited, with subunits displaying high levels of Europeanisation and internationalisation (through bottom-up processes), existing alongside other units mainly engaged in local activities. The consequences of both kinds of dualisation dynamics could be an interesting topic for further analysis.

NOTES

1. Funding from the Ministry of Economic Affairs and Competitiveness (grant CSO2011-29431) is acknowledged.
2. This chapter was mostly prepared when this author was still based at the CSIC Institute for Public Goods and Policies. The information and views set out in this chapter do not necessarily reflect the opinion of the second author's current employer, the European Commission. The EC does not guarantee the accuracy of the data included in this study. Neither the EC nor any person acting on its behalf may be held responsible for the use which may be made of the information contained herein.
3. http://ec.europa.eu/research/era/areas/urpo/urpo_en.htm; http://www.earto.eu/fileadmin/content/04_Newsletter/RPO_Study_Comments.pdf.
4. The first time when a specific chapter on research policy appeared in the treaty was in the Single European Act of 1987 (http://eur-lex.europa.eu/LexUriServ/LexUriServ.do?uri=OJ:L:1987:169:FULL:EN:PDF, article 130f–130q). There had been earlier starts of European research policies going back to at least the third treaty which allowed for the launch of some research programmes in priority areas in the 1960s and 1970s. Both the Euratom treaty and the ECSC contained provisions for research as well as the Roma treaty regarding agriculture. http://ec.europa.eu/research/rtdinfo/special_fp7/fp7/01/article_fp709_en.html.
5. In a case study of La Sapienza, Primeri and Reale (2012) argued that FP participation by individual researchers had limited impact on the Europeanisation of the organisation as a whole.
6. The scientific visa package consists of one directive http://eur-lex.europa.eu/LexUriServ/LexUriServ.do?uri=CELEX:32005L0071:EN:NOT and two recommendations: http://eur-lex.europa.eu/LexUriServ/LexUriServ.do?uri=CELEX:32005H0762:EN:NOT and http://eur-lex.europa.eu/LexUriServ/LexUriServ.do?uri=CELEX:32005H0761:EN:NOT. Denmark and the UK have opted out of the directive, which is binding for other countries. In March 2013 the European Commission proposed a new visa directive.
7. http://ec.europa.eu/euraxess/index.cfm/rights/recommendation.
8. This applies, essentially, to the academic ones at a medium level of research endowments and autonomy.
9. http://www.esf.org/about-esf.html.
10. The CEA is the French Alternative Energies and Atomic Energy Commission.
11. In December 2014, TNO sold its share to the regional government of Kärnten – due to a changing financial situation. http://kaernten.orf.at/news/stories/2684715/

REFERENCES

Annerberg, R., I. Begg, H. Acheson, S. Borras, A. Hallen, T. Maimets, R. Mustonen, H. Raffler, JP. Swings, K. Ylihonko, (2010) *Interim Evaluation of the Seventh Framework Programme Report of the Expert Group*, Report prepared for the European Commission, DG Research, European Research Area, 7th Framework Programme, Luxembourg: Publication Office of the European Union, http://ec.europa.eu/research/evaluations/pdf/archive/other_reports_studies_and_documents/fp7_interim_evaluation_expert_group_report.pdf [Accessed on August 21, 2013].

Arnold, E., K. Barker and S. Slipersæter (2010), *Research Institutes in the ERA*, Technopolis Group, http://ec.europa.eu/research/era/docs/en/research-institutes-in-the-era.pdf [Accessed on August 17, 2015].

Barker, K.E., D. Cox and T. Sveinsdottir (2012), 'Reshaping European Metrology Research – the Role of National Research Managers', *R&D Management*, 42 (2), 170–80.

Banchoff, T. (2002), 'Institutions, Inertia and European Research Policy', *Journal of Common Market Studies*, 40 (1), 1–21.

Bartell, M. (2003), 'Internationalization of Universities: A University Culture-based Framework', *Higher Education*, 45 (1), 43–70.

Berger, M. and R. Hofer (2011), 'The Internationalisation of Research Technology Organisations (RTO) – Conceptual Notions and Illustrative Examples from European RTOs in China', *Science Technology Society*, 16 (1), 99–122.

Boden, R., D. Cox and M. Nedeva (2006), 'The Appliance of Science? – New Public Management and Strategic Change', *Technology Analysis and Strategic Management*, 18 (2), 125–241.

Boden, R., D. Cox, M. Nedeva and K. Barker (2004), *Scrutinising Science: The Changing UK Government of Science*, Houndmills, New York: Palgrave-Macmillan.

Boekholdt, P., J. Edler, P. Cunningham and K. Flanagan (2009), *Drivers of International Collaboration in Research*, final report. Report prepared for the European Commission, DG Research, International Cooperation, Luxembourg: Publications Office of the European Union.

Bozeman, B., J.S. Dietz and M. Gaughan (2001), 'Scientific and Technical Human Capital: an Alternative Model for Research Evaluation', *International Journal of Technology Management*, 22 (7/8).

Chou, M.H. (2012), 'Constructing an Internal Market for Research through Sectoral and Lateral Strategies: Layering, the European Commission and the Fifth Freedom', *Journal of European Public Policy*, 19 (7), 1052–70.

Cox, D., P. Gummett and K. Barker (eds) (2001), *Government Laboratories. Transition and Transformation*, Amsterdam: IOS Press.

Crow, M.M. and B. Bozeman (1998), *Limited by Design. R&D Laboratories in the US National Innovation System*, New York: Columbia University Press.

Dewey, P. and S. Duff (2009), 'Reason before Passion: Faculty Views on Internationalization in Higher Education', *Higher Education*, 58 (4), 491–504.

Drori, G.S., J.W. Meyer, F.O. Ramirez and E. Schofer (2003), *Science in the Modern World Polity. Institutionalizations and Globalization*. Stanford: Stanford University Press.

Ebersberger, B. and J. Edler (2009), 'Internationalization of Public Research

Organizations. Context, Strategies and Effects', *Atlanta Conference on Science and Innovation Policy 2009*, https://smartech.gatech.edu/handle/1853/32320.

Edler, J. (2003), 'Change in European R&D Policy as a Complex Consensus-building Process', in J. Edler, S. Kuhlmann and M. Behrens (eds), *Changing Governance of Research and Technology Policy: The European Research Area*, Cheltenham, UK and Northampton, MA, USA: Edward Elgar, 98–132.

Edler, J., D. Frischer, M. Glanz, and M. Stampfer (2012), 'The Impact of the ERC on Universities and Public Research Organizations', http://www.eurecia-erc.net/wp-content/upLoads/EURECIA-ImpactOnResearchOrganisations.pdf.

Edler, J., D. Frischer, M. Glanz and M. Stampfer (2014), 'Funding Individuals-Changing Organisations: The Impact of the ERC on Universities', in Whitley and Gläser (eds), *Organizational Transformation and Scientific Change: The Impact of Institutional Restructuring on Universities and Intellectual Innovation (Serie Research in the Sociology of Organizations 42)*, Bingley: Emerald Group Publishing Limited, 77–109.

European Commission (EC) (2007), Commission staff working document accompanying the Green Paper 'The European Research Area: New Perspectives', COM (2007)161, http://ec.europa.eu/research/era/pdf/era_swp_final.pdf.

European Commission (2011), *Innovation Union Competitiveness Report 2011*, Brussels: European Commission.

Gassmann, O. and M. von Zedtwitz (1999), 'New Concepts and Trends in International R&D Organizations', *Research Policy*, 28 (2–3), 231–50.

Guzzetti, L. (1995), *A Brief History of European Union Research Policy*, Office for Official Publications of the European Communities.

Hicks, D. (2012), 'Performance-based University Research Funding Systems', *Research Policy*, 41 (2), 251–61.

Jonkers, K. and L. Cruz-Castro (2010), 'The Internationalisation of Public Sector Research through International Joint Laboratories', *Science and Public Policy*, 37 (8), 559–70.

Kaiser, R. and H. Prange-Gstoehl (2010), 'A Paradigm Shift in European R&D Policy? The EU Budget Review and the Economic Crisis', *Science and Public Policy*, 37, 253–65.

Katz, J.S. and B.R. Martin (1997), 'What is Research Collaboration', *Research Policy*, 26 (1), 1–18.

Krücken, G. and F. Meier (2006), 'Turning the University into an Organizational Actor', in Gili, S.D., J.W. Meyer and H. Hwang (eds) *Globalization and Organization. World Society and Organizational Change*, Oxford: Oxford University Press, 241–57.

Langfeldt, L., H. Godø, A. Gornitzka and A. Kaloudis (2012), 'Integration Modes in EU Research: Centrifugality versus Coordination of National Research Policies', *Science and Public Policy*, 39 (1), 88–98.

Lepori, B., P. van den Besselaar, M. Dinges, B. Poti, E. Reale, S. Slipersaeter, J. Theves and B. van der Meulen (2007), 'Comparing the Evolution of National Research Policies: What Patterns of Change', *Science and Public Policy*, 34 (6), 372–88.

Malhotra, N. and C.R. Hinings (2010), 'An Organizational Model for Understanding Internationalization Processes', *Journal of International Business Studies*, 41 (2), 330–49.

March, J.G. (1994), *A Premier on Decision-Making*, New York: Free Press.

Martinez, C., J. Azagra-Caro and S. Maraut (2013), 'Academic Inventors and

Scientific Impact: The Institutionalization of Research in Pasteur's Quadrant', *Industry and Innovation* 20(5), 438–55.

McGuinness, N. and C. O'Carrol (2010), 'Benchmarking Europe's Lab Benches: How Successful has the OMC been in Research Policy', *Journal of Common Market Studies*, 48 (2), 293–318.

Nedeva, M., D. Braun, J. Edler, D. Frischer, M. Glanz, J. Glaser, P. Laredo, G. Laudel, T. Luukkonen, M. Stampfer, D. Thomas, and R. Whitley (2012), *Understanding and Assessing the Impact and Outcomes of the ERC and its Funding Schemes (EURECIA)*, Final Synthesis Report, Brussels: ERC.

Nedeva, M. and M. Stampfer (2012), 'From "Science in Europe" to "European Science"', *Science*, 336 (6084), 982–3.

Nedeva, M. (2013), 'Between the Global and the National: Organising European Science', *Research Policy*, 42 (1), 220–30.

OECD (2010), *Performance based Funding for Public Research in Tertiary Education Institutions*, Paris: OECD.

OECD (2011a), *Public Research Institutions. Mapping Sector Trends*. Paris: OECD.

OECD (2011b), *Public Sector Research Funding*. Policy brief, The Innovation Policy Platform. https://www.innovationpolicyplatform.org/sites/default/files/Public%20Sector%20Research%20Funding_0_0.pdf (author's contribution).

OECD (2011c), *Public Research Organisations*. Policy brief, The Innovation Policy Platform. https://www.innovationpolicyplatform.org/sites/default/files/Public%20Research%20Organisations_0_0.pdf (authors' contribution).

Olsen, J.P. (2002), 'The Many Faces of Europeanization', *Journal of Common Market Studies*, 40 (5), 921–52.

Paradeise, C., E. Reale, I. Bleiklei and E. Ferlie (eds) (2009), *University Governance: Western European Comparative Perspective*, Dordrecht: Springer.

Primeri, E. and E. Reale (2012), 'How Europe Shapes Academic Research: Insights from Participation in European Framework Programmes', *European Journal of Education*, 47(1), 104–21.

Sanz-Menéndez, L. and S. Borras (2001), 'Explaining Changes and Continuity in EU Technology Policy: the Politics of Ideas', in S. Dresner and N. Gilbert (eds), *Changing European Research System*, Aldershot: Ashgate Press, 28–51.

Sanz-Menendez, L. and L. Cruz-Castro (2003), 'Coping with Environmental Pressures: Public Research Organizations Responses to Funding Crisis', *Research Policy*, 32 (8), 1293–308.

Senker, J. (2000), 'Introduction to a Special Issue on Changing Organization and Structure of European Public Sector Research Systems', *Science and Public Policy*, 27 (6), 394–6.

Slipersaeter, S. and D.W. Aksnes (2008), 'The Many Ways of Internationalization: Patterns of R&D Funding and Collaboration', in Å. Gornitzka and L. Langfeldt (eds), *Borderless Knowledge: Understanding the "New" Internationalisation of Research and Higher Education in Norway*, Dordrecht: Springer.

Stokes, Donald E. (1997), *Pasteur's Quadrant. Basic Science and Technological Innovation*, Washington D.C.: The Brookings Institution.

Stromquist, N.P. (2007), 'Internationalization as a Response to Globalization: Radical Shifts in University Environments', *Higher Education*, 53 (1), 81–105.

Van den Besselaar, P., A. Inzelt, E. Reale, E. De Turckheim and V. Vercesi (2012), *Indicators of Internationalisation for Research Institutions: a New Approach*, A report by the ESF Member Organisation Forum on Evaluation:

Indicators of Internationalisation, http://www.fteval.at/upload/Indicators_of_Internationalisation_for_Research_Institutions.pdf.

Van der Meulen, B. (2002), 'Europeanization of Research and the Role of Universities: An Organizational-Cultural Perspective', *Innovation: The European Journal of Social Science Research*, 15 (4), 341–55.

Von Zedtwitz, M. and O. Gassmann (2002), 'Market versus Technology Drive in R&D Internationalization: Four Different Patterns of Managing Research and Development', *Research Policy*, 31 (4), 569–88.

Whitley, R. (2003), 'Competition and Pluralism in the Public Sciences: The Impact of Institutional Frameworks on the Organisation of Academic Science', *Research Policy*, 32 (6), 1015–29.

Whitley, R. (2008), 'Universities as Strategic Actors', in L. Engwall and D.L. Weaire (eds), *The University in the Market*, London: Portland Press, 22–37.

Whitley, R. (2010), 'Reconfiguring Public Science: The Impact of Governance Changes on Authority and Innovation in Public Science Systems', in R. Whitley, J. Gläser and L. Engwall (eds), *Reconfiguring Knowledge Production*, Oxford: Oxford University Press, 3–47.

10. *Quo vadis* European science?
Linda Wedlin and Maria Nedeva

INTRODUCTION

There is little doubt that the policy, governance, structures and organisation of science at the European level has been changing dramatically and rapidly over the last couple of decades. Notions regarding the role of European-level funding and support for research and the interactions between the European and national funding have been re-framed. Policy and governance rationales have been extended to signal the broad integrative ambition of research funding while placing emphasis firmly on the excellence of research. Last but not least, the existence of long-established organisational forms have been brought into question (for example, the ESF) and novel organisations with audacious goals, and budgets to match, have emerged (the ERC).

In parallel, national research spaces have been undergoing profound transformation as well. As higher education and research systems have become both larger and politically more visible in many countries, governance efforts have increased and new and revised systems for evaluating, funding and managing research and science have emerged. These include, but are not restricted to, an increase in performance-based funding principles and mechanisms, development of quality assurance systems, and a global spread of university ranking systems. Such systems represent an increasing influence also of globalised models and ideals for university and science governance, and an adherence to a market rationale characterised by ideals of (largely global) competition and excellence. Some of these changes have resulted from targeted policy action and shifting policy objectives and rationales. Others may, not unlikely, have occurred as a response to the change at European level.

While these transformations have attracted the excited attention of students of science and research policy, science studies scholars and political scientists, there is, we believe, a mismatch between the all-encompassing change we are witnessing and the fragmented research accounts attempting to enhance its understanding. Research accounts are fragmented in three ways. Firstly, these accounts focus on certain aspects of change like governance, funding or organisations. Secondly, the accounts, as a rule, are contained within specific levels of social and political aggregation, for example, national, regional, European, and so on. And thirdly, the research underpinning the interpretations of change originate in different research fields and are framed by their respective assumptions and methodological and analytical demands.

While the research on issues regarding the changes of the support for science and research at European level is generally conceptually and empirically sound, its fragmented nature presents serious issues of analysis and interpretation. Hence, the chief ambition of this book is to take a step, however small this may be, towards laying the foundation for a conceptual synthesis and the alignment of the analytical perspectives of several related but distinct research fields studying the science system and its dynamics.

To this effect, following in the tradition of two emergent, integrative conceptual developments – one of these offering a broad framework for unpacking the dynamics of science as the interactions between research spaces and research fields, and the other offering a framework for the analysis of complex and multi-faceted changes of science policy and governance – we suggested that the empirical change we are witnessing at European level can be seen as a process of global transition from one relatively stable stage in the development of the European research space (Science in Europe) to a different stage, one that we termed European Science.

Now we would like to get back to the three questions asked at the beginning of this book and address these in turn.

IS A EUROPEAN-LEVEL RESEARCH AND SCIENCE SPACE DEVELOPING?

Turning to our starting points, the first question is whether there is, in fact, a European-level science and research space developing? Based in our definition of a research space – the funding and policy environments within which the rules of knowledge production, knowledge legitimacy and knowledge use are negotiated – we have outlined the development and change of policies and policy rationales, governance (particularly relating to funding) mechanism, and a changing organisational setting for knowledge development (science and research) at the European level. Each of these aspects has been treated extensively, separately or in combination, in the chapters of this book. It is, however, when we put these transformations together that we see the cumulative effect of such changes: the forming of a European research space that sets the framework, increasingly, for knowledge development and organisation. This space defines, in turn, the activities and the actors within it, thus constituting a formative process of its own.

We have noted how, over time, the European research space has stabilised around: a) policy and governance rationales, including not only complementarity and collaboration but also competition; b) funding rules, including not only applied and close to application research but also developing and creating the European science base, and emphasis on scientific excellence; and c) the reframing of rather diffused organisations into the establishment of the European Research Council as a central, and increasingly powerful, research funding organisational player.

The contributions in this volume have provided evidence not only that changes in the three dimensions have come about, but also how the different aspects of such changes are intricately related and intertwined. In the following, we will try to reformulate slightly the contributions of the respective chapters, in terms of how they contribute to, describe and explain the development, and essence, of the European research space. We do so, however, without the intention of reducing their distinct contributions set within their respective frameworks and analytical purposes.

A first observation that we can make from the contributions to this volume, is the centrality of the ERC for the development and shape of the European research space. The ERC represents, in essence, a new governance mechanism (target of intervention focused on basic research by means of investigator-driven research funding allocation). As such, it adds to a generally expanding set of governance principles and tools available in the European research space. It was particularly shown, in Chapter 4, how this mechanism represented something new and distinct at the European level, which clearly sets an important framework for other research funding actors and organisations at both European and national levels. This new mechanism thus has the potential to alter the relations and create tensions between the actors in the larger European funding landscape.

But the ERC would not in and of itself provide the basis for a European research space, and all the remaining chapters of the volume have, to varying extent, shown how the development of the ERC was interrelated with change in the two other dimensions: the policy rationales and the organisational architectonic. In Chapter 3, for instance, Luukkonen showed how the ERC was not just a result of the significant changes in policy rationales for supporting and funding science at the European level, it was also instrumental in making these shifts possible. Becoming a carrier of ideas of excellence and competition, the ERC helped to reframe, and perhaps also refuel, the ERA debate, thus contributing to reshape the policy rationales for science and research intervention more broadly. The ERC, and the arguments underpinning it, became both the target of the new policy rationales and the mechanism to bring it forward.

The ERC has also been shown to be central to the development of a partly revised organisational architectonic for science and research governance in Europe. Apart from being an interesting new organisation of its own – with its own premises, its own staff, its own governing council and structures, and the possibility to appoint its own secretary-general for instance – the development of the ERC is part of a larger reorganisation of the research governance capacity of the EC. This change was analysed in Chapter 5. We noted here how the executive governance capacity of the European Commission is highly path-dependent and characterised by layering. Thus representing, in one sense, a completely new form of organisation (an agency) for science/research and EC interaction, the ERC is also in another sense still embedded in the formal organisational structures of DG Research and the rest of the EC. Thus, Gornitzka argues that continuity runs parallel to change, as new policy instruments get developed and are added to existing governance frameworks and structures. We learn from this that change in policy rationales and governance mechanisms are intertwined, and are largely dependent on the organisational capacities to bring them to bear.

A second observation is that while the ERC has been central to the evolving European research space, it is by no means the only new mechanism in the European governance "palette", nor is it the only change in the organisational architectonic of this space. Another significant change is the increasing importance of organisations and actors involved in policy-making, standard-setting, and evaluation of science and research at the European level. By focusing explicitly on the policy rationales underpinning much of the change in the evolving European research space – most significantly the increasing focus on competition, excellence and quality – several contributors in this volume direct our attention to new organisational actors and processes shaping the institutional conditions for science.

In this vein, Wedlin and Hedmo (Chapter 6) note how a diverse set of organisations involved in quality assurance, standard-setting, ranking practices and the like, have become important actors in this European research space. They appear to have a dual role: influencing and legitimising governance processes and mechanisms developed at the European level (such as taking part in the Bologna process) and setting standards and developing mechanisms to measure, assess and evaluate the practices of research and teaching activities and organisations in the European space. As witnessed by the recent involvement of the EU in ranking practices, with the initiation of the U-Multirank comparison in 2014, such mechanisms provide specific tools with which to promote the idea of a European idea of excellence and competition. The result appears to be the forming of a more coherent set of standards for evaluating the quality, excellence and success of science and research endeavours, most distinctively organised at the European level (through new organisations, or with the involvement of European-level actors and organisations).

Engwall notes in Chapter 8, on a comparable note, how very old organisations in the science field – the academies, many of them with a royal charter – have begun to organise on a European level both to contribute to the setting of such standards and to influence the forming of the "policies for science" increasingly shaped in the European space. He argues more specifically that the academies are made up of a particular part of the scientific community, namely the elite. As such, they are particularly prone to be influential also in debates on "science for policy", that is, having a voice in policy issues related to their respective areas of expertise.

A third observation emanating from our contributions is how the changes in the European science and research space also go beyond, and are closely intertwined with, developments in related policy fields as well as with processes that go beyond the scope of Europe. The dynamics of the changes in policy rationales and organisational set-up of the EC in the area of science was clearly interlinked with changes in the adjacent field of higher education and training (see Chapters 3 and 5). This was further evidenced by the strength of the rhetoric of excellence and quality, coupled with that of competition, which have become central parts of the policy agenda for higher education as well as for research: a largely global policy agenda but with a European twist (see Chapter 6).

This interrelation is most clearly visible, however, in the contributions highlighting the organisational dynamics that these changes entail for research performing organisations within the European research space. For these organisations, European developments may have more or less direct implications for how they organise and change. Particularly, as argued convincingly in Chapter 7, university hierarchies are becoming "penetrated" by new networks of actors that gain influence in university structures and decision-making, mainly through the increasing influence of new funding mechanisms, evaluations and organisational routines for quality assurance. The power of the new elites, formed both in the national but also by processes in the European research space, is thus significant, and shapes relations between researchers, funding agencies, the ERC and other actors in the national as well as the European research spaces. It may also influence the relations between researchers and their universities.

One difference between the European-level research space and the national research spaces is that there are still no European research organisations – universities and research institutes – as such (although there are institutes of the European Commission, but these are very few to count as a developing part of the research space). This is an important point, since the research performing organisations are the ones providing the organisational link to the research and science activities. But in the final contribution of the book, Cruz-Castro and colleagues show how the development of the European-level funding instruments and procedures can have a role to play in shaping the agenda for the internationalisation of existing, nationally oriented, research institutes, thereby, at least potentially, filling the role as research performing organisations at European-level organisations. While limited autonomy and managerial discretion over resources may be obstacles to such strategic internationalisation efforts of these institutes, funding from an independent European-level funding organisation, particularly won in competition, may provide impetus for increasing international and European orientation of these research organisations.

WHAT ARE THE IMPLICATIONS OF THIS DEVELOPMENT?

The result of the changes elaborated above is the creation of a European-level research space that in many ways is comparable to, and sometimes even in competition with, the national research spaces. The contributions have demonstrated that the construction of an increasingly salient space for science rationalisation, science support and science organising in Europe has taken place over time and involved many actors as well as many interrelated processes of change. We can also note that this process is, to a great extent, still under way.

This is important as we turn to assess the implications of this development. While the implications are potentially both significant and numerous, they are perhaps not yet clearly visible. The chapters in this volume have, however, pointed us in the direction of some of these effects, showing, for instance, how the European research space is likely to influence the establishment and shape of standards for quality and excellence, how it may play a role in forming elites, how it alters organisational strategies for internationalisation and recruitment, and how it could potentially contribute to shifting powers between different actors and actor groups in, and among, research organisations.

Meanwhile, the implications of the new European research area need to be explored empirically in all its diversity. In this volume, we have focused on setting the framework for such empirical and analytical work. Given this framework – with the focus on the development of a new research space at the European level – we can specifically point to two areas that should be of particular concern in future efforts to understand the impact of the European research space. Those are the implications of such changes on 1) the relations between actors and organisations within the European research space, and 2) the relations and dynamics between and across different research spaces.

On the first note, it has been argued throughout this volume that the development of the European research space creates and reshapes relations between actors and organisations in this new space: relations among and between funding organisations, governance bodies, interest organisations, academies and research performing organisations that occupy this new space. The establishment of the ERC is here a case in point: it is altering the relations within the EC as well as between the EC and other funding bodies, changing relations between the EC and researchers (engaging them as panel member, as applicants, and as stakeholders in European policy-making), and changing practices and procedures for assessing quality and excellence. It also influences relations between individuals and organisations, and between groups of individuals within organisations. Most notably, the ERC reframes researchers and research organisations as competitors, creating partly new dynamics in the science systems. For instance, the establishment of exclusive networks for ERC grantees, and the competition for ERC grants, and grantees, have created new dynamics in the status systems of academics as well as research organisations.

On the second note, we begin to see the implications of the evolving European space in the changing relations between this space and adjacent research spaces. Most notably, this is seen in the relations between the European space and the various national research spaces to which it is closely interlinked. This is perhaps most evident in the potential tensions created between the ERC and national funding agencies, which can have both a mutually supporting and a competing relationship. Also national governments and other governance actors are implicated by the chang-ing relationships to European actors, for instance through the forming of standards and guidelines for national quality assurance systems to which national actors have to relate.

As the European research space continues to evolve, the dynamics of these changing relationships further unfold, and are likely to influence the future development of this space. Thus with the changing relations in focus – between and among actors in the research space as well as between and across different research spaces – further empirical studies are needed to analyse and understand the continuing development of the European research space, how and why it is changing, and the implications of such changes for science and research and for the future governance of this important area of society.

TOWARDS A NOVEL RESEARCH AGENDA?

The research we have included in this book can be seen as bridging the existing research agenda – a research agenda characterised by fragmentation – and a novel one which places at its centre the understanding of science dynamics and the complex interactions between the social and institutional conditions of science on the one hand, and the particular characteristics of science and research on the other. This means that future research attention ought to better conceptualise and account for the effect of the changing conditions of science (policy, governance, structures, institutions and organisations) on the epistemic properties of knowledge; that is, how policy and governance – and the wider institutional conditions for science and research – shape and impact the way in which knowledge is produced and organised as well as on the knowledge being produced. For policy, an important implication of such a stance would be to investigate the way in which the characteristics of different research areas and fields (knowledge communities and properties of knowledge) may demand different social and institutional conditions. The forming of the future European research space along such a path would undoubtedly be the beginning of a new era for science policy more generally.

Index